PENGUIN BOOKS  W9-BTC-822

Oldman's Guide to Outsmarting Wine

For over fourteen years, Mark Oldman has taught his lively Outsmarting Wine™ courses to thousands of budding wine enthusiasts in New York City and California. Mark began his wine journey in 1990, when as a student he founded the Stanford Wine Circle, a popular university club hosting tastings with California wine legends, earning him the nickname "Bacchus on the Campus" in *Wine Spectator* magazine.

Mark's pro-consumer approach and commitment to education have animated all of his professional endeavors. When not involved with wine, he serves as copresident of Vault, Inc. (www.vault.com), the leading media company for career information, which he cofounded in 1997. He is also a licensed attorney and the coauthor of several books, including the bestselling *Best 109 Internships* and *The Internship Bible*. Holding a B.A., an M.A., and a J.D. from Stanford University, he currently serves as one of the youngest members of the Stanford Board of Trustees.

COURSES, CUSTOM EVENTS, AND MORE

■ For more information about Mark's upcoming appearances and wine courses, please visit www.MarkOldman.com.

■ Mark teaches a variety of wine courses and seminars for corporations, organizations, universities, and alumni groups. Contact: info@MarkOldman.com.

Oldman's Guide to Outsmarting Wine

108 INGENIOUS SHORTCUTS
TO NAVIGATE THE WORLD OF WINE
WITH CONFIDENCE AND STYLE

Mark Oldman

PENGUIN BOOKS

PENGUIN BOOKS

Published by the Penguin Group

Penguin Group (USA) Inc., 375 Hudson Street,

New York, New York 10014, U.S.A.

Penguin Books Ltd, 80 Strand,

London, WC2R 0RL, England

Penguin Books Australia Ltd, 250 Camberwell Road, Camberwell,

Victoria 3124, Australia

Penguin Books Canada Ltd, 10 Alcorn Avenue,

Toronto, Ontario, Canada M4V 3B2

Penguin Books India (P) Ltd, 11 Community Centre, Panchsheel Park,

New Delhi – 110 017, India

Penguin Group (NZ), Cnr Airborne and Rosedale Roads, Albany,

Auckland, New Zealand

Penguin Books (South Africa) (Pty) Ltd, 24 Sturdee Avenue,

Rosebank, Johannesburg 2196, South Africa

Penguin Books Ltd, Registered Offices:

80 Strand, London WC2R 0RL, England

First published in Penguin Books 2004

10 9 8 7 6 5 4 3 2 1

Copyright © Mark Oldman, 2004

All rights reserved

LIBRARY OF CONGRESS CATALOGING-IN-PUBLICATION DATA

CIP data available

ISBN 0-14-200492-8

Printed in the United States of America

Set in Filosofia Regular with Franklin Gothic

Designed by Judith Stagnitto Abbate/Abbate Design

"I drink to th' general joy o' th' whole table."
—Shakespeare, *Macbeth*

Contents

Introduction

"I know nothing about wine" is the classic sheepishly exasperated refrain uttered in wine shops and restaurants, at dinner parties, and anywhere else corks are popped. Whether you're a habitué of Michelin three-stars or a connoisseur of Subway sandwiches, chances are you've experienced a Maalox moment when faced with making a decision about wine. It's one of those universal knowledge deficiencies—like remembering friends' birthdays or knowing the right dance moves—that haunt people throughout their lives.

The wine and restaurant industries are partially to blame. How do you experiment with new types of wine when restaurants mark them up at least three times over retail price? Even if you can afford to broaden your wine horizons in a restaurant, there's not always someone there to guide you. Although some restaurants employ wine-savvy servers, many of them have no background in wine or just aren't that approachable if they do. The situation can be just as difficult in wine shops. For every customer-focused wine store, there are others run by imperious or indifferent owners who care more about moving stock than educating their clientele. Even if you ignore the shopkeeper, it's difficult to decipher the multiplicity of wine label types, with some wines identified by grape variety, others by region of origin, and still others by brand name.

Compounding the problem is wine's Grey Poupon aura, which makes it needlessly difficult to master. Do restaurants employ scotch stewards? Do we decant tequila? Do beer guzzlers feel compelled to memorize vintage charts? And it's not just what you do with wine; it's what you say. Can a wine really be "diffident" and "flintaceous" or smell like "gooseberries" and "tomato leaves"? Snobs would have you believe you need a Ph.D. in linguistics to truly enjoy wine.

Oldman's Guide to Outsmarting Wine cuts through this needless confusion like a samurai sword. The idea for it came from my students, who, over the fourteen years I've taught wine courses, have urged me to "put this stuff in a book." The book mirrors my teaching style, which is always focused on providing an approachable answer key of quick, easy-to-implement nuggets of wine wisdom. Having attended countless wine tastings, devoured virtually every wine book on the shelves, and talked with innumerable wine pros, I derive enormous pleasure from serving as a human filter for budding wine enthusiasts by distilling wine information down to its essentials. And because wine is not my primary business, I bring an independent perspective to the task. I am beholden to no winery, distributor, wine shop, publication, or restaurant.

There is no shortage of wine books on the market, and I recommend some of the excellent ones in the last chapter. But even the good ones require several readings to glean basic principles. *Oldman's Guide to Outsmarting Wine* gets to the heart of the matter with unambiguous answers to practical wine questions. It is not a coffee table book, a reference book, or an in-depth study of a particular wine region. If you want to learn the chemistry behind malolactic fermentation or the history of the Côte d'Or, please look elsewhere.

But if you "know nothing about wine" and want to rectify that swiftly and painlessly, this book will help. I have covered the subjects most useful to my students and me and have done so with the kind of brevity that makes these principles easy to remember. This book contains 108 streamlined shortcuts, each followed up by a few explanatory paragraphs. They are carefully designed to impart just enough wine knowledge to conquer dinner parties, business dinners, gift selection, wine handling and storage, and visits to the wine shop and wine country.

Even better, this book will vastly increase the number of bullets in your vinous holster. Because most people are hopelessly resigned to falling back on the same old bottles in stores and restaurants, I've designed every section of this book with an eye toward expanding your wine options. You'll learn the basic grape and regional styles as well as a slew of secret alternatives, with many sections loaded with Mark's Picks wine recommendations. To make your wine decisions even easier, my Faithful Fifty lists supply you with dozens of time-tested bottles that will deliver big pleasure at small cost. Finally, to broaden your perspective even more, I've included On My Table profiles—the personal wine picks and insights of several of the world's most accomplished wine enthusiasts, from Francis Ford Coppola to Rémi Krug.

Consider me your wine sherpa, helping you navigate the perilous but rewarding elevations of vinous knowledge. If my goal is achieved, this book will allow you to do more than just enjoy wine. You will become so confident that you'll feel as though you've gotten the better of it. You will *outsmart* wine.

Key

CHEAT SHEET To help you remember the driving principle of each entry, the Cheat Sheet sums things up in a pithy sentence or two.

LABEL DECODER Even experts lose sight of whether a wine's name refers to its grape or its place of origin; the Label Decoder will supply the answer.

OUTSMART THE TABLE Designed to entertain and enlighten, Outsmart the Table provides a bit of supplementary color to each entry and gives you something scintillating to say around a table of guests.

TALK THE TALK A key reason wine intimidates us is that we can't pronounce all of those tricky European names. Talk the Talk supplies the pronunciations for hundreds of major wine words and producer names.

MARK'S PICKS Each Mark's Picks sidebar offers a list of recommended producers for a particular wine type, based on years of gauging the preferences of my students, my wine friends, and myself. It is designed to be not a complete list of quality producers but a gateway to your exploration of a particular wine category. I have tried to emphasize options that are affordable and widely available—but be advised that even these bottles are sometimes difficult to find given America's byzantine distribution laws. In addition, the On My Table profiles interspersed throughout the book provide hundreds of other interesting picks.

FIT FOR FEASTING While the guiding principle of food-and-wine pairing should be always to follow your own taste, it's helpful to know about the foods that tend to flatter certain wines. Fit for Feasting provides a sampling of these recommendations, with emphasis on general categories, but also specific dishes, especially ones that have traditional (e.g., red Burgundy and roast chicken) or regional (e.g., Gewürztraminer and Muenster cheese) significance. By no means should you feel constrained by these or anyone else's food recommendations—let your palate ultimately be the judge.

ON MY TABLE SURVEY I've found the best way to expand your wine horizons is first to hear about what *other* people drink. So I set out to discover what some of the world's most interesting and accomplished wine lovers drink in their leisure time. The result: the On My Table survey, the personal wine preferences of oenophiles around the world. Interspersed throughout the book, these profiles are designed to inspire the development of your own wine passions. They constitute a veritable Noah's Ark of prominent wine enthusiasts: winemakers, winery owners, star chefs and restaurateurs, award-winning sommeliers, leading importers, academics, auction house legends, merchants, wine educators, and celebrity collectors. I wanted you not only to become familiar with the names and preferences of these wine heroes but also to catch their excitement about wine's ability to, in the words of Herman Melville, "open the heart . . . and thaw it right out."

Each On My Table profile supplies a respondent's favorite wine type, followed by a sampling of specific producers. Consult the Appendix for a full list of On My Table participants, as well as the fascinating trends that emerged from this survey.

Oldman's Guide to
Outsmarting Wine

The Opener

1 The Faithful Fifteen:
Fifteen Top Producers for Value

When it comes to dispensing wine advice, I don't hide the ball. So let's start things off by answering the question that *everyone* asks: where are the best values?

Although I cover buying strategies in depth later on, including my Faithful Fifty lists of the world's best wine deals, I couldn't wait to give you my Faithful Fifteen producers. These are the wineries offering wine that is consistently delicious, widely available, and affordably priced (often below $15 a bottle). They have served my friends, my students, and me so well over the years that they deserve to be recognized, if not memorized.

Here are the Faithful Fifteen producers, followed by some of the wines that make them such an impressive source for value.

Apollonio (Italy)
  (Copertino, Primitivo, Salice Salentino)

Bonny Doon (California)
  (Ca' del Solo Big House White, Red;
    Vin Gris de Cigare; Vin de Glacière)

Chateau Ste. Michelle (Washington State)
  (Chardonnay, Pinot Gris, Riesling, Merlot, Syrah,
    Ice Wine)

Columbia Crest (Washington State)
  (Sémillon-Chardonnay, Chardonnay, Cabernet
    Sauvignon, Merlot, Syrah, Ice Wine)

Concha y Toro (Chile)
  (Casillero del Diablo wines, including the Chardonnay, Sauvignon Blanc,
    Cabernet Sauvignon, Merlot, Carmènere)

Georges Duboeuf (France)
(all types of Beaujolais)

Hess Collection (California)
(Hess Select Chardonnay, Cabernet
Sauvignon)

Paul Jaboulet (France)
(Côtes-du-Rhône Parallèle 45, Crozes-
Hermitage)

Lindemans (Australia)
(Chardonnay Bin 65, Cabernet Sauvignon
Bin 45, Shiraz)

Pepperwood Grove (California)
(Chardonnay, Viognier, Syrah, Merlot)

R.H. Phillips Winery (California)
(Chardonnay, Sauvignon Blanc, Viognier EXP,
Syrah EXP)

Rancho Zabaco (California)
(Zinfandel, Pinot Grigio)

Ravenswood (California)
(Zinfandel, Cabernet Sauvignon)

Rosemount (Australia)
(Chardonnay, Shiraz, Shiraz-Cabernet,
Grenache-Syrah-Mourvedre)

Zardetto (Italy)
(Prosecco)

OUTSMART THE TABLE
In your home, designate a "house"
white, red, and bubbly—and call them
that.

On My Table | **MARIO BATALI** is one of the most influential chefs of our time and the owner of several cutting-edge restaurants, New York's Babbo being the most famous.

Prosecco
  Mionetto

Red Burgundy—Chambolle-Musigny
  Georges Roumier and Ghislaine Barthod—"I love the soft and feminine Burgundies because they go so well with the braised winter food I cook."

Southern Rhône—Châteauneuf-du-Pape (red and white)
  Henri Bonneau, Les Cailloux

White Burgundy—Chablis
  François Raveneau, Moreau, Laroche

Tocai [lively, full-bodied white from the Friuli region of northeastern Italy; not to be confused with Tokay–Pinot Gris from Alsace or Tokaji Aszú from Hungary]
  Schiopetto, Bastianich, Marco Felluga

Primitivo
  A-Mano, Sinfarossa, Felline

Brunello
  Cerbaiona, Col d'Orcia, Barbi—"Special wine for special occasions."

Appreciating Wine

We begin our journey with a few simple principles that will forever improve how you judge a glass of wine. As you read on, you'll realize that the dirty little secret of wine appreciation is that there's just not that much to it. Swirl your wine, breathe deeply, take a taste, and think about what comes to mind. Does it smell like fruit or flowers or spices? Fermented grape juice can evoke everything from apricots to violets—but you have to train your nose to make these associations. Does the wine smell a bit sweet like vanilla? That's evidence of oak. Is there a tingle around the sides or tip of your tongue? Acidity. Is there a puckering dryness on your tongue or inner cheeks? Tannin. Does the wine taste "hot"? Alcohol. Awareness of these and other principles provides a helpful lens through which to assess wine—so that you can then communicate your preferences to wine merchants, servers, and others charged with fulfilling your libational happiness. ■

2 Educate Your Nose

"*How did* strawberries get in the wine?"

When one of my students asked this question as I was describing Pinot Noir, her naïveté generated snatches of snickering in the class. But I thought it was a reasonable question, because to the uninitiated the vocabulary of wine appreciation seems less about grapes and more about the inventory of a fruit stand.

As you embark on your wine journey, be assured that it takes experience and dedication to begin to see what the pros perceive in wine. As when learning French or the piano, you need discipline, concentration, and faith that it will eventually get easier. You have to *want* to detect the subtleties in wine—they won't come to you. The payoff is that even just a little bit of effort will push you light-years ahead of most casual wine drinkers—and turn the daily obligation of eating into a ritual of pleasure and fascination.

Much of the initial difficulty of wine tasting is that we're not used to *thinking* while we smell and taste. When we eat, we're frequently like cows grazing in a pasture, glassy eyed and oblivious to the nuances of what is in our mouths. If we like a steak, we think it's "good" or "delicious"—not that it's "juicy with a funky, charred, minerally character." We're especially unfamiliar with using the nose to make more detailed discriminations—which makes scrutinizing wine that much more difficult, because, as we discuss in the next shortcut, most of taste is in fact smell.

Moreover, we're not accustomed to homing in on specific components in wine—such as distinguishing the grass from the grapefruit in Sauvignon Blanc or the earthiness from the berry aromas in red Burgundy. It's like listening to music: if you're not trained to look for the twang and guttural growl of the bass guitar, you may never notice it. But if someone demonstrates what the bass sounds like by itself, that element becomes infinitely easier to identify when layered into the whole.

Even if we do detect aromas and flavors in wine, we don't necessarily know how to express those sensations. Think about it: there are innumerable ways to describe what you see, hear, and touch—but where is our vocabulary for smell? It usually doesn't venture far beyond "good," "bad," "sweet," or "Who's smoking the Mary Jane?"

Your mission, then, is to construct your own sensory vocabulary for wine. Begin by becoming familiar with the descriptors that experts use. This terminology relates primarily to the aromas and flavors that naturally spring from grape juice after it undergoes fermentation. For example, fermented Cabernet Sauvignon grapes yield wine that is usually aromatic of blackcurrants and plums, while Sauvignon Blanc is often described in terms of lemon and herbs. Wine terminology also describes nongrape essences such as vanilla (from wine's contact with oak barrels), baked bread (from the yeast used in the fermentation process), and leather or mushrooms (from the secondary aromas that develop as certain wines age). To provide a common vocabulary for these kinds of words, one enterprising expert—retired viticulture professor Ann C. Noble—fashioned them into something called the Wine Aroma Wheel. Long a favorite tool of wine-tasting classes, the wheel includes more than a hundred popular descriptors, helping narrow down impressions from the general (like "fruity") to the specific (such as "blackberries," "raspberries," "strawberries").

Winespeak isn't limited to the concrete, of course. Wine is often associated with gender ("an aggressive, muscular Barolo," or "a gentle, perfumed Volnay"), class ("a well-bred Bordeaux," as opposed to a "rustic

Primitivo"), and, of course, plenty of sex ("a lush, full-bodied, hedonistic Meursault"). Such associations are limited only by your imagination; a Chardonnay once reminded me of a "frozen yogurt shop" because, as I later realized, the wine was redolent of the vanilla scent that always filled that store. It is, of course, possible to take wine descriptions a bit too far. And, for your entertainment, I include on page 10 a list of some of the more florid and bizarre terms I have encountered over the years.

As for the classic descriptors, this book will introduce you to dozens of them. But just knowing them is only the beginning. You then need to figure out which of these words make sense to you and educate your nose to recognize those aromas. This is as simple as smelling the real article—a lemon, a jar of blackcurrant preserves, the crushed pepper on your salad—and then looking for those aromas in the wine itself. Become a "student of smells," paying attention to everyday aromas like the fruit you eat, cedar in a closet, or the smell of pavement after it has rained. Doing so, you will more easily isolate the individual components in the wine—like the bass guitar twangs in our music analogy.

Another helpful technique is to smell different wine types side by side, noticing the subtle aromatic differences among, say, a Cabernet Sauvignon, a Pinot Noir, and a Beaujolais. Finally, it's valuable to compare your own impressions against those of the experts. How do the descriptions of seasoned tasters like famed wine critic Robert Parker or the editors of *Wine Spectator* match up with your own? Eventually your own sensory repertoire will take shape—and you'll be able to describe your wine preferences with precision and flair.

CHEAT SHEET

Wine appreciation needn't be stuffy or onerous—but you must be willing to train your nose and develop your own sensory vocabulary.

OUTSMART THE TABLE

• Although the terms are used synonymously by most people, aroma technically refers to the simple, intrinsic smell of a particular grape type, while bouquet is supposed to refer to the more complex smells that develop in wine with years of bottle age. For our purposes, the difference isn't important.

• For more on the Wine Aroma Wheel, visit www.wineserver.ucdavis.edu/Acnoble/waw.html.

Thirty Poetic (and Perplexing) Wine Descriptors

The following are unusual wine descriptions I've heard
over the years—use them at your own risk!

THE GREAT OUTDOORS

Heathery
Meadow flowers
Seaweed
Mown lawn
Burning autumn leaves

INDUSTRIAL

Ash
Lead pencil
Flint
Kerosene
Candle wax
Creosote

EXOTIC

Lychee nuts
Chamomile tea
Nettles
Quince
Lanolin
Bacon fat
Vaucluse truffles

PERPLEXING

Tatsoi
Jangly
Septembral

DOWNRIGHT WRONG

Old running shoes
Wet dog
Cat's pee
Crushed earthworms
Sweat
Beef blood
Dirty hot tub
Waterlogged Buick Riviera
Fungal
Excremental

On My Table | **FRANCIS FORD COPPOLA** is one of America's great filmmakers and the founder of the award-winning Niebaum-Coppola Estate Winery in Napa Valley, California.

Shiraz
Rosemount, Lindemans

Cabernet Sauvignon (and other reds) from Napa
Swanson, Staglin

3 The Three Steps of Wine Appreciation, or Don't Give Short Shrift to the Sniff

If *you* remember anything from this book, know that you should never give short shrift to the sniff. In fact, as we'll soon cover, it is the most important aspect of wine appreciation.

With that in mind, here are the three classic steps that wine tasters use:

1. THE LOOK In a step called "eyeing" the wine, tasters tilt a glass of wine away from them, preferably against a white surface, and take a good look at the wine. Besides the aesthetic pleasure of admiring your wine (such as the twenty-four-karat glow of an Australian Chardonnay or the pitch-black mystery of a Petite Sirah), a wine's appearance can give you an idea of its bottle age. White wine gains color as it ages, often becoming golden and eventually a deep yellow-brown. A red wine sheds color as it evolves, showing a purplish tint in its youth, which turns ruby and finally a faded red-brown hue after several years. Of course, a wine's color also varies with its particular grape type; a Pinot Noir, for example, starts life with a kind of ruby translucence, while Syrah is characteristically darker and opaque.

Although you may feel compelled to consider a wine's "legs"—the streaky droplets wine leaves on a glass—Shortcut 4 will disabuse you of this unnecessary ritual.

2. THE "NOSE" Your olfactory sense is mission control for wine appreciation. While the mouth is a relatively ignorant sensory organ—basically capable of perceiving only things that are sweet, sour, bitter, and salty—your nose is a veritable Geiger counter of sensitivity, able to detect thousands of nuances. So most of our sense of taste is actually smell—which is why Alfalfa of the Little Rascals held his nose before being force-fed castor oil.

"WITHOUT VISUAL CUES FROM THE LABEL AND THE WINE COLOR, YOU WILL BE AMAZED AT HOW MUCH MORE YOU NOTICE IN THE AROMA."

—*Ann C. Noble, professor of viticulture*

To get a good hit of a wine's aromas, you must first aerate the wine—expose it to oxygen—by swirling it in the glass. It's easier to perform this so-called taster's twitch if you swirl the glass with its base resting on a table and when the glass is no more than half full. Then, after swirling the wine, insert your nose well into the glass and take several quick sniffs. This is when you start looking for the whole range of essences mentioned in the previous shortcut—from aromas of fruit and flowers to things like vanilla, earth, and pepper. Tasters refer to the aromas or bouquet of wine as its *nose*, as in "I notice a lot of blackberries on the nose."

3. THE TASTE Let's not kid ourselves here—the smell may be mission control, but the taste is the money shot—the real payoff. As you roll the wine on your tongue, ask yourself if any of the scents echo in its taste. Some will, but remember, it's far easier to smell these nuances than it is to taste them. As the coming chapters explain, you'll also want to assess a wine for its weight or body (light, medium, or heavy), acidity (sharp, moderate, or low), dryness (bone-dry, off-dry, or sweet), and, with red wine, its level of tannin (gum-numbingly high, moderate, or low). As you sit with the wine, you should consider its aftertaste or finish (long or short), balance (harmonious or out of proportion), and complexity (does the wine have a lot to say?). The pros often use the word *palate* to refer to a wine's taste, as in "On the palate, the wine is full-bodied, tannic, and complex."

We'll clarify these concepts ahead, but if you're asking why it's necessary to consider such a laundry list of factors, the answer is, well, it's not. However, if you wish to be able to describe the style of wine *you* really like—so that you can then communicate your preferences to wine servers and other purveyors of vinous pleasure—learning about the basic components of wine is well worth the effort.

CHEAT SHEET

Although proper wine tasting involves three steps, nothing is more important than getting good, deliberate sniffs of the wine.

OUTSMART THE TABLE

- Never judge a wine by the first sip— allow some time for you and the wine to settle down and get acquainted.
- Always hold a glass by its stem, so as not to warm or smudge the bowl.

4 Ignore a Wine's Legs

Legs, also known as *tears*, are the film that collects inside a glass after you swirl your wine. I tell my students to think about how paint looks when it drips down a wall—those are a wine's legs.

Legs are easy to identify, but they aren't easy to interpret. In general, prominent, slow-dripping legs tend to indicate a wine that's of some viscosity and thus more likely to taste fuller bodied. A generation ago, some wine pros declared legs an indication of a wine's quality, and before long, every bell-bottomed barfly was looking to see whether a wine had nice legs.

Although the notion of legs has persisted in the popular imagination, these days you won't hear experts equate legs with quality. At best, a wine with slow-dripping droplets may tip you off to a fuller mouth feel, but there are plenty of exceptions to this rule. You'll learn much more about a wine from actually nosing and tasting it than you will from ogling its droplets.

CHEAT SHEET

Slow-dripping droplets, or legs, can indicate a fuller-bodied wine, but not much else.

OUTSMART THE TABLE

In Spain, a wine's legs are called *lagrimas* (tears); in Germany, they are *Kirchenfenster* (church windows).

On My Table | **ALAN RICHMAN** is one of the world's leading chroniclers of gastronomy and a multiple winner of the James Beard Foundation Award for his contributions to *GQ* magazine.

Sauvignon Blanc from California, New Zealand, France, and South Africa
U.S.: Rochioli. Sancerre: Crochet. New Zealand: Craggy Range. South Africa: Mulderbosch.

Pinot Noir from California
Siduri

Red Burgundy
Lignier, Dujac

Zinfandel
Martinelli, Seghesio

Champagne
Mumm de Cramant Blanc de Blancs

Gewürztraminer
Alsace: Zind Humbrecht. New York: Standing Stone. New Zealand: Lawson's Dry Hills.

Riesling from Germany, California, and Alsace
Germany: Dr. Loosen, Selbach-Oster. California: Smith-Madrone. Alsace: Trimbach, Zind Humbrecht.

5 Dry Wine Is Technically Unsweet, but . . .

CHEAT SHEET

In wine, dry is the opposite of sweet, but dry wines can sometimes seem a bit sweet. This impression of sweetness comes not so much from unfermented (i.e., residual) sugar as from the natural fruitiness that results from the fermentation of intensely ripe grapes, as well as the wine's contact with oak barrels.

ven if you don't know much about wine, you probably order your wine "dry." Somehow, somewhere, ordering "a glass of dry wine" became the politically correct thing to do, even if some people don't know exactly what *dry* means or they normally like sugary beverages like cola and frozen margaritas.

Let's set matters straight: dry is technically the opposite of sweet, so you can think of a dry wine as being unsweet. A truly dry wine occurs when all of the natural sugar in grapes converts to alcohol during fermentation. Sweet wine, in contrast, gets that way because not all of its sugar is allowed to convert to alcohol. The unfermented sugar left in the wine is called *residual sugar* and is the reason dessert wines taste sweet on the tip of your tongue. Wines that are *off-dry*, such as many Rieslings, have only a moderate amount of residual sugar, so they are semisweet but usually dry enough to be enjoyed with a meal.

Where it gets tricky is that many wines that are fermented dry can nevertheless give the impression of sweetness. In fact, many bestselling "dry" wines, from bubbly to Chardonnay to Zinfandel to Shiraz, can seem a bit sweet. This sweet sensation comes not from residual sugar but from the fermentation of extra-ripe grapes. When grapes get intensely ripe—as they often do in warm climates like California and Australia—they can produce wine that gives a sensory impression of sweetness. Vegetables like corn or tomatoes have the same impact: although we don't think of them as sweet per se, at their ripest and most succulent they can seduce the palate with sensations of sweetness. Dry wine can also seem a bit sweet from contact with oak barrels, which imparts a sweet vanilla dimension to wine.

6 Acidity Is a Lemon Squeeze for Food

Miss, *may* I get a plate of lemons?"

If I can only tell you how many times I've heard this while dining out with my friend Adrian. Every chance he gets, he orders lemons with his food. Not just with fish, either. Omelets, tacos, spaghetti—everything he eats gets a hit of lemon.

At first I thought Adrian had some sort of citric obsession—you know, a lemon-colored car, crates of Lemon Pledge in his closet, and posters of ripe lemons in his bedroom.

But as I learned more about wine, I realized that his lemon lust makes perfect sense. A squeeze of lemon is like acidity in wine: it heightens the flavor of food.

Acidity is naturally present in wine and is most noticeable in tart whites like Sauvignon Blanc and light reds like Beaujolais. You know it by the tingle on the edges and tip of your tongue as well as a mouthwatering sensation in the cheeks and back of the throat. Don't confuse acidity with tannin (Shortcut 8), the drying sensation perceptible in big red wines. When describing a wine with noticeable acidity, tasters often use terms like *racy, juicy, tart, tangy,* and *zesty.*

Like everything else in wine, acidity should be in balance. If a wine doesn't have enough acidity, it can taste dull and lifeless— "flabby" in wine parlance. It is also what makes off-dry and dessert wines refreshing, counterbalancing their sweetness and preventing them from tasting syrupy. On the other hand, when a wine has too much acidity, it imparts a sharp, sour, almost salty sensation.

How much acidity a wine has depends on things like its grape type, soil, and climate. Cooler climates, such as France's Chablis region and New Zealand's Marlborough region, tend to produce wines with more pronounced acidity. Winemakers can reduce the acidity in wine by inducing *malolactic fermentation.* That's a

> "FINE WINE IS FOOD FOR THE TABLE; IT'S MEANT TO BE DRUNK AND ENJOYED, NOT ENDLESSLY STUDIED.... REMEMBER, WHAT *YOU* LIKE IS THE MOST IMPORTANT THING. *DE GUSTIBUS NON EST DISPUTANDUM* [THERE'S NO DISPUTING YOUR TASTE]."
>
> —*Jack Stuart, winemaker, Silverado Vineyards*

scary phrase that simply refers to a secondary fermentation that takes place in many wines. When a wine undergoes malolactic fermentation, its sharp malic acids (the same biting acids present in green apples) are converted into lactic acids (the creamy soft acids in milk), making the wine softer and smoother. Now when you hear about a wine's "malo" in winery tasting rooms, you'll know that it's just a chemical reaction that tones down the wine's acidity.

As my lemon-loving friend has demonstrated, however, you don't want to suppress all of a wine's acidity. Not only is tanginess a flavor booster for food, it can actually make certain foods taste better. An acidic wine like Chianti pairs so well with acidic foods like tomato sauces and tangy cheeses because the tart tastes in the wine and the food subdue each other. The net effect for your taste buds is a bit sweet—a pleasing sensation. A wine's tanginess is also useful with creamy sauces, helping to cut through their richness and cleanse your palate. The one pitfall to avoid is pairing acidic wine with sweet food—a combination that clashes on most people's palates—such as having Sauvignon Blanc with birthday cake.

Finally, acidity is the primary reason that a tiny percentage of white wines can actually improve with age, becoming more complex and interesting as the years roll on. Acidity acts the same way that tannin does in red wine, serving as the wine's "structure"—a gradually diminishing preservative that allows an ageable white like a *grand cru* Puligny-Montrachet or a fine German Riesling eventually to scale celestial heights.

CHEAT SHEET

Acidity in wine is your friend, amplifying the flavor of food and giving the wine zest and, in exceptional cases, ageability.

OUTSMART THE TABLE

As we'll cover in Shortcut 84, coldness emphasizes a wine's acidity. That's why serving fine dessert wines ice-cold will bring out their tartness, which is needed to balance their sweetness.

7 Oak Gives Wine Hints of Vanilla and/or Smoke

Is the broccoli buttered?"

Ordering a vegetable like broccoli off a menu is always a gamble. It can come lightly buttered, its crunch softened by a light coating of *beurre blanc*. Or it can be swimming in a buttery lagoon, its very vegetability smothered by a creamy canopy.

So it is with oak and wine. Oak is an add-on winemakers use to enhance a wine's natural fruit, adding a sweet scent and a creamy texture to the wine. Applying it excessively or with the wrong grape type, however, creates a heavy-handed wine that deadens the palate and clashes with food.

So how do you know that oak is in play? Its signature scent is that of vanilla, but it can also smell like butterscotch, caramel, cinnamon, nutmeg, coconut, smoke, or burned toast. Chardonnay from California and Australia is famous for its oakiness, while many of the world's great reds, Cabernet Sauvignon and red Bordeaux, see a lot of time in oak, too. Mature Cabernet Sauvignon and red Bordeaux are often described as redolent of cedarwood, a "cigar box," or, as a wine friend once said, "a sleepless night at the Cohiba factory." Australian Shiraz and Spanish Rioja are sometimes infamous for their heavy contact with strong-scented oak.

"OAK IS THE LAZY WAY TO GET FLAVOR. IT IS TO WINEMAKING WHAT ADVERBS ARE TO WRITING."

—Jay McInerney, novelist and wine writer

Oak adds not only aromas but also flavors that echo these scents, as well as greater viscosity and creaminess. Because tannin naturally occurs in oak wood, contact with oak barrels can also give some reds a bit more tannic impact.

An even easier tip-off to oak is a label mention such as *Oak Aged* or an allusion to barrels, as in *Barrel Fermented, Barrel Aged,* or *Barrel Selection*. These terms describe how a wine gets oaky in the first place. One way is to ferment it in oak barrels, rather than stainless-steel tanks, which, unlike oak, don't add any flavor to the wine. The other source of oakiness is aging in oak barrels *after* fermentation, typically over a period of six months to two years (and sometimes longer), to give a wine more complexity.

The type of oak used determines the impact it makes. New barrels have a much stronger effect than used ones; American oak is considered more aggressive and somewhat less refined than its French counterpart. Another consideration is the degree to which the inside of the barrel has been charred, which gives wine a toasty, smoky character.

Oak barrels don't come cheap. A top-of-the-line barrel from France will set a winery back $600 or more. So if you're wondering how producers of your favorite $10 Chardonnay can afford the expense of oak barrels, the answer is that they can't. They instead resort to the effective but decidedly unromantic use of oak chips, contact with which can oak up thousands of gallons of wine for the price of one precious oak barrel.

CHEAT SHEET

The vanilla, butterscotch, or smoky essence in your wine comes from its contact with oak barrels.

OUTSMART THE TABLE

You've fallen hopelessly into the well of wine geekdom when you start talking about the provenance of the oak wood used with a particular wine. Such oakaphiles will debate the merits of oak from France's Limousin forest versus that from Nevers and Alliers, not to mention looser-grained American and Slovenian oak.

8 Tannin, the Pucker in Your Mouth, Is Red Wine's Natural Preservative

I call it "Château Leep-tohn."

Before I teach about tannin, I boil about a hundred Lipton tea bags in a deep pot, stirring the bags like a witch presiding over her magic cauldron. After it cools, I serve a taste of this massively concentrated tea to my students, telling them it is an old, rare Bordeaux called—what else?—Château Lipton.

As soon as the concoction hits their lips, they know they've been playfully duped. I then ask them to shout out how it feels in their mouths. Inevitably I hear some amalgam of "bitter," "dry," "puckering," and "yuck!" used to describe the sensation of tannin.

I found my tea trick to be the ultimate way to demonstrate tannin—an invisible chemical compound in tea, the skins of walnuts, and the skins, seeds, and stems of grapes. It is noticeable in red wine because when red wine is made, grape skins are fermented with the juice, thereby imparting tannin (and red color) to the wine. White wine isn't allowed to ferment with its skins, so it has only imperceptible levels of tannin.

Because tannin is also present in wood, wine can get some of its tannic character from aging in oak barrels. Certain grape types, Cabernet Sauvignon being the classic example, are known for producing tannic wine, while others, Pinot Noir for example, are often only slightly tannic.

If tannin is bitter, why even suffer it? Its raison d'être is to serve as a naturally diminishing preservative, giving wine what tasters call *structure*, which, along with acidity, is the chief reason some wines improve with age. I tell my students to imagine an ageable, tannic wine as being born with a jacket of bitter tannin. As the wine gets older, it sheds that tight jacket as its tannins slowly precipitate out as sediment, leaving the wine with more complexity and a softer texture. Tannin is also useful for giving a rich wine some oomph—a bit of bite that balances out a wine's ripe fruit flavors and cleanses the tongue of fats and oils during a meal. Without an undercurrent of tannin, certain wines can taste dull or out of balance.

You should ultimately assess all red wines for their tannic impact and decide how much tannin you like. After you take a sip of wine, run your tongue along the roof of your mouth. Does the wine leave any noticeable dryness on your tongue? Does the wine give your tongue a dry but powdery-soft coating, indicative of soft tannins? Or is it very tannic, with a bitter, almost painful numbing dryness on your tongue, cheeks, and gums? In the last case, the proteins and fats in certain foods may help ease the pain. Just as milk softens the astringency of tea, meat and cheese tend to diminish the sensation of tannins in wine; blue-veined cheeses like Roquefort are especially helpful here. Nuts such as walnuts and pecans, which contain tannin themselves, are effective neutralizers, too. A tannic brute might also soften somewhat with an hour of aeration in a large decanter.

CHEAT SHEET

Resulting from a wine's contact with grape skins during fermentation, tannin is the gum-drying bitterness you find in certain red wines.

OUTSMART THE TABLE

It makes sense that tannin often gives you a sense of *leathery* dryness, because tannins are also used in converting cow hides into your favorite pair of leather gloves.

9 A Wine's Alcohol Content Hints at Its Body

Starting *with* our first, regretful realization that "liquor is quicker," we learn to distinguish between the differing alcohol levels of beer, wine, and hard liquor. What we aren't prompted to do, however, is distinguish between the different alcohol levels in wine. Alcohol content—noted in small print on the label—can reveal important things about the wine's weight and taste, not to mention how quickly it will get you trolleyed.

Most wine varies between 10 percent and 14 percent alcohol, with some notable exceptions. This level depends mostly on the ripeness of the grapes at harvest. During fermentation, yeast transforms grape sugar into alcohol, which means that the more sugar the grapes contain, the more alcohol exists in the finished wine. It follows, then, that warmer growing regions like California and Australia, where grapes get ripe and sugary, make wine that's higher in alcohol—sometimes hitting 14 percent or more.

Grapes in cooler climates such as Germany and northern France don't get nearly as ripe—a fact reflected in the generally lower alcohol content of these regions' wines. In difficult vintages, winemakers in cool regions may even resort to *chaptalizing* the wine—adding sugar to the grape juice before fermentation to give the resulting wine an extra 1 or 2 percent alcohol content.

A wine's alcohol content is a good indicator of its body. A wine's body is simply how heavy it feels in your mouth. Wine educators often compare light-bodied wine to skim milk, medium-bodied wine to whole milk, and full-bodied wine to a rich, mouth-filling taste of half-and-half. Connecting the dots, then, a wine that promises 10 percent alcohol should be relatively light on your palate, whereas a 14 percent blockbuster—such as many California Zinfandels—will slosh between your cheeks like a mouthful of chicken soup. When a wine has that much alcohol, it needs to be balanced by a good amount of fruit flavor, or it can leave a coarse, hot, burning sensation on the palate.

CHEAT SHEET

The higher a wine's alcohol percentage, the fuller its body is likely to be.

OUTSMART THE TABLE

- Giving a highly alcoholic red a slight chill will tone down its "hot" taste.
- The low alcohol content of off-dry German Rieslings (8 to 9 percent) and lightly sweet Moscato d'Asti (5 percent) results from the fact that winemakers stop their fermentation early, preventing all the sugar from converting into alcohol; this unfermented or "residual sugar" makes the wine sweet.
- The high alcohol in port and other "fortified" wines (17 to 21 percent) comes from the addition of brandy during production.

10 Assess Every Wine for Balance, Complexity, and Finish

Wine tasters are always looking for a wine's fruit sensations, as well as evidence of oak, tannin, acidity, and alcohol. Awareness of these components can help you identify three hallmarks of great wine: balance, complexity, and finish.

BALANCE A balanced wine has nothing excessive or deficient when judged against other wines of its type. For an oaky Chardonnay to be balanced, its sweet-vanilla essences must be equaled by a sufficient amount of ripe fruit. Similarly, the sweetness in a dessert wine needs to be counteracted by a slash of acidity. Even massively concentrated wines can be balanced if their fruit, acidity, tannin, and alcohol are integrated such that no one element dominates. Tasters use terms like *harmonious* and *symmetry* to describe wines that are well balanced.

COMPLEXITY Even if a wine is balanced, it won't necessarily have complexity. *Complexity* refers to a wine's ability to show a range of pleasing aromas and tastes. Whereas inexpensive, everyday wines are mostly simple, one-dimensional affairs, better wines intrigue you with a panorama of nuances. Some great red Burgundies, for example, can offer a shifting kaleidoscope of berries, violets, rose petals, smoke, earth, and Asian spices—all of which are subtle, beguiling, and apparent only after you sit with a glass for a while. A fine Viognier can treat you to an Edenic bouquet of peaches, apricots, and flowers like honeysuckle and orange blossom. Don't fret if such gradations are not immediately apparent to you; it takes experience and concentration to appreciate them in a complex wine; see Shortcut 2.

FINISH Do certain songs resonate with you after the music has stopped? Like great music, some wine tends to reverberate with you after you've experienced it. This is a wine's finish, which means its aftertaste or, poetically, its lingering farewell. While the sensation of everyday wine may evaporate from your palate in just five to ten seconds, the flavor of better wine can linger for thirty seconds or more and, in exceptional cases, over a minute. A wine's finish is judged not only by its length—how long the taste lingers in your mouth—but also by the balance of components and complexity in the wine's finish. Is the finish too alcoholic (i.e., "hot") or too acidic? Is the aftertaste smooth and velvety, or gritty with bitter tannins? Are you getting just one flavor or a variety of compelling nuances? These are the things tasters look for on the finish.

On My Table | **MORLEY SAFER** is the longtime co-anchor of CBS's venerable *60 Minutes* news magazine and the man behind "The French Paradox," the groundbreaking story that revealed the health benefits of moderate wine consumption.

Red Bordeaux

Lubéron [primarily red and rosé wine from around Provence in southern France]

Chianti

Champagne

More from Morley: "The thing that I feel is most important about buying and drinking good or even indifferent wine is: there are no rules. Do not listen to anyone who claims that you *must* have a particular wine with a particular food. They are talking rubbish. Drink what you enjoy. Period."

11 *Terroir:* A Wine's Sense of "Somewhereness"

With *no precise* definition in English, the French wine concept of *terroir* can be elusive. The best shorthand I've encountered for it comes from wine writer Matt Kramer, who says that certain wines taste like they come from *somewhere*—and thus exhibit a sense of "somewhereness." These wines—often described in connection with French Burgundy—are said to reflect the particular parcel of land from which their grapes come, as well as all of the natural conditions of that land, such as the soil type, angle of slope, and microclimate.

The homespun analogy I offer my students is to tomatoes. I ask them to imagine that if they bit into a tomato grown on Johnson's Farm in my hometown of Martinsville, New Jersey, they would be able to identify a consistently unique taste. The taste of the tomato would express not just the essence of this type of fruit but also the particular plot of land it came from—its *terroir,* or the sum total of the natural conditions, such as Martinsville's clay soil, gentle hills, ample August sunshine, high humidity, and so forth. The personality of this parcel of New Jersey land would be reflected in the taste of the tomato to such an extent that a tomato grown a mile away might taste slightly different.

In Burgundy, winemakers cannot say enough about *terroir.* Their job, they will tell you, is not to imprint their own personality on a wine, such as through the excessive use of oak barrels, but to express the *terroir* of each individual vineyard with as little human tinkering as possible. Respect for *terroir,* it is said, means that a winemaker steps aside and lets nature determine the character of a wine as much as possible. An admirable concept, no doubt, but as critic Robert Parker has stressed, respect for *terroir* does not give winemakers license to shirk their responsibilities. At least as important as *terroir* is a winemaker's energy and ingenuity in making decisions about when to harvest the grapes, how to ferment them, whether to filter the wine, and other matters. *Terroir,* then, can be thought of as one factor in determining a wine's character, especially in rarefied locations like Burgundy, but it shouldn't be given the overriding importance it sometimes is.

CHEAT SHEET

Terroir refers to the unique personality given to a wine by its soil and other natural conditions in which the grapes were grown. It is most often associated with fine wine from Burgundy and Bordeaux but also is used in connection with other regions such as Alsace and Germany.

OUTSMART THE TABLE

Those who consider *terroir* all-important in determining a wine's character are sometimes branded *terroir-ists.*

TALK THE TALK

terroir *tare-WARE*

Related to the concept of *terroir* is the term *goût de terroir,* or "taste of the soil," also often used in connection with wine from Burgundy and other regions. You'll often hear wine enthusiasts invoke it to describe a wine's earthiness, which gets tasters speaking of things like tilled soil, mushrooms, and wet leaves. Mature red wine can sometimes "give up the funk" even more, with hints of aged beef or manure—a gaminess that many connoisseurs quietly appreciate.

Vintage Rearing: Survey Respondents

on Their First Wine Experiences

"I received a few drops of Krug on my lips a few hours after birth and before mother's milk (like all Krugs)."

—Rémi Krug, Champagne Krug

"I was brought up with wine. My parents would give me a little bit of wine with water during our dinner, and I grew up looking at wine as liquid food. As a result, when I went to college and watched my classmates overindulging in beer, scotch, etc., I was surprised."

—Robert Mondavi

"I drink only wine with a meal—not alone as a cocktail or an aperitif. Growing up, wine was always on our table, and as kids we could try it if we wanted to—often with some water or even ginger ale. So to me, wine and the family at table are forever linked."

—Francis Ford Coppola

"My grandfather gave me sips of the Widow [Veuve Clicquot], his favorite Champagne, when I was a child, but, at a more adult level, [what hooked me was] the first night I arrived to live and work in Paris, on a hot night in July 1965, a bottle of Nuits-St.-Georges [red Burgundy]. I have loved that earthy, vibrant taste ever since."

—Serena Sutcliffe, head of Sotheby's wine department

"At age fifteen, I was deep into my first kitchen apprenticeship at a two-star Lyon restaurant called Gerard Nandron. One day on our way back from a catered event, Chef Nandron and I stopped off to visit [famed chef] Paul Bocuse at his restaurant. The man himself poured us a bottle of Château Grillet [rare Viognier from the northern Rhône]. I don't recall the exact vintage, but I do remember it seemed very old to me at the time. . . . Well, I returned to work drunk but was hooked for life on great wine."

—Daniel Boulud, celebrity chef

"When I was ten, during a recorking of our treasure, I tasted Gräfenberg Rieslings from the nineteenth century—vintages my great-grandfather, the founder of Weil, had [enjoyed]."

—Wilhelm Weil, winemaker, Weingut Robert Weil

"Champagne. I loved it since I was a child and drank the remains of glasses from my parents' dining table one evening. They found me standing on my head with a big smile. It still makes my world turn upside down—in a happy way."

—Arthur von Wiesenberger, writer on gastronomy and water master

"Being Tuscan, I was born with wine, and there families don't go to the wine store to buy it; they go directly to the small producers and get great prices and wonderful wine."

—Sirio Maccioni, owner, Le Cirque 2000

Basic Grapes

In this section, we cover eight classic wine types—each named after its grape of origin, because New World (i.e., non-European) wine regions like the United States and Australia tend to label wine by grape type (or *varietal* in wine parlance). We encounter the eager-to-please Chardonnay grape, then the grassy penetration of Sauvignon Blanc, and finally the feathery and floral Riesling, the last being the favorite white in the On My Table survey of wine lovers. We then turn to two marquee reds—Cabernet Sauvignon and its softer sister, Merlot—and finish with three other primary reds: food-fabulous Pinot Noir, peppery, lovable Zinfandel, and spicy, dark, deep Syrah. ■

WHITE

12 Chardonnay: The World's "It" Wine

When I'm around wine experts, it sometimes seems like Chardonnay is the piñata wine: everyone likes to beat on it because of what's sweet inside. My survey respondents weren't shy about taking Chardonnays to task for "all looking alike and making wine drinkers' lives quite boring" (vintner Etienne Hugel) and being "overripe, overoaked, over-everything [such that they] tire the palate and destroy a meal" (vintner Mike Havens).

On the other hand, Chardonnay remains not only the most popular white wine in America but also the *only* white wine for many drinkers. Its vanilla-bean bouquet, creamy texture, and overall inoffensiveness make it as comforting as a spoonful of applesauce—and thus a starting point in our wine journey for many of us. For me, tasting a ripe California Chardonnay is like hearing the first few bars of the Beach Boys' "California Girls": a dreamily sweet ride down the palm-lined boulevard of my past.

This is not a bad thing in and of itself, but the problem, as echoed by my panel of wine experts and an increasing number of consumers, is the raft of mediocre "McChardonnays" flooding the market. Chardonnay is such a popular wine type that wineries can get away with churning out big, blowsy butterballs that taste more like an oak two-by-four than the wide range of delicious fruit flavors this grape can muster. In the warm climate of California, the Chardonnay grape ripens to yield wine of considerable weight and fruitiness, enough to stand up to the vanilla-tinged influence of oak fermentation and aging. In the spirit of America's *Supersize Me* culture of excess, however, many winemakers throttle up the oak influence, sometimes to hide the inferior quality of their fruit

"I BECAME HOOKED ON CALIFORNIA CHARDONNAY WHEN I FIRST VISITED CARMEL IN 1976 FOR FIVE WEEKS. THE ATMOSPHERE OF CARMEL AND THESE NEW WINES FOR MY PALATE OPENED UP A DIFFERENT WORLD FOR ME. [I HAD] STAG'S LEAP, KISTLER, TREFETHEN . . ."

—Greg Norman, pro golfer and winery owner

and almost always to cater to the throngs of consumers who don't know any better.

While disappointing examples still crowd the shelves, quality winemakers are more frequently reining in their use of oak and striving to make Chardonnay with better balance. But even with a lighter touch, California Chardonnay is almost never bashful. Though a range of styles exists, the dominant one is still a showy display of fruit aromas and flavors, often a cascade of peach, pineapple, and mango, though subtler renditions shade toward apples, pears, and lemons. When oak is used judiciously, it imparts a vanilla or smoky dimension that enhances the fruit rather than obscuring it. Better versions of Chardonnay have enough acidity to counterbalance its signature creaminess and perceived sweetness.

Because it's easy to grow and to sell, Chardonnay shows its buttery face in wine regions around the world. The flamboyance of California Chardonnay contrasts with its counterpart in France, where the cool climate and winemaker restraint yield Chardonnay of greater subtlety. The template for France, and indeed the world, is White Burgundy, which is almost always 100 percent Chardonnay; its clean, nutty, appley fruit, crisp acidity, and hint of earthiness stir the souls of collectors everywhere. In contrast, Australian Chardonnays tend to resemble the California style with their one-two punches of tropical fruit and oak, but often at less expense. While the last decade has seen more wineries moderate their use of oak, you'll still see plenty of toasty butterscotch bombs from Down Under. Another good source of inexpensive Chardonnay is Chile, whose style also tends to be ripe and oaky.

A common criticism of Chardonnay is its propensity to overwhelm food. There is truth in this; a monster-style California Chardonnay, for example, can steamroll the delicate flavors of a light fish preparation. At the same time, the legions of Chardonnay drinkers across the land don't seem to be complaining about the wine's

CHEAT SHEET

If any white wine embodies a "big," almost Texan spirit, it is the dominant style of California Chardonnay: big weight, big alcohol, and big hints of tropical fruit and oak.

LABEL DECODER

Chardonnay is a grape.

MARK'S PICKS

Under $20: *U.S.*—Beaulieu Vineyard (BV), Bogle, Chateau Ste. Michelle, Columbia Crest, De Loach, Gallo of Sonoma, Hess Select, La Crema, Meridian, Pepperwood Grove, R.H. Phillips, Zaca Mesa. *Non-U.S.*—Concha y Toro, Kim Crawford, Lindemans, Greg Norman Estates, Oxford Landing, Rosemount, Wynns.

$20 and Over: Au Bon Climat, Beringer Private Reserve, Cakebread, Chalone, Grgich Hills, Kistler, Marcassin, Robert Mondavi, Silverado.

FIT FOR FEASTING

Fattier fish (swordfish, salmon, tuna, etc.); lobster with butter; soft-shell crabs and crab cakes; fried oysters; rich seafood soups (lobster bisque, chowders); pasta with butter and cream sauces (e.g., risotto, fettuccine Alfredo); grilled and smoked preparations; dishes with fruit/tropical sauces (e.g., mango salsa, coconut milk); Thai dishes with peanuts; roast and fried chicken; chicken noodle soup; veal; sautéed sweetbreads; dishes with corn (e.g., corn bread, creamed corn, popcorn); macadamia and other rich nuts; rich dips like guacamole; steak.

outsize personality. Whatever your view, it is always helpful to play to Chardonnay's butter, weight, and hint of sweetness. If you're going to have fish, opt for fattier types in heavier sauces, like salmon with lime butter or aïoli. Think rich: creamy chowders, fried foods, guacamole, lobster with butter, sweetbreads, shrimp and grits. Heavier styles of Chardonnay even have the requisite bulk to stand up to red meat, so if you're going to drink white with a cabal of carnivores, Chardonnay couldn't be a better choice. The off-dry fruitiness in many Chardonnays also pairs well with tropical sauces such as mango salsa and coconut milk. And with sweet yellow corn, who needs butter when you have a creamy Chardonnay? On second thought, add an extra dollop.

On My Table | **GREG NORMAN**, the golf champion known to millions as the "Great White Shark," also applies his golden touch to winemaking through his Australia-based Greg Norman Estates portfolio.

Chardonnay
Kistler, Grgich Hills, Lewis, Greg Norman Estates [Australia]

Shiraz
Greg Norman Estates—"Smoothness and deep blueberry flavor."

Cabernet Sauvignon
Opus One, Devil's Lair [Australia]

13 Sauvignon Blanc: Grapefruity
Tart and Freshly Mown

Mown.

This is actually a word, I discovered, when I first started studying the grape Sauvignon Blanc. Almost every book I read and seminar I attended described Sauvignon Blanc as redolent of freshly mown grass. Silly as it sounded then, I, too, use this descriptor when I teach this grape because more often than not it's accurate. Likened to cut grass, bell peppers, asparagus tips, or even mint, Sauvignon Blanc usually has a green herbaceousness that gives it one of the most instantly recognizable aromas in wine.

This is not to say that Sauvignon Blanc always has an aggressively grassy smell. In fact, a common criticism among the wine-impassioned is that many American Sauvignon Blancs are essentially "defanged," stripped of their natural grassiness and acidity to make them more marketable to Chardonnay-obsessed Americans. It is true that in the warmer climes of California you tend to find rounder styles of Sauvignon Blanc, especially when winemakers employ softening techniques like oak fermentation or aging or malolactic fermentation (see Shortcut 6). The result is a medium-bodied white with fruity aromas such as melon and peach and a noticeable but restrained degree of grassiness and acidity. White Bordeaux, discussed in Shortcut 21, offers another typically tamer version of Sauvignon Blanc, in part because the grape is blended with the rounder, richer grape Sémillon.

To see Sauvignon Blanc play its rightful role as the sensory penetrator, look no farther than France's Loire Valley for Sancerre, a style of Sauvignon Blanc so popular that it merits its own shortcut (24). You'll also find grassy, vibrant styles of Sauvignon Blanc from Chile, South Africa, and New Zealand—the last being so exciting that we focus on it in Shortcut 48.

It's difficult to visit a wine shop without also seeing Fumé Blanc, a designation that sometimes makes my students wonder if it means Sauvignon Blanc with smoky aromas. Not so; it actually is just a synonym for Sauvignon Blanc, dreamed up in the 1960s by Robert Mondavi when his Sauvignon Blanc sales

CHEAT SHEET

A liberatingly lighter and less expensive alternative to Chardonnay, Sauvignon Blanc is citrusy and herbal. American Sauvignon Blanc is often tamer than versions from France (notably Sancerre and Pouilly-Fumé) and New Zealand.

LABEL DECODER

Sauvignon Blanc is a grape.

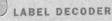

OUTSMART THE TABLE

I've heard the English speak of Sauvignon Blanc as having "a hint of gooseberries and tomato (pronounced *tow-MAH-tow*) leaves." Use of this description may bring bodily harm in certain circles.

TALK THE TALK

Sauvignon Blanc   *Soe-veen-yohn Blahnk*

MARK'S PICKS

U.S.: Benziger, Brander, Château Potelle, Duckhorn, Frog's Leap, Geyser Peak, Hogue, Honig, Kenwood, Kunde, Matanzas Creek, Robert Mondavi, R.H. Phillips, Raymond, St. Supéry, Voss, Wente.

Chile: Casa Lapostolle, Concha y Toro.

FIT FOR FEASTING

Great versatility, especially with fish and white meat of all kinds; herbed sauces or crusts (e.g., saffron, tarragon, dill); citrus sauces; yogurt and other tangy sauces; pesto; tomato dishes (tomato and mozzarella salad, gazpacho, tomato sauces); sushi; fried calamari; green veggies (e.g., bell peppers, peas); "problem" veggies such as artichokes and asparagus; goat cheese and other tangy cheeses; softer cheeses like Brie and Camembert.

needed a boost. Always the marketing maven, he combined the tail ends of both Pouilly-Fumé, a Loire region producing Sauvignon Blanc, and Sauvignon Blanc. Sales of the tonier-sounding Fumé Blanc rocketed, and this alternative name for Sauvignon Blanc was soon appropriated by a host of other wineries.

Forever in the shadow of prom-king Chardonnay, Sauvignon Blanc is often overlooked in restaurants and shops—which makes it an excellent value. And it is difficult to find a better wine for seafood, as Sauvignon Blanc's citric snap provides a cleansing dash to the fattiest of fishes. The wine's food friendliness and appetite-stoking crispness also qualify it as one of the best all-around matches for hors d'oeuvres at a cocktail party. And don't forget to take it along on picnics, as its lemony zinginess makes it a dry, grassified lemonade for adults.

14 Riesling: Tragically Neglected Paragon of Feathery Finesse

Ask most people about Riesling and you're likely to get a yawn or a "yecchh." Flashbacks of Blue Nun hangovers, cryptic labels, and the misperception of Riesling as solely a sweet, heavy wine are enough to send many wine drinkers on a one-way trip back to the familiar terrain of Planet Chardonnay. But invoke Riesling with wine pros, and they'll start drooling like hounds outside a butcher shop. This is because experts have had the opportunity to learn that Rieslings are incredibly aromatic, magically food friendly, and, at their best, light as a feather.

First you must disabuse yourself of the notion that fine Riesling has anything to do with the oceans of cloyingly sweet jug wine from Germany. This is not to say that all Rieslings are now dead-dry. Some are, and others are quite sweet, but you'll often encounter Riesling that's off-dry—that is, lightly sweet. This is problematic, because most people have gotten so accustomed to a dry white wine that they've never allowed themselves the opportunity to see how delightful a wine with a little sweetness can be. What makes German Riesling special is that it isn't sugary sweet like a cheap white Zinfandel or a raspberry wine cooler. Instead, Germany's cool-climate location—about as far north as Newfoundland, Canada—gives it a swath of springy acidity that balances out its dulcet tones. Like a fountain spray on a hot summer day, Riesling's acidity is its revitalizing counterbalance.

To overcome Riesling resistance, do what I ask my students to do: refocus your taste buds. When you see a glass of Riesling, don't expect the usual dry taste you'd get in a similar-looking Chardonnay or Pinot Grigio. *Instead, visualize lemonade.* That's right—imagine that your glass of Riesling will have some of the flavor components of a glass of deliciously tart lemonade: a bit sweet, but also light and refreshingly crisp. (No, Riesling won't taste like lemonade, but it can have that simultaneously sweet

"NOTHING MATCHES RIESLINGS FOR THEIR WONDERFUL ABILITY TO PAIR WITH A MYRIAD OF FOODS."

—*Charlie Trotter, celebrity chef*

and tangy quality that's so refreshing.) Once you've recalibrated your expectations this way, it's easier to appreciate how Rieslings can balance a little sweetness with pure, clean, crispness.

Not all Riesling is created equal, or equally sweet. In fact the distinction between sweetness and ripeness confounds many would-be Riesling lovers. Except for dessert-style examples, most German Riesling isn't sweet in the sense that it has a lot of residual sugar—that is, sugar left in the wine after fermentation stops, as in sugary white Zinfandel. Rather, German Riesling can give the *impression* of sweetness when made from well-ripened Riesling grapes. So the slight sweetness you'll often encounter in German Riesling isn't due to a large dose of unfermented sugar but to the natural fruitiness that results from ripe grapes.

German wine authorities are so focused on ripeness that they classify the best Rieslings according to the ripeness of their grapes at harvest. This ripeness designation often, but not always, correlates to the level of sweetness and body in the bottled Riesling. *Kabinett* signifies normally ripe grapes, while *Spätlese* indicates riper grapes and *Auslese* even riper still. Accordingly, Kabinetts are typically light to medium bodied, usually with little or no sweetness, while Spätleses are a bit richer and more expensive, with some sweetness. Ausleses are the priciest and often rich and sweet enough to be served with dessert. Even riper styles of Riesling exist—Beerenauslese, Trockenbeerenauslese, and Eiswein—which are some of the world's most delectable and expensive dessert wines.

Unlike a typical Chardonnay, German Rieslings are rarely fermented or aged in oak barrels, so there are no oak-wrought vanilla essences to compete with the wine's natural fruitiness. Instead you get the Riesling grape in all of its bare-chested glory, with a floral nose and delicate flavors of apples, honeysuckle, or peaches. And never forget: bringing up the rear should be a scintillating shiver of acidity that makes your mouth water.

Being so unloved and therefore relatively low in demand, German Rieslings are generally very affordable, with a slew of excellent bottles to be had in the $10-to-$20 range. Don't be put off by the plethora of strangely named wineries, many of which sound like some crazy Teutonic version of *ER* because of the inexplicable number of them named after doctors, such as Dr. Loosen and Dr. Thanisch. Even if they aren't licensed to carry stethoscopes, many German producers deserve the doctor title just for their ability to consistently make bewitchingly flavorful yet light wine.

Riesling's acidity allows it to accomplish something few whites can do: improve with age. While most Rieslings are made to be drunk within five years of release, some bottles are able to improve for decades, taking on nuances of butter, honey, or even kerosene (the last being surprisingly appealing). Acidity also makes Riesling a chef's dream, ready to gently flatter a seemingly endless range of lighter dishes, making it arguably the most versatile white wine with food. As covered in Shortcut 69, a well-chilled, off-dry (Spätlese) bottle of Riesling will even let you scale the food-and-wine equivalent of Mount Everest—spicy ethnic food—taming exotic fires be they satay, samosa, or spareribs.

While Germany rules the roost for Riesling, other countries have also had success with this varietal. Best known and beloved are the Rieslings from Alsace, France, which tend to be bone-dry with more weight and alcohol than their German counterparts (see Shortcut 25). Austria is also a favorite destination for Riesling, achieving a similarly dry-and-weighty type of Riesling with plenty of zingy acidity. Despite its reputation for Chardonnay butter bombs, Australia is also a notable source for Rieslings, especially the tropical-fruit-scented versions from the country's Clare Valley (try Annie's Lane and Pike's). America has also successfully cultivated the grape, but it remains more a novelty than the raison d'être for most stateside wineries.

TALK THE TALK

Riesling	*REES-ling*
Kabinett	*Kab-ee-NET*
Spätlese	*SCHPATE-lay-seh*
Auslese	*OUSE-lay-seh*
Beerenauslese	*BEER-en-OUSE-lay-seh*
Trockenbeerenauslese	
	TROH-ken-BEER-en-OUSE-lay-seh
Eiswein	*ICE-vine*

MARK'S PICKS

Germany

Gunderloch	*GOON-deh-lohkh*
Fritz Haag	*Hahk*
Dr. Loosen	*LOW-zen*
J. J. Prüm	*Proom*
Selbach-Oster	*Zell-bok-Oh-stir*
J. & H. A. Strub	*Stroob*
Dr. Thanisch	*TAH-nish*
Robert Weil	*Viyl*

U.S.: Bonny Doon (Pacific Rim Riesling), Chateau Ste. Michelle (Johannisberg Riesling), Columbia Winery (Cellarmaster's Reserve), Hogue.

FIT FOR FEASTING

Ideal as an aperitif, with hors d'oeuvres, or with a universe of lighter food types, especially spicy Indian/Asian food; chutneys and other spicy-sweet relishes; dishes with fruit sauces (e.g., duck à l'orange); seafood of all kinds; pork dishes; and deep-fried foods (e.g., tempura). Fully sweet Rieslings should be served at the end of the meal.

On My Table | **WILHELM WEIL represents the fourth generation of the family that founded Weingut Robert Weil of Rheingau, Germany, one of the world's great estates.**

Red Bordeaux
Cos d'Estournel, Latour, Margaux, Palmer, Tertre-Rôteboeuf

Red Burgundy
Comte Georges de Vogüé, Leroy, Armand Rousseau

White Burgundy
Marc Colin, J-F Coche-Dury, Comtes Lafon, Leflaive

Riesling
The top producers from the great Danube, Rhine, and Moselle Rivers

Sauvignon Blanc from Austria and New Zealand
"The pure smell and fruity taste—like a drug."

Cabernet Sauvignon from California
Ridge

RED

_____

15 Cabernet Sauvignon: Scaling the Heights with Blackcurrants and Tannin

I f *there's* one descriptor I reflexively associate with Cabernet Sauvignon, it's blackcurrants—so much so that in my classes I pass around a big jar of blackcurrant jam to sniff so my students never forget the connection. Beyond blackcurrants, you may detect other dark fruits like plums or black cherries, as well as spices like pepper and cinnamon, and chocolate or coffee. The intensity of the Cabernet grape suits it for oak barrels, which give the wine hints of vanilla and smoke and often a cedary, cigar box character as it matures. On your palate Cabernet is lush and full-bodied, often accompanied by a puckery tug of tannin.

Cabernet Sauvignon is considered the greatest red grape of them all. It is what put California wine on the map, keeps red Bordeaux the envy of the world, and often puts the "super" in many Italian Super Tuscans. The manifestation of Cabernet most of us know, however, is a far simpler affair. Your average $15 California Cabernet is fashioned to be Merlot's doppelgänger—with gobs of dark fruit, sweet oak, and soft tannins. While there's no crime in buying into the immediate gratification of this style, it often lacks the nuance and personality that finer examples of Cabernet can deliver, such as those beguiling hints of chocolate or crème de cassis or mint that wash over your palate as you sit with a glass. You typically have to pay over $20 and often much more to find Cabernet of this breed.

On the subject of ageabilty, Cabernet has a better track record for aging than any other grape. While simpler versions of New World Cabernet are ready out of the gate, better ones often need a few years of bottle age and can improve for at least another decade or two. In the best years, superior examples of red Bordeaux are even more ageable, achieving their peak

CHEAT SHEET

Cabernet Sauvignon is dry and full bodied, with notes of black fruits like blackcurrants and plums and oak-derived hints of vanilla or cigar box. Basic versions offer sweet, plump, uncomplicated fruit and soft tannins, while the best premium examples are densely concentrated and spectacularly complex, with enough tannin to improve for decades.

LABEL DECODER

Cabernet Sauvignon is a grape.

OUTSMART THE TABLE

Much has been made of "cult wine"— that is, wine whose production is so small and quality so high that it has achieved a cultlike following of connoisseurs. The term often refers specifically to a handful of California Cabernets that skyrocketed to fame in the last two decades and can fetch up to $1,000 or more per bottle on the auction block. Typically included in this elite club is Araujo (*Ah-RAH-ho*), Bryant Family, Colgin, Dalla Valle, Grace Family, Harlan Estate, and Screaming Eagle.

several decades down the line and in exceptional cases emerging from a century of slumber with surprising flavor and grace.

Cabernet's vast popularity means you'll have a panoply of options in wine shops in the $10-to-$20 range. Chile and Washington State offer particularly good values. Premium Cabernet starts at about $20 and can command well over $100 per bottle. You'll notice that the labels of the best Cabernets boast of a "mountain" in their name—as in Dunn's Howell Mountain, Pride Mountain, Mount Veeder—because mountain grapes tend to be the most flavorful, producing rich, intensely concentrated, tooth-staining wine.

Given its grandeur, you might think Cabernet would be an easy partner for food. Yet this often isn't the case, because Cabernet's powerful flavors can bludgeon the flavor out of lighter preparations like fish and pasta dishes. But if you're a meat eater, a bottle of Cabernet will push all the right buttons. Not only do robust meats such as a porterhouse steak or lamb stew match Cabernet's brawny body, but the proteins and fat in meat subdue Cabernet's tannic bitterness, making the wine taste smoother and fruitier. Proteins and fat are also the reason dry cheeses can soften up an edgy Cabernet, doubly so for the super-stinky charms of blue-veined counterparts. Dishes with peppercorns are also a good match; my stomach growls with desire as I think of how a pepper steak heightens the flavor of a young, bold Cabernet. Some people also find a ripe, generous version of Cabernet a luscious partner for chocolate, this normally hard-to-pair sweet treat seduced by Cabernet's sweet-seeming fruit and spicy oak. Finally, while the big names in Cabernet are often served with rich fine cuisine, don't overlook the opportunity to pair a simple, flavor-packed bottle of Cabernet with barbecue fare like hamburgers and ribs.

MARK'S PICKS

Under $20: *California*—Carmenet, Coppola Black Label Claret, Estancia, Gallo of Sonoma, Hess Select, Kendall-Jackson, J. Lohr, Meridian, Ravenswood, Sterling, St. Francis. *Washington*—Chateau Ste. Michelle, Columbia Crest, Hogue. *Chile*—Caliterra, Casa Lapostolle, Concha y Toro, Haras de Pirque, Los Vascos, Santa Rita "120," Miguel Torres Santa Digna. *Australia*—Wolf Blass, d'Arenberg High Trellis, Lindemans Bin 45, Greg Norman Estates, Rosemount.

$20 and Over: Beaulieu Vineyard (BV), Beringer Knights Valley, Cain, Chateau Montelena, Diamond Creek, Dominus, Dunn, Heitz, Hess Collection, Robert Mondavi, Mount Veeder, Niebaum-Coppola Rubicon, Joseph Phelps, Pine Ridge, Pride Mountain, Ridge, Shafer, Staglin, Stag's Leap Wine Cellars.

FIT FOR FEASTING

Heavier meats (steak, lamb, game, short ribs, sausages); peppercorn sauces (steak au poivre); walnuts, pecans, and other nuts; rich sauces; firm, dry cheeses (Dry Jack, Manchego, Parmigiano-Reggiano, Cheddar, etc.); Maytag Blue and other blue-veined cheeses; chocolate.

16 Merlot: Cabernet's Softer Sister

can't say I was surprised the first time I laid eyes on a bottle of Marilyn Merlot at my local liquor store. It was only a matter of time before someone linked a wine of broad appeal with America's most appealing broad.

Like the starlet, a bottle of good Merlot is generally soft, sensuous, and uncomplicated—offering the ripe, jammy fullness of a fine Cabernet Sauvignon without its complexity or tannic backbite. It is the wine equivalent of Monroe's sultry, dulcet voice singing "Happy birthday, Mr. President"—not intellectually engaging but a delight nonetheless.

Wine drinkers across America apparently agree, as Merlot continues to be *the* reach-for red for most casual wine drinkers, the red equivalent of the omnipresent "glass of Chardonnay." So popular is Merlot that some producers have rushed to cash in on its fame, flooding the market with watery or downright bitter wines, many as soothing and sensuous as a sumo wrestler with a blond wig and beauty mark. If you choose carefully, however, you at least can find affordable bottles of Merlot fulfilling the Hippocratic oath of "doing no harm" with broad swaths of black fruit and a soft, round texture. Many pros, however, fault inexpensive Merlots for their one-dimensional personality.

If you're willing to pay for it, Merlot can slip into something more intriguing. North of about $25, the finest renditions of Merlot open the curtain on more hedonism than a scene from *Caligula*. We're talking deep flavors of concentrated, mega-ripe black fruit (plums, blackcurrants, blueberries) mingled with layers of tobacco, chocolate, cinnamon, or cloves. The sensation is succulent, ripe, with lots of velvet in the enduring aftertaste. Tannins are usually soft, but some of these finer bottles have some astringency. Overall, for Americans craving flamboyantly fruity tastes without too much bitterness, upscale Merlot is

CHEAT SHEET

Often called "Cabernet without the pain," Merlot is medium to full bodied, redolent of black fruit, oak, and chocolate, rounded out by softer tannins than Cabernet Sauvignon. Its commercial success has led to a myriad of dull, flavorless bottles in the lower price range, so choose carefully.

LABEL DECODER

Merlot is a grape.

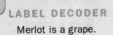 OUTSMART THE TABLE

- At its best, Merlot is no joke: Pomerol's Château Pétrus, one of the world's most expensive wines, is virtually 100 percent Merlot.
- Value-minded Merlot junkies tend also to love Carmenère (Car-men-air), a grape variety popular in Bordeaux long ago and now the pride of Chile. Expect a dark, plummy, smooth affair, often for as little as $10 to $15, especially if you can locate Concha y Toro, Viña Carmen, or Santa Ema—all from Chile.

nirvana. Others find it too luscious for its own good, like a warm comforter you've spent too long under.

Merlot may be an American passion, but it is hardly an American grape. The most widely planted grape in France's Bordeaux region, it is primarily a blending grape used to round out Cabernet Sauvignon's sharp corners—an essential ingredient in most of the famous red Bordeaux you hear about. In Bordeaux's Pomerol and St.-Emilion districts, however, it is often the dominant grape, and there it makes wine of greater subtlety and earthiness than its American equivalent—but no less hedonistic once you appreciate its understated grace. Shortcut 30 reveals more about wine from these areas.

You'll have no trouble finding Merlot at your local shop, but beware the bargain bin, which is a minefield of uninspired industrial Merlots. On the lower end, the best bang for your buck often emanates from the fertile soils of Washington State, Australia, and Chile.

With its flavor profile so similar to that of Cabernet Sauvignon, Merlot will flatter the hearty, meaty foods that work so well with Cabernet. Steak, rack of lamb, game meats, hamburgers, and sausages are perfect partners— even better if the meat is heavily charred, as the bold fruit and oak intensity of Merlot can handle deep flavors from flame broiling.

Given its relatively soft tannins, the vast majority of Merlot is made to drink immediately. In a good year, however, the finest examples can improve for fifteen years or longer.

MARK'S PICKS

Under $20: *California*—Estancia, Gallo of Sonoma, Markham, Meridian, Pepperwood Grove.
Washington—Chateau Ste. Michelle, Columbia Crest, Hogue.
Chile—Casa Lapostolle, Chateau Los Boldos, Concha y Toro, Viña Carmen.
Australia—Marquis Philips, Greg Norman Estates Cabernet-Merlot blend, Rosemount.

$20 and Over: *California*—Beringer Howell Mountain, Duckhorn, Havens, Luna, Joseph Phelps, Pride Mountain, Robert Sinskey, Swanson.
Washington—L'Ecole No. 41, Leonetti, Northstar, Seven Hills, Walla Walla Vintners, Woodward Canyon.

FIT FOR FEASTING

By itself as a soft sipping wine, or with red meat such as steak, rack of lamb, game meats, hamburgers, and sausages; flame-broiled fare; roasts of all kinds; substantial pasta dishes; veal; hearty casseroles; goose pâté and rich terrines; rich sauces; cranberry and other ripe berry sauces; hard, dry cheeses; blue-veined cheeses.

17 Pinot Noir: A Juicy Berry Kiss

If the god Dionysus bestowed on me a secret laboratory in which to build the perfect wine, I would sit there, pushing buttons and turning dials, until a wine of this profile emerged:

- Beautifully aromatic, with essences of berry fruits, flowers, and smoke
- Silky texture, long finish, and an absence of bitter tannin
- Light and crisp enough to pair with a universe of foods and please fans of both red and white wine

My dream wine is Pinot Noir, or actually Pinot Noir at its best. The problem is that when this wine doesn't rise to the level of dreaminess, it can send you to the depths of frustration. In fact, winemakers often consider it a "headache wine," its fragile grape requiring labor-intensive winemaking techniques and a relatively cool climate. What this means is that you'll often pay more for Pinot Noir than other varietals, sometimes with disappointing consequences.

To foster the grape's potential, better Pinot Noir producers in the United States forgo the relative warmth of Napa Valley for the cooler climes of California's Sonoma Coast, Russian River Valley, Carneros (straddling Napa and Sonoma), and certain areas of Santa Barbara, as well as Oregon's Willamette Valley. The result, while varying somewhat with the specific region, producer, and year, is often a fruity, strawberry- or cherry-inflected scent, framed by tangy acidity and a silky texture. Often called a "feminine wine" because of its delicacy, Pinot Noir has a strawberry-and-flowers perfume, accompanied by a light to medium body, low tannin, and a shimmering ruby translucence that makes it one of the most fetching wines in a glass. Some versions show a bit more muscle, with more pronounced tannins and a black plum and black cherry character. Although it is a dry wine, Pinot Noir from the New World may give a slight impression of sweetness, derived from the ripeness of the grape and from oak aging.

American Pinot Noir differs from red Burgundy, Pinot Noir's universal benchmark from its historic homeland. As described

"I MAKE CABERNET BUT DRINK PINOT NOIR."

—Jack Stuart, winemaker, Silverado Vineyards

in Shortcut 32, red Burgundy is a more restrained manifestation of the grape, with less pronounced ripe berry aromas and more of the characteristic tilled-soil earthiness the French call *goût de terroir* (see Shortcut 11). More ageworthy than American Pinot Noir, red Burgundy after a few years is more likely to carry scents of mushrooms, leather, incense, savory spice, and sometimes even a funky barnyard smell. Red Burgundy is also fiendishly inconsistent, far more so than American Pinot Noir, such that the same village in the same year can be home to one wine that is sublime and another that is barely fit for a saucepan. Producers count for a lot in Burgundy, and knowing the good ones, like those mentioned in Shortcut 35, can help navigate this frustrating fog.

What it lacks in complexity and grandeur American Pinot Noir makes up in reliability. For those willing to pay at least $20, it is relatively easy to find the juicy berry kiss that is good Pinot Noir, but pickings are slim below $20. Three delightful exceptions to remember are Gallo of Sonoma, Meridian, and Saintsbury's Garnet bottling. With its small production runs, Oregon Pinot Noir is harder to get, but the extra effort is worth it for its more Burgundian, less flamboyant style. Value seekers should locate Rex Hills' Kings Ridge, a gem at about $20.

While the finest red Burgundies and a few American Pinot Noirs have enough muscle to improve for ten years or more, most Pinot Noirs are best out of the gate and start to fade after five years or so. With its mouthwatering acidity, lighter body, and ripe fruit, Pinot Noir is a front-runner for the title of world's best wine for food. It deftly straddles the foods associated with both red and white wine, as flattering with heavier fish like grilled salmon as it is with pork, chicken, or duck. In fact, if Pinot Noir were on death row, roast chicken would be its final meal, so perfectly does the cherry smokiness of the wine highlight a crisp and juicy bird. Mushrooms, with their earthy, meaty character, are also a famous match. Richer Pinot Noirs can handle roasts, stews, and the funky perfume of truffles.

CHEAT SHEET

An ideal wine for food, Pinot Noir is usually light to medium bodied, with bright berry fruit flavors, perhaps some smoke, mouthwatering acidity, and a smooth, sometimes satiny, texture.

LABEL DECODER

Pinot Noir is a grape.

TALK THE TALK

Pinot Noir   *Pee-noh N'ware*

MARK'S PICKS

California: Au Bon Climat, David Bruce, Buena Vista, Calera, Chalone, De Loach, Gallo of Sonoma, Meridian, Robert Mondavi, Ramsay, Saintsbury Garnet and Carneros, Sanford, Steele, Villa Mt. Eden.

Oregon: Adelsheim, Archery Summit, Domaine Drouhin, Elk Cove, King Estate, Panther Creek, Ponzi, Rex Hill.

FIT FOR FEASTING

Incredibly versatile, including poultry of all kinds, notably roast chicken, turkey, and duck; robust fish such as salmon, swordfish, and tuna; veal; pork; bacon and other smoky foods; grilled fare; mushroom dishes; tomato-based sauces. Richer styles match well with truffles and roasts, stews, and game; goat cheese and other tangy cheeses; soft cheeses such as Brie.

18 Zinfandel: The Great American Tooth Stainer

> "THE ALL-AMERICAN GRAPE, AND IT TASTES LIKE IT, TOO.... THIS IS ROCK AND ROLL IN A GLASS, LOUD AND UNSUBTLE, LIKE BLACKBERRY JUICE WITH A BIG ALCOHOLIC KICK. PERFECT WITH FRIED CHICKEN. THIS IS SOMETHING THEY CAN'T DO IN EUROPE. DRINK IT YOUNG...."
>
> —*Jay McInerney, novelist and wine writer*

I have a public service request of you.

Find some people who drink only white Zinfandel—it shouldn't be difficult—and bestow on them a bottle of good Zinfandel, the red stuff, the real McCoy.

Being used to pink wine, they may not take to Zinfandel's potent personality at first. But showing them the real deal is an investment in their cultural enlightenment, like offering someone who's never left Paris, Texas, an airplane ticket to the true City of Light.

The difference is that Zinfandel is fully fermented with its grape skins, unlike white Zinfandel, whose skins are pulled out before they can make the wine red and rich (see Shortcut 20). While real Zinfandel can vary from relatively light to almost portlike, its dominant style is a full-throttle, heady swirl of ripe blackberries and raspberries and even prunes or dates, along with hints of pepper, spice, smoke, and chocolate. Tasters also speak of Zinfandel as "brambly," which refers to bramble fruits like blackberries and raspberries but always makes me think of the smoky, leaf-pile aromas of autumn.

"No Wimpy Wines," reads the motto of Zinfandel favorite Ravenswood Winery, an ethos executed faithfully by the varietal's mouth-filling heft and massive alcohol, the latter sometimes topping a room-spinning 15 percent. While you may notice some tannin, Zinfandel usually has less astringency than fellow heavyweight Cabernet Sauvignon. Overall it offers a lovable, jammy excursion—built for immediate gratification. Is it any wonder that Zinfandel has its own fan clubs and bumper stickers and acronyms—not the least of which is Château Potelle's "VGS," short for "Very Good . . ." (you get the picture).

Such American-style exuberance suits Zinfandel's status as the one "Great American Wine." To be sure, Zinfandel didn't originate in the United States as some folks once thought—DNA testing traced its origins to Croatia and also revealed that it is the same grape as Italian Primitivo (see Shortcut 55). But with a few exceptions, America is the only country to cultivate the grape and label it Zinfandel. In fact, the grape has been in America since the mid-1880s, which is good news for wine drinkers, because it means that finer examples often come from ancient vines, a fact you'll see trumpeted on labels as *Old Vines*. Although it has no legal meaning, *Old Vines* generally refers to vines that have been in existence for several decades, often for forty years or more, though definitions vary. While these gnarled beasts may seem inhospitable to making good wine, their low yields produce concentrated fruit, which in turn makes intensely flavorful wine.

Zinfandel is widely available in stores, but as with Merlot, there are plenty of disappointments on the lower end. To get the whopping power and complexity this grape can muster, you usually have to throw down at least $20. Your dinero will be well spent on one of the many offerings from Ridge Vineyards, widely considered the benchmark for Zinfandel.

Regarding Zinfandel and food, my advice is to grab a calendar and circle July 4, because there isn't a better wine for a meat-intensive barbecue, especially if you're looking to buy American on this holiday. The combination of charcoal-grilled meats with the smoky, peppery quality of Zinfandel will bring pyrotechnics of the gastronomic sort. Hot coals, of course, are not needed to enjoy Zinfandel—any preparation of steak, roast beef, or lamb will flatter the wine, as will lighter meats like veal chops, pork roast, roast duck, and Thanksgiving turkey. The spiciness and good acidity in Zinfandel also make it an enticing partner for pizza or spaghetti and meatballs.

CHEAT SHEET

A burly, exuberant, quintessentially American wine, Zinfandel is immediately likable for its flush of berry fruit, surge of pepper, and moderate tannins.

LABEL DECODER

Zinfandel is a grape.

OUTSMART THE TABLE

- Pros invoke the three Rs when citing Zinfandel's best producers: Ridge, Ravenswood, and Rosenblum. A fourth R, Rancho Zabaco, represents one of the best values in Zinfandel.
- Those craving an intensely brawny style of Zinfandel (or Syrah) should keep a weather eye for bottles from Amador County, a region nestled in California's Sierra Foothills, east of Sacramento. Amador wineries like Renwood, Monteviña, and Sobon turn out full-throttle, kneepads-needed Zin monstrosities.

MARK'S PICKS

Under $20: Rabbit Ridge, Rancho Zabaco Dancing Bull, Ravenswood's Vintners Blend, Seghesio Sonoma County.

$20 and Over: Château Potelle, Cline Cellars, De Loach, Gallo of Sonoma, Martinelli, Ravenswood, Ridge, Rosenblum, St. Francis, Steele, Storybook Mountain, Joseph Swan, Turley Cellars, Whitehall Lane.

FIT FOR FEASTING

Hearty red meat dishes, such as steak, lamb chops, grilled sausages, and stews; lighter meats like veal chops, pork roast, fried chicken, roast duck, and Thanksgiving turkey; anything smoked or charcoal grilled; pizza; spaghetti and meatballs; heavy sauces seasoned with garlic or herbs like rosemary, sage, and oregano; Dry Jack and other firm, dry cheeses.

You can even introduce it to hearty, spicy fare such as chili, paella, or creole dishes—though gonzo, high-alcohol versions may set your tonsils ablaze.

Most Zinfandels are meant for immediate consumption, although finer renditions may improve after release. While Zinfandel doesn't have the age-ability of a red Bordeaux or Hermitage, it's safe to predict that the brawniest versions—as indicated by their deep flavors, firm tannins, and high price tags—can evolve over a decade or more.

On My Table | **ROBERT MONDAVI** is America's living icon of wine, a dogged visionary who single-handedly created the American market for fine wine.

Red Bordeaux and Cabernet Sauvignon from regions all over the world

Pinot Noir

Fumé Blanc/Sauvignon Blanc

Muscat (dessert style)

19 Syrah: The Inky Abyss

The red grape Syrah boasts a big, spicy personality that provides a refreshing change from the usual mainstays of wine. The wine it produces equals if not eclipses Merlot's jammy softness but also brings to the table a pleasing pepperiness and often lusher, deeper flavors. For me, Syrah is the inky abyss, a big, dark lunar eclipse of a wine that dares you to plumb its indulgent depths. Increasingly a fashionable choice for those weary of one-dimensional Merlots, Syrah is prized for its ripe surges of raspberry and black fruit, black pepper and smoke, swooningly high levels of alcohol, and tannins that rarely flagellate you as Cabernet Sauvignon's can. As exuberant as it is in its American manifestation, Syrah can be even bigger and fruiter in Australia, where it is called Shiraz. (Shortcut 44 is devoted to Australian Shiraz, a wine so pleasurable I nickname it the "plush ripey.")

No discussion of Syrah is complete without paying homage to its homeland, France's northern Rhône Valley. Here soil, climate, and winemaking technique conspire to make a less immediately lovable style of Syrah, as seen in the bitter tannins and mineral notes of a young Hermitage or Côte Rôtie. (Remember, most French wines are labeled not by grape but by location, or *appellation*, so you just have to know that northern Rhône wines are based on the Syrah grape.) With sufficient aging, the best wines of the northern Rhône reveal a marvelous medley of roasted fruit, earth, and sometimes enticingly funky traces of leather, bacon fat, or game. Shortcut 37 provides the lowdown on the northern Rhône, and Shortcut 38 details the southern Rhône, where Syrah is often one of several grapes used in the delicious, sun-ripened wine.

Inspired by the success of Syrah in the warm climes of the Rhône Valley, a posse of American vintners started planting the grape in the similarly sunny climate of

CHEAT SHEET

A sexy beast of a wine, Syrah warms the mortal soul with ripe, rich fruit and manageably moderate tannins. Syrah from the New World is typically fruitier and softer than its counterpart in the northern Rhône.

LABEL DECODER

Syrah is a grape. It is called Shiraz in Australia.

OUTSMART THE TABLE

Most casual drinkers wrongly assume Syrah and Petite Sirah (sometimes spelled Syrah) are the same grape. Syrah has long been considered one of the world's noble grapes, while DNA testing has shown Petite Sirah to be but a humble French grape called Durif. Despite their difference, both Syrah and Petite Sirah make intense, mouth-filling red wine, the latter flourishing in California under the care of such wineries as Bogle, Turley, and Rosenblum.

MARK'S PICKS

Under $20: Chateau Ste. Michelle, Cline, Hogue, Pepperwood Grove, R.H. Phillips, Qupé Central Coast, Rabbit Ridge.

$20 and Over: Araujo, Beaulieu Vineyard (BV), Bonny Doon, Cline, Columbia Crest, Dehlinger, Havens, Jaffurs, L'Ecole No. 41, Ojai, Joseph Phelps, Qupé, Shafer, Swanson, Viader, Zaca Mesa.

FIT FOR FEASTING

Robust winter fare, including hearty winter stews, short ribs, steak; lamb; game (e.g., boar, venison); anything smoked or charcoal grilled; pepper sauces.

California in the early 1980s. The compelling results of these so-called Rhône Rangers demonstrated the potential of Syrah and other Rhône varieties in the United States—and a movement was born. Most high-quality Syrah sells in the $20-to-$40 range, although cult favorites like Viader and Araujo will easily top $60 if you can even find these rare specimens.

When turtlenecks appear, it's prime time to serve Syrah, a perfect choice for hearty, cold-weather food. Any type of substantial meat dish, including stews and game meats, is ideal. Peppery dishes, so good with any robust red, reach new heights in the company of a spicy Syrah.

Given its relatively recent rise to fame, American Syrah has yet to establish a track record for ageability. While it's safe to assume that most versions are best drunk within a few years of bottling, the heftiest bottles in the best years might improve for a decade or more.

On My Table | **CRAIG JAFFURS**, a former aerospace executive, is making some of the best wine in Santa Barbara, California, including consistently wonderful Syrah.

Syrah

Ojai Vineyard

White Rhône

Château de Beaucastel Vieilles Vignes Châteauneuf-du-Pape—"The best example of pure Roussanne in the world. Its purity and minerality show the potential of this grape."

Northern Rhône—Hermitage

Chave Hermitage—"Powerful, focused, and it evolves over time. More spicy than my wines. We can't make anything like it in California."

Southern Rhône—Gigondas

"Wines [from the] Grenache grape can be fabulous. They have power and tannin and fruit and depth—these may be my favorites!"

PINK

20 White Zinfandel: The Bee Gees of Wine

It *seems like* everyone who knows about wine (or wants to) loathes white Zinfandel, while the rest of the world loves it. You might call it the Bee Gees of wine: castigated by the cognoscenti, loved by legions. The truth is that both camps are justified: some white Zinfandels deserve to be shot into space, while others have earned their rightful time and place.

Before discussing the good and the bad, let's tackle a common source of confusion. Despite its infamous hue, white Zinfandel is not the product of pink grapes. It comes from your standard-issue Zinfandel, a grape that normally makes rich and spicy red wine (see Shortcut 18). *White* Zinfandel is what results when the dark skins of Zinfandel grapes are removed from their juice before they can fully impart their color or complexity to the wine. It can also be made by simply mixing a bit of red wine into a tank full of white, the favored method of jug wine factories. Either way, the resulting wine can vary in color from pale pink to flaming flamingo. It is light bodied, with strawberry or even red-candy aromas, and somewhat sweet, which comes from residual sugar left in the wine after fermentation.

"IT'S REQUESTED ONLY ON SATURDAY NIGHT."

—Chris Shipley, the wine director of New York's '21' Club, referring to the propensity of less sophisticated out-of-towners for ordering white Zinfandel during weekend visits

It's hardly a surprise that our Jolly Rancher–fied nation has made sweet-and-simple white Zinfandel one of the most popular wine types in America. Profit-maximizing winemakers like it, too, because it's relatively cheap to make, requiring no special handling like aging in expensive oak barrels. High demand and low production costs have spawned a host of greedy producers inundating the market with a sea of, well, wine behaving badly. To maximize profits, some use leftover grapes or mix in inferior grape types, such as Thompson seedless. Others make wine with so much residual sugar that it tastes as if you could blow bubbles with it. And you wondered why you were so hung over after that wedding last year?

Better examples of white Zinfandel hold their sweetness in check, avoiding the sugary "Hawaiian Punch" afflicting so many mass-produced versions. The better stuff also has enough acidity to balance out its sweetness.

In some shops you'll find white Zinfandel in its own section, while elsewhere it will be categorized as rosé or blush. These two terms are synonymous; *blush* was invented in the 1970s when American marketers worried that the term *rosé* sounded too fusty and old-fashioned.

Being the shorts-and-sandals wine that it is, white Zinfandel doesn't require much food planning. Chill up a bottle and knock it back at a party, picnic, or anywhere you'd normally be drinking cranberry juice or sangria.

CHEAT SHEET

More the libationary equivalent of Barry Gibb than Johann Bach, white Zinfandel is, at best, easy drinking and refreshing and, at worst, liquefied bubble gum.

LABEL DECODER

Although Zinfandel is a red-wine grape, *white* Zinfandel is made such that it is, ironically, neither red nor white but pink.

OUTSMART THE TABLE

White Zinfandel was invented in the late seventies to satisfy a heavy demand for lighter wine while there was a low supply of white-wine grapes.

MARK'S PICKS

Beringer, De Loach, Kenwood, Robert Mondavi.

FIT FOR FEASTING

Pretty much everything; see Shortcut 45.

Basic Regional Styles

We *now cover* basic regional styles—the classic wines that, for the most part, are named not for their grape but for their region of origin, as is common in Europe (or the "Old World" to insiders). On the white side, we encounter the minerally, crisp charms of white Burgundy (made from the Chardonnay grape) and the racy herbaceousness of Sancerre (from the Sauvignon Blanc grape), among others. Moving to the reds, we see regional styles such as red Bordeaux (usually dominated by the Cabernet Sauvignon grape), red Burgundy (from the Pinot Noir grape), Chianti (primarily from the Sangiovese grape), and Rioja (mostly from the Tempranillo grape).

While there are many exceptions, you'll often find that European wine tastes are more subtle than those from the United States and other New World locations. This means that while the typical California Chardonnay tastes ripe and full bodied, with tropical fruit scents like pineapples and peaches, its counterpart from France or Italy will likely be less intense, with subtle citrus or apple essences. Similarly, Cabernet Sauvignon from Europe won't be a lush, plummy affair like so many Californian Cabs; it's a more restrained wine, with berry and currant nuances. One type isn't necessarily better than the other: it's just that European wine often isn't as immediately accessible to New World palates.

One reason for this difference is environmental. The cooler, sun-challenged climes of France, Italy, and Germany produce grapes that are relatively acidic and spare—which makes wine that tastes leaner and crisper. In contrast, the warmer, sun-drenched climates of California and Australia yield more sugary grapes that make full-blown, flavor-packed wine.

Another reason for the Old World/New World difference is stylistic. Pioneers and iconoclasts at heart, American and Australian vintners some-times strive for bold flavors by experimenting with new farming practices, bolder-style oak barrels, and unusual grape combinations. Taking the opposite tack, European winemakers are famous for letting the wine's natural environment, or *terroir* (see Shortcut 11), shape the wine's taste. These traditionalists stay out of the way and let a particular region's weather and soil nurture the grape varieties that, through centuries of trial and error, have proven best suited to the land. With Mother Nature—not the winemaker—at the wheel, there is nothing to stop Europe's cooler climate and challenging soil from producing wine that is more likely to whisper than shout. ■

WHITE

21 White Bordeaux: The Debonair White

First impressions of wine are sometimes final impressions since a disappointing experience can prompt one to dismiss an entire category forever. Most people aren't going to risk their night's wine on something that betrayed them before.

This was my experience with white wine from the Bordeaux region of France. After a few instances of doling out $30 for little more than lemon water with a fancy label, I banned this wine category faster than a vegan shuns mutton cakes.

What rescued white Bordeaux from my vinous blacklist was the passionate enthusiasm of my survey respondents. Rock musician Geddy Lee called it "structured honey." Astrophysicist Neil deGrasse Tyson spoke of a "cornucopia of fruit flavors structured by a steel frame." And David Andrew, Costco's former global wine buyer, "drinks it daily if [he] can get away with it" because he loves "its combination of acidity with a fat, lanolin quality."

Intrigued, I tried several other producers and started to see the light. Better examples had an unmistakable duality, showing both lemony zest *and* honeyed richness. This is because white Bordeaux (also called *Bordeaux Blanc*), like red Bordeaux, usually comes from a blend of grapes—Sauvignon Blanc and Sémillon. The Sauvignon Blanc grape, as we discussed in Shortcut 13, asserts itself with crisp acidity and a cut-grass herbaceousness. The Sémillon grape, in contrast, arrives on the scene with a completely different box of tricks—notes of honey and figs, earthiness, and a soft, round texture. When these grapes are blended together, and the wine is aged in oak barrels as is common for white Bordeaux, the result can light up your sensory dashboard with citrus fruits, melon, honey, minerals, vanilla, and a faint hint of

CHEAT SHEET

White Bordeaux combines Sauvignon Blanc with Sémillon to produce, at its best, a wine of citric zestiness, wet-stones minerality, round texture, and subtle smokiness.

LABEL DECODER

White Bordeaux refers to any white wine from France's Bordeaux area. Graves is the region where most of the best white Bordeaux originates. Pessac-Léognan is the best subregion of Graves.

OUTSMART THE TABLE

A native of Graves, the eighteenth-century French philosopher Charles Montesquieu, whose ideas influenced the writing of the U.S. Constitution, once wrote that "the air, the grapes, the [Bordeaux] wines from the banks of the Garonne and the humor of the Gascons, all are excellent antidotes to melancholy."

grassiness. But don't expect the piercing daggers of a Sancerre from France's Loire Valley; rather, the addition of Sémillon and oak aging rounds out its sharp edges and leaves a trail of creamy softness that's hard to resist.

Because Bordeaux is so celebrated for its red wine, novices are surprised to discover that white wine even comes from this famous region of southwestern France. The best stuff originates in Bordeaux's Graves district, which is also home to red wine as well as the world's most famous dessert wine, Sauternes, covered in Shortcut 62. Graves's northern subregion, Pessac-Léognan, is where you can find the finest dry whites, so look for that name on labels.

Finding white Bordeaux isn't always easy. Overshadowed by mass-appeal whites like Chardonnay and Pinot Grigio, it is an afterthought at most wine shops, if it makes it to the shelves at all. As with red Bordeaux, there are two levels, regional and château. Retailing in the $8-to-$15 range, regional-level bottles carry the name of a general region, like *Bordeaux* or *Graves*, and sometimes have a brand name, such as *Mouton Cadet Blanc*. Some are crisp and refreshing, while many others are no more thrilling than an anonymous carafe of Pinot Grigio.

For finer white Bordeaux, seek out a particular château of Graves, especially one from Pessac-Léognan. For $20 to $50, you can find dependable players like Château Bouscaut, Château Carbonnieux, Château Olivier, and Château La Louvière. If you're shooting for the top, there is Château Haut-Brion Blanc, from the same estate that produces the famous red first growth, as well as the celebrated Domaine de Chevalier and Château Laville-Haut-Brion. Depending on the vintage and where you shop, treasures like these can cost anywhere from $80 to several hundred dollars. In a great vintage, they stand alongside the tiny minority of whites that can improve with age, gaining heft and an enthrallingly figgy, honeyed character.

TALK THE TALK

Graves	*Grahv*
Pessac-*Léognan*	
	Peh-SACK-Leh-OH-NYAHN

MARK'S PICKS

$20 to $50:

Blanc de Lynch-Bages	*Lansh-BAHJ*
Château Bouscaut	*Boos-KOH*
Château Carbonnieux	*Kah-bahn-YUH*
Château de Fieuzal	*Fee-uh-ZAHL*
Château La Louvière	*Lah Loo-VYEHR*
Château Olivier	*Oh-lee-VYAY*
Château Pape-Clément	*Pahp-Cleh-MAHN*

$50 and Over:

Château Haut-Brion Blanc	*Oh-Bree-OHN*
Château Laville-Haut-Brion	
	Lah-veel Oh-Bree-OHN
Domaine de Chevalier	*Shuh-val-YAY*

FIT FOR FEASTING

Lobster, oysters, and other shellfish; richer fish; white meat; pasta; grilled or smoked preparations (e.g., smoked salmon); bisques and other creamy fare; herb and citrus sauces; chèvre and other tangy cheeses.

There's something unmistakably sophisticated about white Bordeaux. With its complex taste and aristocratic labels, having fine white Bordeaux at a dinner party is like bringing along an impeccably dressed friend whose Old World charm is leavened by a rapier wit. Being the debonair white that it is, it is fitting to match it with finer fish and seafood preparations—so consider it for celebrations and anniversaries.

22 White Burgundy: French Chardonnay, Lean and Elegant

If you were making a movie starring Tom Hanks, wouldn't his participation be the first thing you promoted?

Producers of white Burgundy are in a similar situation, making wine solely from the Tom Hanks of wine grapes—Chardonnay—whose appeal is the closest the wine world has to a bankable superstar. But instead of clueing in consumers to this star power, the French mostly continue to label white Burgundy (and most other wine) only by its location of origin or *appellation* and not also by grape type. If only they slapped a shiny *Chardonnay* sticker on every bottle of white Burgundy exported out of this famous region of eastern France, things would be so much clearer.

Or would they? New World Chardonnay and white Burgundy share the same grape, but they sometimes seem a world apart in personality. Chardonnay from California and Australia tends to be fat, round, buttery, and tropically scented, contrasting with the lean, clean, appley elegance of white Burgundy. The latter is more Chyna Phillips; the former, more Carnie Wilson, *before* gastric surgery.

White Burgundy's leaner take on Chardonnay can be attributed to the region's cool climate and unique soil, as well as the tendency of winemakers to exercise more restraint in their use of oak. All these factors combine to create medium- to full-bodied wine whose edges of acidity and earthiness make it a joyous partner for food, especially with lighter dishes that are sometimes clobbered by the buttery heft and gonzo fruit of California Chardonnay. White Burgundy's understatement and zestiness make it a perfect accompaniment for fish, poultry, and pasta of all kinds.

"CORTON-CHARLEMAGNE LOUIS JADOT 1971 IS THE BEST WHITE WINE PRODUCED BY MY FATHER. IT IS HARMONIOUS, NEARLY A SIN. I HAVE DRUNK IT ALREADY THIRTY-SEVEN TIMES, AND THE TWENTY BOTTLES REMAINING WILL BE DRUNK IN MY PRESENCE."

—*Pierre-Henry Gagey, president, Louis Jadot*

Generalizations about white Burgundy are perilous, however, since it has a range of styles from the light lemony scowl of a Chablis to the rich nutty power of a Meursault. Let's take a closer look at three main sources of white Burgundy:

CÔTE DE BEAUNE (COAT DUH BONE) Here in the southern half of Burgundy's famous Côte d'Or ("golden slope"), you find the greatest white wines of white Burgundy, namely Meursault, Puligny-Montrachet, Chassagne-Montrachet, three villages I nickname the Golden Trinity, as well as a vineyard called Corton-Charlemagne. Unlike most other white Burgundies, these wines are fermented and aged in oak barrels—which contributes to their lush, full-bodied, hedonistic disposition. Their bright acidity and stony earthiness, combined with relatively subtle fruit, however, help keep them from being the one-dimensional butter bombs we sometimes see from the New World. Finer versions easily cost $50 and sometimes more than triple that. Shortcut 23 provides the full scoop on this regal Golden Trinity.

CHABLIS (SHAH-BLEE) No relation to the deceptively named jug wine, real Chablis is considered the purest expression of the Chardonnay grape because it typically has little or no oak to compete with its fruit character. Located seventy miles northwest of the main part of the Burgundy region, Chablis has a cool climate and chalky soil that create a Clint Eastwood scowl of a wine, bringing to mind things that make your mouth tingle—lemons, limes, green apples—and things that make your nostrils flare—wet stones, minerals, and chalk. Such sourness can be offputting at first, but serve it with shellfish and you'll see why Chablis is considered such a clean, scintillating lemon squeeze of a wine.

Chablis has three quality levels promising more flavor and weight the higher you go. The basic level, *Chablis,* is made from grapes anywhere in the Chablis region and rings up in the $20 range. Next up is *Chablis premier cru*, which comes from one of about forty *premier cru* vineyards and costs in the $20-to-$50 range, a relative bargain compared to the $100 or more fetched by some *premier cru* bottlings from the Côte de Beaune. The highest level is *Chablis grand cru*, made from grapes in only one of seven *grand cru* vineyards and priced between $40 and $90. Although Chablis typically has little perceptible oak, some winemakers like to offer their better-quality Chablis a brief flirtation with wood.

Because consumers still confuse real Chablis with the jug wine of the same name, many stores don't stock a lot of it. Ask your favorite wine merchant for recommendations or track down Chablis from Louis Michel (Mee-SHELL), René & Vincent Dauvissat (Dew-vee-SAH), François Raveneau (Rah-vuh-NO), Christian Moreau (More-OH), Verget (Vehr-ZHEH), Jean Collet (Koe-LEH), Jean Dauvissat (Dew-vee-SAH), and William Fèvre (Fehv).

MÂCONNAIS (MAH-KOE-NAY) The mere mention of this region should get you thinking "good value," as prices can be considerably lower than in Burgundy's more prestigious locations. The best bet here is Macon-Villages, a clean and simple wine, if sometimes a bit dull, that typically sees nary a splinter of oak. At around $10 a bottle, it is a good call for large groups content to quaff a simple, refreshing white. The most famous wine of the Mâconnais is Pouilly-Fuissé, which is like a Mâcon-Villages but with a bit more flavor and intensity, although not always. Many people think that Pouilly-Fuissé's slightly more engaging character just isn't worth its $20-to-$45 price tag, which it commands largely on the basis of its famous name. Dependable producers for Mâcon-Villages and Pouilly-Fuissé are Jadot (Jah-DOE), Verget (Vehr-ZHEH), Bouchard (Boo-SHAR), and Louis Latour (Lah-TOOR).

Burgundy's "Golden Trinity": Intensity and Restraint with Sex Appeal

"[WHITE BURGUNDY DISPLAYS] THE PURITY OF THE CHARDONNAY GRAPE AT ITS FINEST. NO OVEROAKED BUTTER BOMBS HERE—YOU CAN TASTE THE EARTH AND FEEL THE HISTORY OF CENTURIES OF WINEMAKING WHEN DRINKING GREAT WHITE BURGUNDY. THERE IS MORE BREED, STYLE, LENGTH, AND SUBTLETY THAN ANY OTHER WHITE WINE IN THE WORLD."

—John Kapon, president and auction director, Acker, Merrall & Condit

Can a white wine be sexy?

Reds, of course, have a long history of making pulses race. But what of white wine? Isn't most of it light and casual, more a refresher than a seductress?

Not when you're talking about the complex charms of white wine from Burgundy's Côte de Beaune, about as majestic as white wine can get. You see, the best wine from this region—most, but not all, of which comes from the neighboring villages of Meursault, Puligny-Montrachet, and Chassagne-Montrachet, a trio I nickname the Golden Trinity—shows what happens to the Chardonnay grape when it is grown in the unique soils of Burgundy. There, it is vinified with a deft, disciplined hand reflecting centuries of experience. Whereas Chardonnay from the New World can sometimes be clumsily oaky, the best whites from the Côte de Beaune offer intense aromas and flavors without tasting heavy. They're oaky, with shades of vanilla and toasted nuts, but not overtly sweet. They're fruity, but subtly so, evoking a lush mélange of baked apples, honey, and sometimes tropical fruits. Their signature quality is a slight taste of the soil, or *goût de terroir* (see Shortcut 11), that reminds tasters of minerals or wet stones. They're full bodied, often with a soft, voluptuous texture, but they don't seem leaden, because of the vibrant current of acidity that runs through them. Finally, the best examples have an enduring aftertaste, resonating on your palate like the sumptuous beats of Ravel's *Bolero*.

With such a profile, is it any wonder that Côte de Beaune whites are the world's model for Chardonnay? With more acidity than the typical New World Chardonnay, they are also a better choice with food. Rich varieties of seafood (e.g., salmon, bass, tuna, lobster) in heavy sauces will ring gastronomic bells alongside the wine's heft and butteriness. The slash of acidity in these wines also lets the finest examples do something few white wines can do—get better with age. In the best years, certain *premiers crus* and *grands crus* get more complex and interesting with up to ten years of bottle age, in special cases longer than that.

Speaking of *grands crus*, wine from the Côte de Beaune, like all wine in Burgundy's fabled Côte d'Or district, is ranked according to the location of its vineyards; the higher the rank, the greater the wine's quality potential, as explained in Shortcut 34. Wine at the Village level comes from grapes in and around particular villages, including, for our purposes, Meursault, Puligny-Montrachet, and Chassagne-Montrachet. Village-level wine generally rings up between $20 and $40. Things get more interesting at the *premier cru* level, which is wine made from grapes in *premier-cru*-ranked vineyards, such as Meursault's Les Charmes vineyard or Puligny-Montrachet's Les Folatières. Expect to pay between $35 and $90 for these gems. The top level is *grand cru*, sourced from just one of a handful of rarefied *grand-cru*-ranked vineyards. Priced vertiginously from $80 to multiples of that, *grands crus* include the legendary Le Montrachet and Chevalier-Montrachet.

As we cover later in our exploration of red Burgundy, these designations can take you only so far in distinguishing good bottles of Burgundy from the deluge of disappointments in the market. Because of the region's mercurial weather, the wine's year of vintage is also determinative, a topic expanded on in Shortcut 94. Nothing, however, trumps the importance of the producer, whose energy and integrity can make or break a wine. The following is a summary of the Côte de Beaune's Golden Trinity of villages, along with recommended producers.

MEURSAULT (MUHR-SOE) The northernmost village of the Golden Trinity, Meursault is the most immediately likable of the three, typically a rich, round affair with hints of toasted nuts, butter, and fruits like peaches. As Burgundy expert Allen Meadows writes in his survey response, Meursault is a "richly satisfying wine . . . comforting . . . expressive . . . and intensely enjoyable." Meursault has no *grand cru* vineyards but plenty of illustrious *premiers crus* like Les Charmes and Les Genevrières.

Favorite Producers: R. Ampeau (An-POE), Coche-Dury (Kosh-Dew-REE), Domaine des Comtes Lafon (Kohnt Lah-FOHN), A. Grivault (Gree-VOE), Guy Roulot (Roo-LOW).

PULIGNY-MONTRACHET (POO-LEE-N'YEE MOAN-RAH-SHAY) South of Meursault lies Puligny-Montrachet, Burgundy's most celebrated village for white wine. Although styles vary, tasters speak of its harmonious balance and steely, minerally character. It includes the famous *grand cru* vineyards of Le Montrachet and Bâtard-Montrachet, both of which, confusingly enough, straddle the boundary between this village and neighboring Chassagne-Montrachet.

Favorite Producers: Drouhin (Drew-AHN), Jadot (Jah-DOE), Latour (Lah-TOOR), Leflaive (Luh-FLAYV), Ramonet (Ram-moe-NEH), Sauzet (Soe-ZEH), Verget (Vehr-ZHEH).

CHASSAGNE-MONTRACHET (SHA-SAHNNE MOAN-RAH-SHAY) The most southerly of the three villages, Chassagne-Montrachet is world renowned but doesn't quite match Puligny-Montrachet's reputation for finesse and balance. While distinctions are slight, its wines are often noted for their big, ripe, fleshy fruit.

Favorite Producers: Blain-Gagnard (Blahn-Gah-NYAHR), Colin-Deléger (Koe-LAHN-Duh-leh-ZHAY), Bernard Morey (Moe-RAY), Ramonet (Ram-moe-NEH), Sauzet (Soe-ZEH).

24 Sancerre and Pouilly-Fumé: Steely Sauvignon Blanc from France

If *Chardonnay evokes* the first few dreamy notes of the Beach Boys' "California Girls," Sancerre channels the menacing synthesized drone prefacing Gary Numan's "Cars." Don't get the wrong idea: Sancerre may be, as the name of its grape, Sauvignon Blanc, suggests, the most *sauvage* of white wines, but you'll like how it mixes a lash of pain with its pleasure.

Many consider Sancerre the purest expression of the Sauvignon Blanc grape. The town of Sancerre resides in France's cool-climate Loire Valley, where the grape doesn't get overly ripe and thus retains a pleasantly piercing degree of acidity. And, unlike some of their American counterparts, winemakers in Sancerre rarely expose their wine to the mellowing effects of oak. This combination of cool climate and winemaker restraint allows Sancerre to fulfill its potential of grassy pungency and tongue-tingling acidity. The best Sancerres are what you'd expect from grapes grown in the region's famously chalky soil: light bodied, citrusy, with prickly acidity and a minerally finish. Sometimes the wine gets so herbaceous and tangy that it achieves a musky quality infamously known as "cat's pee," or, in French, *pipi du chat.*

Slightly less famous than Sancerre is its Loire neighbor, Pouilly-Fumé, which also displays this old-school style of Sauvignon Blanc. I've never noticed an appreciable difference between Sancerre and Pouilly-Fumé, but some say the latter can be a bit fuller bodied and less acidic than the former. Careful: it's easy for the uninitiated to confuse Pouilly-Fumé with Pouilly-Fuissé, which is Chardonnay from the Mâconnais region in southern Burgundy (see Shortcut 22).

Although most Sauvignon Blanc from the Loire is traditionally made without the creamy caress of oak barrels, some winemakers are experimenting with adding an oaky dimension, often with disappointing results. One winemaker who gets it right is Didier Dagueneau. A lion-coiffed dogsledding enthusiast with a fanatical devotion to making quality wine, Dagueneau makes oak-aged

"I MUST HAVE LOVED TO PUT STONES IN MY MOUTH AS A KID."

—Karen King, wine director of New York's Gramercy Tavern, on her love of stony, steely Sancerre

Pouilly-Fumés that are legendary for a level of complexity and creamy richness rarely found in wine from this part of France. Starting at about $60 a bottle, Dagueneau's wines—particularly the Silex and Pur Sang bottlings—make great gifts for wine enthusiasts who think they've seen it all.

Rarities aside, Sancerre and Pouilly-Fumé are a terrific value, inhabiting the lower end of restaurant wine lists and ranging between $12 and $25 in wine shops. Their zesty grapefruit-in-a-glass acidity makes them a turbo booster for food, especially shellfish like oysters and crab and tangy cheeses like goat. Cultivating an herb garden? Drop everything and buy Sancerre by the case, as its herbaceousness partners beautifully with any concoction involving dill, thyme, rosemary, and virtually anything green sprinkled on food. Better yet, locate the nearest croquet lawn, unfold a chair, knock back some Sancerre, and have yourself a grassy good time.

25 Alsace: Whites of Purity and Weight

Want to sound wine savvy in one word? When asked your favorite wine region, raise a randy brow, affect an air of breezy nonchalance, and hiss "Ahl-ZASS." Better yet, say: "Ahl-SAY-shen," taking your time on the middle syllable.

People will know you mean business—not only because of the word's racy resonance but also because you're invoking a long-neglected, insider's region of northern France that somehow manages to combine aspects of several other wine worlds into one compelling package. You see, Alsatian wines are like a schizophrenic traveler: they look German, talk American, and act French.

With long, tapered bottles and Germanic names like Hugel and Trimbach, Alsatian wines give the distinct impression of Germany, whose influence, unsurprisingly, is just a few miles away. But just when you think you've got Alsace pegged as classically European, it tips its hat to the New World, labeling its wines not by their region, as is typical of French wine, but by the grape from which they come, such as Riesling or Gewürztraminer, as we do in the United States. When it comes to flavor, however, Alsace remains faithful to its French roots, showing not the delicate sweetness of German wine or the oaky vanilla scents of American Chardonnay but the richness of a Meursault combined with the unoaked quality of a Chablis or Sancerre. Although they can vary widely depending on the grape and producer, typical Alsatian wines surprise you with more weight and less oak than you expect—bone-dry wine that is both powerful and intense yet with fruit as clean and pure as the small rivers that cut through the nearby Vosges Mountains. Superior examples show layer on layer of complexity with a clean, zesty finish that seems to last forever.

Having never achieved mass appeal, the majority of Alsatian wines are reasonably priced between $12 and $20, with premium bottlings, including those afforded the *grand cru* designation, ringing up at $40 or more. Their obscurity is such that wine shops often lump them into the German section, itself a backwoods category at most shops.

OUTSMART THE TABLE

It may be surprising that Alsace, tucked into the rainy northeastern corner of France, produces wine that is full bodied; the nearby Vosges Mountains, however, run interference on the bad weather, ensuring that grapes get ample sun and therefore produce weightier wine.

TALK THE TALK

Riesling	*REES-ling*
Pinot Gris	*Pee-no GREE*
Gewürztraminer	*Guh-VURTS-trah-mee-ner*
Vendange Tardive	*Vahn-DAHNJ Tahr-DEEV*
Sélection de Grains Nobles	
	Say-lek-SHAWN duh Grahn NOE-bl
Tokaji	*Toh-KAY*

MARK'S PICKS

Lucien Albrecht	*Lew-SYEN AHL-bresht*
Leon Beyer	*LAY-oh Beh-yehr*
Albert Boxler	*Ahl-bare Bohks-lehr*
Marcel Deiss	*Dice*
Hugel	*Hew-GELL*
Josmeyer	*JOCE-meyer*
Schlumberger	*SCHLOOM-ber-ger*
Pierre Sparr	*Shpahr*
Trimbach	*TREEM-bahr*
Zind Humbrecht	*Zeend HOOM-bresht*

Most Alsatians are very dry, although sweeter versions do exist, notably the scarce Vendange Tardive (or VT) style, a luscious heavyweight white that comes from grapes picked extra-ripe (or late harvest) and is typically dry or only moderately sweet. With the exception of Pinot Blanc, all of the grape varieties that follow can be used to make VT, as well an even later-harvest style called Sélection de Grains Nobles (or SGN), which is lusciously sweet and even more expensive than VT.

Rarities aside, here are the major grapes from Alsace:

RIESLING The Rolls-Royce of Alsatian grapes, offering not the lightly sweet delicacy of German Riesling but heft and complexity with rarely any trace of sweetness. You'll detect citrus fruits, green apples, and often peaches, linked with a steely taste of minerals and often joined by what is described, in praise, as a whiff of petroleum, or "petrol." Indeed, unlike most whites, the best Alsatian Rieslings have the complexity and acidity to get better with age, reaching their peak in five to fifteen years.

PINOT GRIS It shares the same grape as Italian Pinot Grigio, but, happily, that's where the similarity ends. In contrast to the sea of wimpy juice pumped out of Italy, Alsatian Pinot Gris is fuller bodied and, at its finest, filled with scents of honey, peaches, almonds, and smoke, bolstered by enough acidity to keep things interesting. Because its former name, Tokay, was often confused with the famous Hungarian dessert wine, Tokaji Aszú, French wine authorities are phasing out the Tokay designation. You may, however, still see *Tokay–Pinot Gris* on labels.

GEWÜRZTRAMINER The wine that gets the girl, Gewürztraminer is a big-personality affair with signature aromas of lychee nuts and rosewater, followed by pepper and a swirl of fruit scents and flavors. So exotic it earns a chapter of its very own (see Shortcut 49).

PINOT BLANC With a name as generic as Pinot Blanc, it is unsurprising that this is the anti-Gerwürz—a mild, apple-scented, light-to-medium-bodied wine that's a welcome refresher on the hammock but rarely merits further contemplation.

FIT FOR FEASTING

Pinot Blanc: Delicate seafood, white meat, and pasta preparations.
Fuller-bodied Alsatians: Somewhat richer fare, such as grilled fish, sausages, and pork dishes; escargots; hollandaise and other rich sauces; onion tarts; bean dishes; creamy, pungent cheeses like Alsatian Muenster.

On My Table | **ETIENNE HUGEL** represents the twelfth generation of the Hugel family, which has been a top name in Alsatian wine since 1639.

Champagne
Pol Roger, Bollinger, Krug

Riesling from Germany
Egon Müller, J.J. Prüm—"Asian food's best friends."

Red Burgundy
Drouhin, Faiveley, Roumier

Alsace
Hugel—"My cheapest supply!"—Trimbach, Weinbach, Zind Humbrecht

Sauternes
Climens, Coutet, Suduiraut, d'Yquem

Rhône (North and South)
Jaboulet, Chave, Perrin

26 Pinot Grigio: The Italian "Safety Blanket" Eclipsed by Its Alter Egos

Imagine a new drink that approximates a glass of ice water with a wedge of lemon. It is made in Italy and adorned with a fancy label. We'll brand this hypothetical beverage *Lemonico.*

Well, Lemonico comes pretty close to Pinot Grigio, the safety-blanket wine loved by millions of Americans. They gravitate to it because it's easy to drink, it's easy to say, and, with its light, clean taste, it serves as a welcome counterpoint to the plethora of leaden, oaky Chardonnays crowding store shelves. Its popularity is also fueled by advertising so relentless it could run for office—and probably win.

This would be fine were it a $4 sipper at an outdoor café. Unfortunately, Pinot Grigio is not a cheap bottle of Lemonico but a "fine wine" retailing between $12 and $25 and multiples of that in restaurants. With apologies if I am denigrating your favorite wine, but you have to ask yourself if it is worth that price, and the calories, to have a wine with so little personality. Drinking Pinot Grigio is often like experiencing an IKEA rug, Ben Stein's voice, or a dose of Paxil: neutral, monotone, and devoid of highs. So many times I have ordered it hoping for a little oomph and gotten only the faint trace of apples or lemons, if even that. Pinot Grigio's blandness is paradigmatic of much of the white wine emerging from Italy, such as Soave and Orvieto, the unfortunate result of Italian winemakers who just don't put the same energy into their whites as they do with their magnificent reds.

CHEAT SHEET
A light, refreshing, but often bland alternative to the heavy taste of Chardonnay, enormously popular Italian Pinot Grigio is outshone by its more interesting, fruit-driven Pinot Gris alter egos in Oregon and Alsace, France.

To be fair, more interesting versions of Pinot Grigio can be had, especially if you focus on the high-quality producers in Italy's northeastern alpine regions of Friuli and Trentino–Alto Adige. You'll sometimes find more flavor and complexity from bottlings by Livio Felluga, Ecco Domani, CAVIT, and Zemmer. Sadly, however, the typical Pinot Grigio displays all of the raciness and intrigue of a wine stuck in second gear.

All hope is not lost, however, for Pinot Grigio's grape—

Pinot Gris—finds better expression in Oregon and France's Alsace region. In the last few decades, Pinot Gris has emerged as the showpiece white of Oregon. Heftier than its Italian counterpart, Oregon Pinot Gris is usually medium bodied, with more pronounced fruit and a spritzy jolt of acidity. Better versions can show some complexity, with layers of pears, apples, or honeydew intermingling with a smidgen of honey or spice, followed by a creamy texture that never loses its clean, vibrant personality. Prices are usually in the $12-to-$18 range, and I can always rely on the bottlings from Ponzi, Chateau Ste. Michelle, King Estate, Adelsheim, and Eyrie, the last being Oregon's original Pinot Gris. With its substantial body and zesty acidity, you may not find a better wine for Oregon's other gastronomic gift—fresh salmon.

Some California vintners are also trying their hand at the Pinot Gris grape, and the resulting wine—often labeled with the Italian name *Pinot Grigio*—can be vibrant with fresh essences of citrus and green fruits. If you can find it, Luna Vineyards, a boutique winery in Napa, consistently makes complex and flavorful Pinot Grigio.

The Pinot Gris grape achieves its greatest potential in the cool but sunny climes of France's Alsace. Here you get something dramatically different, as the region's ample sunlight and unique soil make wine that is full bodied, with essences of peach and citrus fruit and some smoke or nuttiness. Alsatian Pinot Gris (also sometimes called Tokay–Pinot Gris) represents the grape at its most complex and serious, able to stand up to the kind of hearty sausage-and-sauerkraut cuisine for which Alsace is famous. Despite its richness, it is usually bone-dry, although sweeter dessert-style versions exist. You'll pay in the $15 range for entry-level Alsatian Pinot Gris and twice that or more for the finest versions, which taste full bodied and creamy while retaining the purity of fruit and long, clean finish that makes this wine such a joy. Superbrands Trimbach and Hugel are dependable places to start. For more on Alsatian wine, see Shortcut 25.

LABEL DECODER

Pinot Gris is the grape. Its primary regions are Italy; Alsace, France; and Oregon.

OUTSMART THE TABLE

According to *Wine Spectator* magazine, Italian Pinot Grigio is now the number-one imported wine type in America.

MARK'S PICKS

Italian Pinot Grigio:

CAVIT	*CAHV-it*
Ecco Domani	*Doe-MAH-nee*
Franz Haas	*Hahs*
Livio Felluga	*Lee-vyo Fell-LEW-gah*
Peter Zemmer	*ZEM-er*

Oregon Pinot Gris:
Adelsheim, Chateau Ste. Michelle, Elk Cove, Eyrie, King Estate, Ponzi.

California Pinot Grigio/Gris:
Gallo of Sonoma, Luna, Rancho Zabaco.

Alsatian Pinot Gris:

Lucien Albrecht	*Lew-SYEN AHL-breckt*
Hugel	*Hew-GELL*
Josmeyer	*JOCE-meyer*
Trimbach	*Treem-bahr*
Zind Humbrecht	*Zeend HOOM-bresht*

FIT FOR FEASTING

Italian Pinot Grigio and American Pinot Gris/Grigio: Lighter seafood, white meat, and pasta preparations; goat cheese; citrus sauces; capers, green olives, and other briney treats; salads; summer fruits like melon.

Alsatian Pinot Gris: Hollandaise and other rich sauces; scallions, shallots, and other pungent members of the onion family; bean dishes; Brie and other creamy cheeses; Alsatian Muenster cheese.

On My Table | **RAY WALSH**, an ace winemaker and native New Zealander, ensures that King Estate's Pinot Gris and Pinot Noir remain the pride of Oregon.

Pinot Noir

Oregon: Chehalem, Broadley, St. Innocent, Witness Tree. New Zealand: Whither Hills, Nautilus, Pegasus Bay.

Red Burgundy

Domaine Robert Arnoux, Domaine de l'Arlot, Domaine Yvon Clerget, Domaine des Lambrays

Pinot Gris

Alsace: Zind Humbrecht. Oregon: King Estate—"Such a pretty varietal that can express *so* much in the way of fruit and spices."

Shiraz/Syrah

Australia: Penfolds, d'Arenberg. California: Hitching Post.

Champagne/Bubbly

Champagne: Krug, Pol Roger. Oregon: Domaine Meriwether.

Sauvignon Blanc from New Zealand

Kim Crawford, Vavasour, Cloudy Bay

RED

27 Red Bordeaux: As Aristocratic
as Wine Gets

*D*on de da daa . . ."

When I think about Bordeaux, I can almost hear the trumpets of the Twentieth Century Fox fanfare. Fine Bordeaux says you've arrived. Actually, it says you've arrived on a red carpet, in top hat and tails. This is the wine that Thomas Jefferson lusted after, that eighteenth-century writer Samuel Johnson declared essential for the "serious" wine drinker, and that has inspired bottle labels by artists like Picasso and Dalí. And what other wine has its own pet name—*claret*—bestowed on it by the British?

Actually, the red Bordeaux most of us hear about is only 2 percent of the story. As the world's largest wine-growing region, spread out among three rivers in southwestern France, Bordeaux is home to oceans of simple and undistinguished juice. But it's the minority of good stuff that fires the imagination of the wine impassioned, ranging from a delicious $25 *cru bourgeois* to a $1,500 bottle of Château Pétrus.

By law, red Bordeaux is always a blend of up to five grapes, the most common being Cabernet Sauvignon and Merlot, with smaller, supporting roles from Cabernet Franc, Petite Verdot, and Malbec. Such blending allows winemakers to tone down Cabernet's edgy tannins with Merlot's gentle, plummy caress and inject added complexity from the other grapes. It also spreads the agricultural risk, so no vintage depends on the performance of just one grape type. Each Bordeaux winemaker has his or her own recipe for blending grapes together, which helps ensure that each château has a fairly consistent style through the years—at least when compared to the vinous unpredictability in France's other marquee region, Burgundy. Although the term *château* is French for "castle," here it is synonymous with "wine estate"—denoting any winery structure attached to a vineyard.

Although Cabernet Sauvignon is the grape most closely associated with Bordeaux, it dominates the blend only in certain

"DON'T JUDGE RED BORDEAUX WITHOUT FOOD—BY ITSELF IT'S RATHER TANNIC."

—*Michael Broadbent, author and head of auctions, Christie's*

places. On the west side of Bordeaux's Garonne River and its Gironde Estuary, the districts of Médoc (Bordeaux's most famous) and Graves typically use a higher proportion of Cabernet and are thus known to be more tannic and long-lived. This area, dubbed the *Left Bank* by the wine trade, is described in Shortcut 28. The lower-profile area east of the rivers, or *Right Bank*, is home to Merlot-based wines of St.-Emilion and Pomerol. The richer, more generous charms of Merlot make these wines more approachable, as discussed in Shortcut 30.

The aroma and flavor profile of red Bordeaux is consistent with what you'd expect from Cabernet and Merlot, with plenty of blackcurrants, plums, and cassis. Better wines see a good deal of contact with oak barrels, so they are likely also to have subtle vanilla, cedar, or cigar box aromas. In the best years, top châteaux can fashion wine of exquisite intensity and complexity, treating your senses to hints of smoke, coffee, earth, spice, and violets, as well as sometimes pencil lead—a surprising but classic aroma in certain fine Bordeaux. At best, it has the ability to be rich and intensely flavored without seeming heavy—a quality that sets it apart from the over-the-top, fruit-bomb styles you sometimes see in New World Cabernet. Indeed, Bordeaux's cool climate, unique soil, and winemaker restraint are why tasters describe superior versions as paragons of breeding and sophistication, making certain New World Cabernets seem, in contrast, a bit overripe or out of balance. In the end, neither style is necessarily *better*—it is a matter of personal preference.

If you choose the French route, however, don't expect the immediate pleasure you find in many New World Cabernets. Red Bordeaux, especially the best stuff from Cabernet-based Médoc, often enters the world with punishing tannins that diminish only after a decade or more of aging. While some winemakers are catering to current tastes by making wine somewhat more approachable in its youth, the tannic edge of young Bordeaux makes it a risky choice at restaurants, as does,

CHEAT SHEET
The world icon for fine wine, red Bordeaux is all about understated elegance, its blend of Cabernet Sauvignon, Merlot, and other grapes fashioning wine of medium to full body, essences of black fruits, spice, and cedar, and overall more earthiness and restraint than its equivalent from the New World.

LABEL DECODER
Bordeaux is the famous wine region of southwestern France. Red Bordeaux is typically a blend of the grapes Cabernet and Merlot and, to a lesser extent, Cabernet Franc, Petite Verdot, and Malbec.

TALK THE TALK
Bordeaux	*Bohr-DOE*
claret	*KLAR-ett*
château	*sha-TOH*
Petite Verdot	*Peh-teet Vair-DOE*
Garonne	*Gah-RUN*
Gironde	*Jhee-ROND*
Médoc	*May-DOK*
Graves	*Grahv*
Pomerol	*Paw-muh-RAWL*
St.-Emilion	*Sahn-Tay-mee-L'YON*

FIT FOR FEASTING
Heavier meats (steak, game, and especially lamb, a regional favorite); dishes with smoky or grilled flavors; Bordelaise and other rich wine sauces (note: finer, mature Bordeaux are often best with simple, less sauced-up preparations); pepper sauces; mushrooms and earthy foods; firm, dry cheeses; Roquefort and other blue-veined cheeses

of course, its stratospheric pricing. If you do find yourself with a young, astringent Bordeaux, be sure to give it an hour or so of aeration in a decanter (see Shortcut 86) before drinking.

With regard to purchasing Bordeaux, the shortcuts ahead will cover particular châteaux and their classifications. Note, however, that not all red Bordeaux originates from the vineyards of particular châteaux. Wines labeled only by a particular Bordeaux district, such as *Médoc* or *Graves*, signify a step down in quality. Typically $10 to $15, regional Bordeaux comes from grapes grown anywhere in that particular area and is a simple, everyday wine meant to be enjoyed young. The most basic quality level doesn't even point to a subregion but merely says *Bordeaux* and usually a brand name like *Mouton Cadet* or *Maître d'Estournel*. Coming from grapes anywhere in Bordeaux, these so-called proprietary Bordeaux rarely cost more than a ten-spot and have the uncomplicated tastes you'd expect of wine at this price point.

Given its aristocratic cachet, red Bordeaux is perfectly suited for holiday feasts, celebrations, and any other occasion when you want to impress. Its medium to full body makes it an excellent choice with heavier, meat-oriented menus, such as steak, roasts, prime rib, and lamb, the last being a historic favorite among the Bordelaise. Lower-end bottles are gratifying with casual fare like hamburgers and sausages. Spicy or rich sauces can overwhelm the delicate flavors of mature Bordeaux, so keep it simple. Cheeses like Parmigiano-Reggiano and Manchego are good for mitigating a young Bordeaux's tannins and are mild enough to avoid stealing the show from a fragile old bottle of Bordeaux.

As the hysteria surrounding Bordeaux's triumphant 2000 vintage demonstrated, the topic of vintage in Bordeaux generates a lot of excitement, trickling down even to nonconnoisseurs. While vintage does matter more for fine red Bordeaux than for most other wine types, it isn't necessarily the do-or-die factor some think it is. In fact, if, like most people, you crave wine that is immediately drinkable, a great vintage of a top château isn't necessarily what you want, as it will likely have high levels of bitter tannin. For immediate pleasure, it is wiser—and, of course, far more affordable—to buy top châteaux in years that don't get as much hype. Top winemakers using the best equipment and rigorous techniques routinely make delicious wine in less-than-stellar vintages, even if that wine is lighter and less ageable. If your heart is set on sampling the fruits of a great Bordeaux vintage, try buying one of the lesser châteaux, like a *cru bourgeois* covered in Shortcut 31. These wines are often ready to drink far sooner than the big names, and you'll be saving yourself an oak barrel of cash.

On My Table | **SERENA SUTCLIFFE** is an internationally recognized wine writer and expert and head of Sotheby's International Wine Department in London, England.

Red Bordeaux

Pomerol: Pétrus, Trotanoy, L'Evangile, Vieux Château Certan. St.-Emilion: Cheval Blanc, Ausone. Médoc: Lafite, Sociando-Mallet—"A relative bargain; should be classified." Graves/Pessac-Léognan: Haut-Brion and La Mission-Haut-Brion.

White Bordeaux

Haut-Brion Blanc and Laville-Haut-Brion, Domaine de Chevalier

Red Burgundy—"Wild . . . heady . . . sensual."

Domaine de la Romanée-Conti, Charles Rousseau, Comte Georges de Vogüé, Méo-Camuzet, Jean Gros, Chandon de Briailles

White Burgundy

Jean-Noël Gagnard, Ramonet, Domaine Leflaive, Michel Niellon, Louis Latour, Bonneau du Martray

Champagne

Roederer Cristal. Vintage Champagne: Veuve Clicquot, Pol Roger, Moët. Blanc de Blancs: Dom Ruinart, Taittinger Comtes de Champagne, Salon, Jacques Selosse Substance.

Sauternes and Barsac

d'Yquem, Rieussec, Climens, Coutet

German Riesling

J. J. Prüm, Fritz Haag, Egon Müller, Dr. Heger, Didinger

28 For Cabernet-Style Bordeaux: Look to the Médoc and Graves

How *would* you feel if I told you to choose a restaurant or graduate school or vacation destination based on a ranking published over a century ago?

You'd probably tell me to jump back in my horse-drawn carriage and drive off.

In a similar vein, the châteaux of Bordeaux's most famous district, the Médoc, are stratified according to a ranking rendered way back in 1855. For the Paris Exposition held that year, Napoleon asked the wine merchants of the day to rank the top Bordeaux châteaux according to the selling price of their wine. Thus emerged the famous 1855 classification, which organized the top sixty-one châteaux into five tiers, the top being the *premiers crus*, or "first growths," down to the fifth growths. This is what tasters mean when they speak of a Bordeaux as a "first growth" or "third growth." The sixty-one châteaux lucky enough to have their wine included in this old classification get to say *cru classé*, or "classified growth," on the label; thousands of other châteaux can't. With one change, exactly the same classification persists today.

If this system seems inconsistent with our meritocratic, *Consumer Reports* view of the world, well, it is. A lot can happen in 150 years: châteaux change owners, some estates improve, others slack off, new ones crop up. An often cited example is Château Gloria, now a splendid property, but without *cru classé* cachet because it didn't exist in 1855; instead, it wears the lower rank of *cru bourgeois*, a category just below the *cru classé*. With politics and traditions the way they are, this system is unlikely to see the update it needs. Even so, most Bordeaux experts maintain that the 1855 classification remains useful as a general guide to top châteaux and their relative cost.

The 1855 classification pertains only to the châteaux of the Médoc district (as well as one château from Graves—Haut-Brion—which was so famous in 1855 that it was included, too). As we have already learned, the Médoc and Graves compose Bordeaux's informally named Left Bank, where the wines are dominated by the grape Cabernet Sauvignon, in part because that grape is well suited to the gravelly soil of this area.

Bordeaux's heart and soul, the Médoc has four legendary wine-growing subregions or villages: St.-Estèphe, Pauillac, St.-Julien, and Margaux. Although today distinctions between the wines of these appellations have blurred somewhat, for now know that the northernmost villages, St.-Estèphe and Pauillac, have a reputation for wines that are hefty, tannic, and slower to mature. Wine from more southerly St.-Julien and Margaux is known for somewhat less gum-numbing power, with softer tannins and a bit less body. Margaux is perceived as the lightest and most perfumed of the four. Such are broad generalizations based on the unique natural conditions of these areas—their so-called *terroir* (see Shortcut 11). But there are many exceptions, and how a particular wine ultimately tastes also depends on the individual château and vintage year.

To get you started on the better wines of the Médoc and Graves, a subset of popular favorites follows; a quick Internet search will give you the entire 1855 classification if you so desire. Note that the best Graves comes from the region's northern subregion, a separate appellation called Pessac-Léognan. Graves also has its own ranking.

For the Médoc, I offer a selection of its *cru classé* châteaux except the five, exorbitantly expensive first growths—which get their own spotlight in the next chapter. Médoc's more affordable *cru bourgeois* wines, as well as other Bordeaux values, are covered in Shortcut 31. Prices for the wines in the following list generally range from $30 to $70, depending on their reputation and the particular vintage.

CHEAT SHEET

The heart of red Bordeaux is the Cabernet Sauvignon–dominated Médoc district, whose top châteaux are ranked according to five tiers, or "growths," of the classification of 1855. Joining the Médoc on the Left Bank is Graves, a district that favors Cabernet Sauvignon, though not always as much as Médoc.

LABEL DECODER

Médoc is the most famous district of Bordeaux. St.-Estèphe, Pauillac, St.-Julien, and Margaux are Médoc's major subregions or villages. In Médoc, the *crus classés*, "classified growths," refer to the châteaux that made the cut in the 1855 classification.

OUTSMART THE TABLE

Although Graves is home to some wonderful red wine, as well as some of Bordeaux's better values, it is better known for its dry white wine (see Shortcut 21) and world-class dessert wine, Sauternes (see Shortcut 62).

TALK THE TALK

St.-Estèphe	*Sahn-Eh-STEFF*
Pauillac	*POE-yack*
St.-Julien	*Sahn-Joo-LYAN*
Margaux	*Mahr-GO*
Pessac-Léognan	*Peh-sack-Leh-oh-NYAHN*

A Selection of Top Médoc Cru Classé Châteaux, Excluding First Growths

CHÂTEAU	CRU (TIER) + VILLAGE
Château Calon-Ségur (Kah-lawn-Say-GOOR)	Third growth, St.-Estèphe
Château Grand-Puy-Lacoste (Grahn-Pwee-Lah-COST)	Fifth growth, Pauillac
Cheateau Gruaud-Larose (Groo-oh Lah-ROHZ)	Second growth, St.-Julien
Château Lafon-Rochet (Lah-FOHN-Roh-SHAY)	Fourth growth, St.-Estèphe
Château Léoville-Barton (Lay-oh-VEEL-Bar-TOHN)	Second growth, St.-Julien
Château Léoville-Las-Cases (Lay-oh-VEEL-Lahss-KAHZ)	Second growth, St.-Julien
Château Lynch-Bages (Lansh-BAHJ)	Fifth growth, Pauillac
Château Montrose (Mohn-TROS)	Second growth, St.-Estèphe
Château Palmer (Pahl-MAIR)	Third growth, Margaux
Château Prieuré-Lichine (Pree-uh-RAY-Lee-SHEEN)	Fourth growth, Margaux
Château Talbot (Tahl-BOE)	Fourth growth, St.-Julien

A Selection of Top Graves/Pessac-Léognan

Château Bouscaut
(Boos-KOH)
Domaine de Chevalier
(Shuh-val-YAY)
Château de Fieuzal
(Fee-uh-ZAHL)
Château Haut-Bailly
(O-Bah-YEE)
Château Olivier
(Oh-lee-VYAY)
Château Pape-Clément
(Pahp-Cleh-MAHN)

29 Bordeaux's First Growths:
Wine's Immortal Monuments

So *what does* one drink on the presidential yacht, anyway?

Rumor has it that Richard Nixon kept his favorite wine, Château Margaux, for himself, wrapped in a white napkin, while the rest of his guests drank more modest juice from California.

Who can blame Tricky Dick? Château Margaux stands at wine's pinnacle—a first-growth Bordeaux—the kind of wine that naturally evokes one's inner scrooge. It is as monumental as wine gets. If the god of wine, Dionysus, had a favorite bottle, it would probably be a Château Margaux—1945, mind you.

If, like most mere mortals, you lack the resources to regularly enjoy first growths, it's still valuable to know about them. It's one of those obligatory aspects of connoisseurship—like a car buff knowing his Ferraris even if he never owns one.

First growth refers to the famous classification of 1855, which ranked Bordeaux's sixty-one most expensive wines according to their selling price. Originally the top tier—called *premiers crus* or "first growths"—comprised four châteaux: Château Lafite-Rothschild, Château Latour, Château Margaux, and Château Haut-Brion, all being from Bordeaux's Médoc district except the last. The only change ever allowed in this monolithic ranking happened in 1973, when the charismatic Baron Philippe de Rothschild achieved his lifelong dream of coaxing French authorities into elevating his Château Mouton-Rothschild from second growth to first growth. Since that time, it has remained an elite club of five wines—a tantalizingly scarce quantity available to slake the thirst of the world's moneyed sybarites.

It can be dangerous to try to identify consistent differences among the first growths, especially as many of today's top winemakers strive to make wines in a rich, powerful style. Traditionally, differences in *terroir* and the final blend of grapes have designated Château Latour and Château Mouton-Rothschild as the most powerful and ageworthy of the lot. Château Haut-Brion combines power

with a distinctly smoky and earthy dimension, derived in part from the gravelly soil from which it comes. Château Lafite-Rothschild and Château Margaux are known as the most elegant of the five, emphasizing fragrance, subtlety, and delicacy over heft and tannin.

Whether or not those generalizations hold true from year to year, first growths are invariably rich, full bodied, and in the best years sometimes so tannic as to be almost undrinkable in their first decade of life. Such tannic brutality is a virtue, because it is the key element that makes some first growths almost immortal, or able to last for one's lifetime and beyond. Neil deGrasse Tyson, an enthusiastic collector and director of New York's Hayden Planetarium, told me that he opened a bottle of 1900 Château Latour during the millennial New Year's dinner he hosted. Deeming this an "academic exercise" to see how such an old wine would hold up, he said that while it had faded in color, it was "disarmingly rich, concentrated, and intense," with notes of leather and smoke.

First growths don't capture every ray of the spotlight. Mindful of the limitations of the 1855 classification, collectors like to point to a group of slightly-lower-ranked wines whose quality today rivals that of the top rung. This unofficial group of overachievers—informally dubbed the *super seconds*—see the same kind of coddling as the *premiers crus*: rigorous grape selection, expensive new oak barrels, and so forth. Any list of super seconds is likely to include such top châteaux as Cos d'Estournel, Ducru-Beaucaillou, Pichon-Lalande, Palmer, and Lynch-Bages. Don't confuse the super seconds, which are an informal grouping of châteaux unconnected to a specific tier of 1855 classification, with the second growths, which are the second tier of the official classification.

Depending on the vintage, first growths can cost anywhere from $100 to $500 at release. Some consumers, especially those with a penchant for the best of Bordeaux, buy Bordeaux futures from a particular wine merchant. Futures allow one to lock in the opening price for the wine about two years in advance of its release from the winery. While buying futures of top châteaux in the best years can bring considerable savings, there's no guarantee that the wine is going to appreciate in value between the time you purchase the future and the time it is sold in stores. And while it's a good way to secure hard-to-find labels, you never know if the bottles will live up to the initial assessments made by wine journalists before the wine is even bottled.

On My Table | **CORINNE MENTZELOPOULOS** is co-owner of Bordeaux's Château Margaux and is credited with modernizing this celebrated first-growth château.

Red Bordeaux

"The first growths can attain, in their greatest vintages, a certain form of perfection."

Red Burgundy

"Their aromatic finesse is incomparable."

White Burgundy

Champagne

Vintage port

Riesling from Germany—dessert styles

"Those Trockenbeerenausleses have brought us such wonderful moments."

30 For Merlot-Style Bordeaux, Look to St.-Emilion and Pomerol

Everyone *knows* that restaurants make most of their money selling booze, but $62,138 worth of wine for a dinner for six?

According to the *Guinness Book of World Records*, that's how much six bankers paid at a London restaurant a few years ago for the world's most expensive restaurant meal per capita. Held at London's Pétrus restaurant, the dinner focused on three vintages of the wine for which the restaurant was named—Château Pétrus—including a 1945 Pétrus priced at $16,500.

Fetching even more than Bordeaux's first growths, Château Pétrus often wins the distinction of being the world's most expensive wine. Pétrus comes from the Bordeaux district of Pomerol, where, sadly, most of the best wines of this small region, and its neighbor, St.-Emilion, are priced stratospherically, though not all of them are out of reach.

Located east of Bordeaux's rivers, Pomerol and St.-Emilion compose what is known as Bordeaux's Right Bank. While Left Bank districts Médoc and Graves tend to use more Cabernet Sauvignon in their wine, the Right Bank favors the round, soft character of Merlot; in fact, Château Pétrus is almost 100 percent Merlot in most years. This means that, price notwithstanding, a bottle from Pomerol or St.-Emilion can be a better starter Bordeaux for the uninitiated, with the predominance of Merlot instilling less tannic laceration than its equivalent from the Médoc.

Even with Merlot's soft, plummy charm, don't expect a Right Bank wine to mirror your favorite Merlot from the United States. As those familiar with French wine would expect, the region's cool climate, soil, and viticultural traditions bring about wine of more subtlety and earthiness. Many observers consider Pomerol and St.-Emilion Merlot's ideal environment, where the clay soil and chilly maritime climate maximize the grape's potential better than the

MARK'S PICKS

Pomerol: Under $50:

Château Bellegrave	Bell-grahv
Château de Sales	duh Sahl
Château Gazin	Gah-zan
Château Mazeyres	Mah-zyair
Château Rouget	Roo-zhay

Pomerol: $50–$200 and Over:

Château L'Evangile	Leh-vah-jeel
Château Lafleur	Lah-fluhr
Château Pétrus	Pay-TRUES
Château Trotanoy	Troh-tah-nwah
Vieux Château Certan	
	View Sha-toe Sehr-tan

St.-Emilion: Under $50:

Château L'Arrosée	Lah-roe-zeh
Clos des Jacobins	Cloe deh Jah-coe-ban
Château La Dominique	Lah Doh-mee-neek
Château La Gaffelière	Lah Gahf-l'yair
Château Haut-Corbin	Oh-Kohr-bahn

St.-Emilion: $50–$200 and Over:

Château Angélus	Ahn-jeh-lews
Château Ausone	Oh-zon
Château Cheval Blanc	Shuh-vahl BLANN
Château Monbousquet	Mohn-boos-keh
Château Pavie	Pah-vee
Château Troplong Mondot	
	Troh-lohn Mohn-doe

OUTSMART THE TABLE

sunny hills of California. For this reason, Right Bank wine generally garners more awe in wine circles than varietal Merlot from the States. A good Pomerol or St.-Emilion can show a stunning degree of complexity, with a swirl of vanilla, cedar, earth, and chocolate that resonates on your palate for one velvety eternity. The very best combine relatively easy drinkability with enough structure and power to improve for fifteen years or more, but in most cases not as long as Médoc's top dogs.

Both Pomerol and St.-Emilion are relative newcomers on wine's center stage, having achieved fame in the 1980s when critics discovered how well they satisfied the world's emerging demand for kinder, gentler reds. To the casual taster, differences between wines from the two districts are slight, but Pomerol is said to be the richer and lusher of the two, in part because of its soil's heavy concentration of clay. The Cabernet Franc grape tends to play a larger role in the wines of St.-Emilion, often giving them a slightly herbal or cedary dimension.

Given their cachet and relative scarcity, many Pomerols and St.-Emilions go for at least $50 and often more than twice that. Pomerols are particularly expensive. Don't beat yourself up trying to find particular châteaux, because most merchants stock only a handful; let a knowledgeable salesperson steer you to the best bets. St.-Emilion has its own classification system, which is updated every ten years, while Pomerol has never had an official ranking.

On My Table | **T O R I A M O S** is a Grammy-nominated singer-songwriter and Bordeaux lover known for her intense piano arrangements, erotic lyrics, and zealous following.

Red Bordeaux—Médoc

Pichon-Longueville Comtesse de Lalande—"The Comtesse has been at our table sharing her beauty, love, and laughter." Chateau Gruaud-Larose—"Just absolute heaven. This wine is a composition I desire to play."

Red Bordeaux—Pomerol

Château Latour—"This Big Mama shares her bounty with [our chef] Duncan Pickford's *ragoût de boeuf.*"

Red Bordeaux—St.-Emilion

Château Magdelaine—"She blesses and graces our table on winter solistice."

Spanish Reds

Descendientes de J Palacios Corullon [from the little-known Bierzo region, located in the northwest corner of Spain]—"This is a sexy, sweet, provocative Spanish lady."

31 For Budget Bordeaux, Look Beyond the Buzz

With all this talk about first growths and *Guinness Book* records, the notion of a good cheap Bordeaux may seem oxymoronic. And, indeed, if you're stalking bargain reds, you're better off in Australia or Chile or Argentina or southern Italy.

That said, with some research and strategizing, good Bordeaux can be had without resorting to pawn shops or Chapter 11 protection. Here are four ways.

Top Châteaux in Off-Vintages

If you're interested in the top châteaux but don't want to pay their astronomical price tags, try purchasing them in off-vintages—a useful strategy often recommended by wine educators. Many people wrongly assume that all wine will be disappointing in a less-than-stellar vintage, but this is just not the case. Through severe grape selection and other hands-on care, top winemakers often make delicious wine—though it won't necessarily have the ageability or complex, concentrated flavor of the best years.

Cru Bourgeois (of the Médoc) in Good Years

There's a whole world of Bordeaux wine beyond the 1855 classification. Most notably, the next ranking down, called the *cru bourgeois*, includes about three hundred Médoc châteaux that didn't make the cut in 1855. Despite its name, there is nothing *bourgeois* about some of these châteaux; in fact, the best of them would likely get an invite to Médoc's *cru classé* were its ranking ever revamped. In the meantime, we can take advantage of their moderate prices, which typically range between $12 and $25.

A *cru bourgeois* wine may not have the longevity or complexity of a top classified growth, but it can offer a lot of Bordeaux charm, as well as an impressive-looking label, at a fraction of the price. I recently served a magnum of one of my favorites, Château Monbrison, at Thanksgiving dinner—and the table loved it so much we might as well have been drinking a wine several times the price.

A SELECTION OF *CRUS BOURGEOIS*

Château d'Agassac	*dah-gah-SACK*
Château de Pez	*duh PEHZ*
Château de Marbuzet	*Mahr-bew-ZEH*
Château Gloria	*Glow-ree-YAH*
Château Greysac	*GREH-zahk*
Château Lafon	*Lah-FOHN*
Château Larose-Trintaudon	*Lah-ROSE-Trent-oh-DOAN*
Château Les Ormes-de-Pez	*Lay Zohrm-duh-PEHZ*
Château Meyney	*May-NAY*
Château Monbrison	*Mohn-bree-ZOHN*
Château Phélan-Ségur	*Fay-LAHN-Say-GEWR*
Château Siran	*See-RAHN*

Second Wines

Virtually every classified growth and many other châteaux have something called *second wines*—which, echoing *Saturday Night Live*'s "not ready for prime-time players," are made from grapes not good enough for the marquee wine. These aren't bad grapes, mind you—they just lack the concentration and power of a château's *grand vin.* In truly awful vintages, some uncompromising wine-makers will go so far as to relegate all of their grapes to a second (or third) wine.

At best, the advantage of second wines is that they can give you a sense of a château's style at a fraction of the price of the primary wine—like buying a Wolfgang Puck pizza in lieu of eating at Spago. Don't expect, however, close similarities between the *grand vin* and the second wine; most observers see only a hazy congruity, if even that. And, of course, a second wine has nothing to do with the second growths of the 1855 classification, although most of those esteemed châteaux have second wines.

The name of a second wine will often incorporate words from its château's primary wine—such as Château Latour's Les Forts de Latour. Don't be disappointed if you can't find your favorite château's second wine—many are harder to source than their *grand vin.* Some, like Château Mouton-Rothschild's Le Petit-Mouton, are virtually unobtainable in the States.

A SELECTION OF SECOND WINES

SECOND WINE . . .	OF CHÂTEAU . . .
Clos du Marquis (Klow dew Mahr-KEE)	Léoville-Las-Cases
La Dame de Montrose (Mohn-TROS)	Montrose
Les Forts de Latour (Lay Fohr duh Lah-TOOR)	Latour

SECOND WINE . . .	OF CHÂTEAU . . .
Pavillon Rouge de Château Margaux (*Pah-vee-yohn Roozh duh Sha-TOH Mahr-GOH*)	Margaux
Réserve de la Comtesse (*Kohn-TEHS*)	Pichon-Longueville Comtesse de Lalande
Sarget de Gruaud-Larose (*Sahr-geh duh Groo-oh-Lah-ROHZ*)	Gruaud-Larose

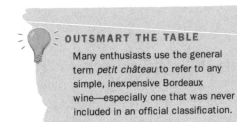

OUTSMART THE TABLE
Many enthusiasts use the general term *petit château* to refer to any simple, inexpensive Bordeaux wine—especially one that was never included in an official classification.

Fronsac and Other Up-and-Coming Regions

There are also some good buys outside Bordeaux's four major red wine districts. If you see Fronsac in a store or on a wine list, know that this is a good region for big, full-flavored, sometimes tannic red Bordeaux retailing in the $15-to-$25 range. Although Fronsac is located just west of Merlot-dominated St.-Emilion, its wine tends to have significant proportions of Cabernet Franc as well as some Cabernet Sauvignon and Malbec. Nearby Canon-Fronsac is said to make wine of slightly finer character. Popular selections include Château Les Trois Croix (Lay Trwah Krwah), Château Canon-Moueix (Cah-nohn-Mwexx), Château Fontenil (Font-neel), and Château La Croix Canon (Lah Krwah Cah-nohn).

Another good deal, and one that is perhaps softer and more immediately approachable, is Lalande de Pomerol, often available for less than $30. A northern satellite of the grand Pomerol district, Lalande de Pomerol produces wines with high percentages of Merlot, delivering some of the soft charm we see in Pomerol, although usually with less body, concentration, and longevity. Quality estates include Château La Fleur de Boüard (Lah Fluhr duh Boew-ahr), Château La Sergue (Lah Sehrg), Château Les Cruzelles (Lay Krew-zell), Château Haut-Chaigneau (Oh-Sheh-nyo), and Château La Fleur-St.-Georges (Lah Fluhr-San-Zhorzh).

32 Red Burgundy: French Pinot Noir, Gloriously Aromatic and Silky

Backwash at $200 a bottle?

There I was, finishing my first barrel sample in the dark, chilly cellar of one of Burgundy's most celebrated domaines. As I went to pour the remnants of my glass into a nearby spittoon, my host, a renowned winemaker, reacted as if I were about to leap off a cliff.

"*Non!*" he barked, grabbing my arm. He then poured the remains of his glass back into the barrel and motioned for me to do the same. I did so reluctantly, wondering if this winery was in the business of hawking backwash at $200 a bottle.

So it was at every domain I visited in Burgundy's Côte d'Or, or "golden slope," where wine is so scarce they won't even waste your last, saliva-saturated drops. (Not to worry: the alcohol supposedly eliminates any impurities.)

Then again, there is sometimes something pleasantly dirty—or at least earthy—about fine Burgundy. You see, although it won't say so on the label, all red Burgundy comes from the Pinot Noir grape, as no other grape is allowed in red wine from this famous region of eastern France. American Pinot Noir, as discussed in Shortcut 17, typically has bright berry aromas and tangy acidity. Its cousin red Burgundy displays a similar profile, but in this sun-challenged locale its aromas are more subtle and often include an underlying hint of earthiness, like mushrooms or forest floor, which increases with age. Mature versions can even exude a slight barnyard or aged-beef gaminess, a quality deemed desirable by many. Some red Burgundy is light bodied and fruity, while others are medium bodied, with richness and noticeable tannin. Either way, the wine typically displays a splendidly shimmery glow, a kind of ruby

> "I TASTED THIS RED BURGUNDY, AND IT GAVE ME GOOSE BUMPS. THAT'S WHEN I REALLY UNDERSTOOD HOW BEAUTIFUL WINE COULD BE. WE REFER TO THAT PHENOMENON AS 'KAREN'S TINGLE TEST'—WHEN A WINE GIVES ME GOOSE BUMPS, IT IS SUBLIME."
>
> —*Karen King, wine director of New York's Gramercy Tavern*

translucence that is a world away from midnight-dark wines like Syrah and Zinfandel. What gets me most is its texture: a silky, satiny coating that seems to leave a talcum trail across your palate.

Fine Burgundy is legendary for its complexity, especially as it ages, with layers of aromas and flavors revealing themselves the longer you sit with the wine. With understatement as Burgundy's hallmark, don't expect such complexity to grab you by the nose. Burgundy's subtlety helps to make it the most intellectually challenging of wines, forever demanding your concentration and imagination. Are those violets you smell? Smoke? Cedar? Freshly tilled soil? Mushrooms? Barnyard? Cola? Asian spices? These beguiling nuances, as well as the intoxicating fragrance of berries and rose petals, instills an almost ecclesiastical reverence in Burgundy's enthusiasts. For no other wine have I heard people speak of epiphanic "Burgundy moments," when they first realized Burgundy was something more than "just wine."

Like the streets of Manhattan or a drug addiction, Burgundy's highs are countervailed by frustrations that border on the intolerable. First, the region's marginal weather means that grapes are sometimes starved for sunlight and can thus yield wine that is hard and flavorless. For historical reasons, vineyard land is maddeningly fragmented, and this hodgepodge makes it important to distinguish between villages and vineyards, vintages, and especially producers. Got that?

Finally, because the region of Burgundy is so small, the supply of wine is minuscule, making Burgundy staggeringly expensive—for wines that are deserving of such pricing and for many that aren't. Without careful selection, it is not uncommon to pay $80 or more for a bottle of flavored acid-water. The cruel reality for the Burgundy enthusiast is that he must often play the part of the lovelorn, enduring a steady diet of the lackluster for the occasional sublime embrace.

That said, there are good bottles to be found, and when you have one, a universe of food opportunities

CHEAT SHEET

For those willing to endure its expense, inconsistency, and perplexing intricacy, red Burgundy at its best offers a celestial berry-earth bouquet, waves of nuanced flavors, and a seductively silky texture.

LABEL DECODER

Pinot Noir is the grape. Burgundy is the famous wine region of eastern France. Red Burgundy is 100 percent Pinot Noir.

OUTSMART THE TABLE

Red Burgundy and cheap "Burgundy" jug wine from California are in no way related; jug wine producers appropriate the Burgundy name to add prestige to their gulping wine.

TALK THE TALK

Bourgogne   *Bor-GUH-nyeh*

FIT FOR FEASTING

A huge range of foods, including roast chicken, dishes with earthy components like mushrooms, truffles, and lentils; richer preparations of fish (especially salmon and ahi tuna), veal, and pork; bacon and other smoky foods; game meats (especially with older Burgundy); tomato-based sauces; most cheeses except the extremely pungent; Burgundian favorites like *coq au vin, boeuf à la bourguignonne*, escargots in garlic butter, and, typically after dinner, the rare cheese Epoisses (not-too-stinky versions with richer styles of red Burgundy).

awaits. Being of Pinot Noir stock, red Burgundy is spectacularly versatile with food, its light-to-medium weight and zesty acidity befriending everything but the very heaviest of dishes. As in other historic wine regions, many of the classic pairings spring from local history, focusing on the kind of simple, hearty "supper fare" consumed by the friendly farmer-vintners who inhabit Burgundy. Just as the vintners wash down *boeuf à la bourguignonne, coq au vin,* and crispy roast chicken with red Burgundy, so should you.

Though not nearly as ageable as the tannic powerhouses of Bordeaux, red Burgundy with the requisite tannin and flavor can improve in its first six to ten years of life. Many bottles don't benefit from any aging, and about a dozen top domains make wine that sometimes can be cellared for twenty years or more. It is generally not a good idea to decant red Burgundy, because excessive exposure to air can dissipate its delicate perfume. You can, though, give the wine a bit of a chill, which will focus its flavors.

On My Table | **GEDDY LEE** is an avid wine collector and lead singer and bassist extra-ordinaire for Canada's most celebrated rock band, **Rush,** which has released twenty-four consecutive gold and platinum records, second only to the Beatles and the Rolling Stones.

Red Burgundy—Chambolle-Musigny, Vosne-Romanée, Volnay
Georges Roumier, Dugat-Py, Jayer, Arnoux, Lafarge

Northern Rhône
Chave, Gentaz-Dervieux, Guigal, Jamet

Southern Rhône
Les Cailloux, Mont-Olivet, Rayas, Beaucastel

Barolo and Barbaresco
Altare, Scavino, Sandrone, Mascarello, Giacosa

White Rhône—"Great with lobster . . . oily and powerful."
Chave, Guigal, Paret, Beaucastel Vieilles Vignes

White Bordeaux
Haut-Brion, Laville-Haut-Brion, Chevalier, Smith-Haut-Lafite

Cru Beaujolais—"There is no better everyday food wine."
Diochon, Thivin, Duboeuf

33 A Sampling of Villages for Red Burgundy

If they didn't know about my interest in wine, visitors to my kitchen might think I had a strange obsession with tracking crime scenes. On my kitchen wall I have two long maps, with flags marking off locations, straight out of a *Kojak* rerun. Instead of marking homicides, however, I track the locations of the Burgundies I've had, as the maps give a microscopic, vineyard-by-vineyard account of this region. A bit extreme, yes, but to master the crazy quilt that is Burgundy, it's helpful to familiarize yourself with the major regions and some of the important villages of Burgundy.

Burgundy's heart and soul is the Côte d'Or, or "golden slope," named for the color of the region's autumn foliage but for many symbolizing the twenty-four-karat prices of the wine produced here. The Côte d'Or is divided into two subregions: the Côte de Nuits and Côte de Beaune, some of whose villages are described here. South of the Côte d'Or is the other region associated with red Burgundy, the Côte Chalonnaise, the more affordable, "value" region for Burgundy wine.

If you're wondering why it's necessary to learn so much geography, it's because location counts for a lot in Burgundy. More than any other wine region, Burgundy is associated with the idea that each parcel of land has its own consistently identifiable character, or *terroir*, that comes from the unique soil, slope, sunlight, microclimate, and other nonhuman factors affecting that land. Many Burgundy winemakers believe that a vineyard's unique *terroir* plays a significant role in determining the wine's ultimate bouquet and flavor. (See Shortcut 11 for more on *terroir*.)

Consistent with this emphasis on location, each village of the Côte d'Or is said to have its own character, which is often described along the politically incorrect lines of gender. Some villages, for example, are known for "masculine" wine—dark, powerful, earthy, gamy, and sometimes surprisingly tannic for Pinot Noir. Others have a reputation for wine that shades to the "feminine"—displaying finesse in its delicate weight, floral aromatics, softer tannins, and satiny texture. Relying too much on these generalizations is risky business since so much also depends on the winemaker's influence as well as the year of vintage and other factors. And with all of this wine coming from the same grape, Pinot Noir, the differences are often subtle and difficult to distinguish even for professional palates.

As an introduction, the following gives red Burgundy's main regions and some famous villages therein, along with some very broad generalizations about these villages' overall character. I have also added some of my favorite producers, but given the wine's scarcity, you're unlikely to find many at your local wine retailer.

CHEAT SHEET

Each of the villages of Burgundy's Côte d'Or is known for a slightly different style that sometimes manifests itself in the wine.

OUSTMART THE TABLE

Vosne-Romanée's Domaine de la Romanée-Conti, shortened to *DRC* by insiders, is Burgundy's most famous producer. Among its *grand cru* vineyards is the eponymous Romanée-Conti, whose four and a half acres yield wine that can fetch over $1,000 a bottle.

A Sampling of Burgundy Villages

REGION: CÔTE D'OR (COAT DOOR) Burgundy's famed center stage, a thirty-five-mile strip that is home to the region's greatest domains and choicest real estate.

SUBREGION: CÔTE DE NUITS (Coat duh NWEE) The Côte d'Or's northern half, generally known for more powerful wine, almost all of it red.

Gevrey-Chambertin (Jeh-VRAY Sham-bear-TAN) Responsible for many of the most coveted red Burgundies. Known for full-bodied, powerful wine that at its best balances rich fruit with firm tannins. Includes the famous *grand cru* vineyard Chambertin.

Favorite producers: Dugat (Doo-GAH), Faiveley (FAVE-ah-lee), Louis Jadot (Jah-DOE), Denis Mortet (Duh-nee More-teh).

Chambolle-Musigny (Sham-BOWL Mu-SIN-yee) Surprisingly soft and elegant for wine from the Côte de Nuits. Rich, spicy, with an emphasis on red fruits. Contains the famous *premier cru* vineyards Les Amoureuses and Charmes as well as the *grand cru* vineyard Musigny, among others.

Favorite producers: Comte Georges de Vogüé (deh VOE-gway), Drouhin (Drew-ahn), Dujac (Dew-zhahk), J. F. Mugnier (Mew-nyay), Georges Roumier (Roo-myay).

Vosne-Romanée (Vone-Rom-ma-NAY) The zenith of red Burgundy, perhaps of all wine. Known for big, velvety wines of superb balance. Its six *grand cru* vineyards include superstars Romanée-Conti and La Tache.

Favorite producers: Domaine de la Romanée-Conti (Raw-ma-NAY-Kawn-TEE), Leroy (Luh-RWAH), Robert Arnoux (Ahr-NOO), Méo-Camuzet (May-oh-Kam-oo-ZEH).

Nuits-Saint-Georges (Nwee-San-ZHORZH) Known for sturdy, spicy, earthy wine, but its southern half can make lighter, more elegant wine.

Favorite producers: L'Arlot (Lar-LOW), Robert Chevillon (Ro-BEAR Shev-ee-YAWN), Leroy (Luh-RWAH), Henri Gouges (GOOJH).

SUBREGION: CÔTE DE BEAUNE (Coat duh BONE) The Côte d'Or's southern half, known for both red and white wines. Compared to those of the Côte de Nuits, the red wine here is generally softer and less powerful.

Savigny-lès-Beaune (Sah-VEE-nyee-lay-BONE) Perhaps the best value in the Côte d'Or, it is home to wine that is light, agreeable, and considerably less expensive than its more prestigious neighbors.

Favorite producers: Bouchard (Boo-SHAR), Simon Bize (See-mon Beez), Bruno Clair, Maurice Ecard (Ay-CAHR), Louis Jadot (Jah-DOE), Leroy (Luh-RWAH).

Volnay (Vole-NAY) The most elegant, immediately likable red Burgundy. Floral, violet-and-lilac aromatics and spicy red fruits make it a great "starter Burgundy." No *grand cru* vineyards, but plenty of *premiers crus*, such as Caillerets and Clos des Chênes, that demand the big bucks.

Favorite producers: Domaine de la Pousse d'Or (Poos DOHR), Michel Lafarge (Mee-shell Lah-FAHRZH), Marquis d'Angerville (DAHN-jehr-veel).

REGION: CÔTE CHALONNAISE (COAT SHAH-LON-NEHZ) The second string for red Burgundy; what these wines lack in complexity and polish they make up for in simple charm and affordability. Two popular villages:

Mercurey (Mair-coo-RAY) Considered the best of the Côte Chalonnaise, Mercurey at its best offers lots of spicy cranberry charm.

Favorite producers: A & P de Villaine (deh VEE-lehn), Chartron et Trébuchet (shar-TRAWN aye Treh-bew-SHAY), Faiveley (FAVE-ah-lee), Juillot (Jhee-yo).

Santenay (Sahn-t'NAY) Less famous than Mercurey but often a good deal in the hands of a reputable producer.

Favorite producers: Bouchard, Vincent Girardin (Van-SAHN Zhee-rahr-DAN), Louis Jadot (Jah-DOE), Bernard Morey (Bear-NAHR More-AY).

On My Table | **ALLEN MEADOWS** is one of the world's leading authorities on the wines of Burgundy and the man behind Burghound.com, a leading online resource for Burgundy information.

Red Burgundy—Vosne-Romanée—"Unequaled for their exotic spice."

Red Burgundy—Chambolle-Musigny—"Perhaps most intensely perfumed [of red Burgundies]."

Red Burgundy—Volnay—"[These wines] most closely resemble Chambolle-Musigny."

White Burgundy—Puligny-Montrachet—"My favorite [*grand cru* here] is Chevalier-Montrachet."

White Burgundy—Meursault—"A 'friendly' wine . . . with a wonderful butter and nut quality."

34 The Best Burgundies Are Ranked by Location, Not Producer

As in Bordeaux, French wine laws have established a pecking order for Burgundy that indicates levels of quality. But while Bordeaux is ranked according to producers, or châteaux, wine from Burgundy's celebrated Côte d'Or is ranked by where its grapes come from. As a general rule, the more specific the location, or *appellation,* noted on the label, the more special the wine is considered, and priced accordingly (i.e., region, village, vineyard).

But even the most geographically specific of designations doesn't guarantee a great-tasting wine—much still depends on the producer, the vintage, and other factors. That said, French law requires higher-ranked wines to have lower vineyard yields, which means, for instance, that a *grand cru* wine is hoped to taste more concentrated and flavorful than a village-level bottling. Winemakers also apply more effort to their higher-ranked wines, selecting the grapes more carefully, using new oak barrels, and coddling them in other ways. But there are never guarantees in Burgundy, and a lower-ranked wine in the hands of a top producer can outshine a higher-ranked wine from a middling producer.

On the next page are the quality designations of the Burgundy's most famous vineyard area, the Côte d'Or.

CHEAT SHEET
French law ranks the wine of Burgundy's Côte d'Or according to the location of its grapes.

OUTSMART THE TABLE
Despite giving rise to some of the world's most expensive wines, the spirit of the Burgundy area is not nearly as formal as that of Bordeaux. Whereas Bordeaux is about stately eighteenth-century châteaux and aristocratic pretenses, Burgundy has a looser, friendlier feel that springs from its agricultural roots.

Côte d'Or Quality Levels

LEVEL	HOW IT APPEARS ON THE LABEL
Generic $10–20	**general region** e.g., Bourgogne or Côte de Beaune/Nuits Villages

Made from grapes anywhere in the entire region of Burgundy—not just one particular village or vineyard therein. Affordable but often undistinguished. Safest to stick with big producers like Bouchard.

Village $20–45	**village name** e.g., Gevrey-Chambertin or Volnay

Made from grapes in or around a particular village. This is where Burgundy starts to get interesting, but the market is flooded with disappointing examples.

Premier Cru $35–90	**village + vineyard** e.g., Volnay Les Amoureuses or **village + *premier cru* (or 1er cru)** e.g., Volnay *premier cru*

Made from grapes in *premier cru*–ranked vineyards within a particular village. Often a big leap up in quality from village wine, but only in the hands of a good producer.

Grand Cru $80–sky's the limit	**only the vineyard** e.g., Le Musigny, La Tache, Le Chambertin

Made from grapes grown in one of the Côte d'Or's thirty-three *grand cru* vineyards, the most prime vineyard land in Burgundy, perhaps the world. Like Aristotle or Eminem, it needs only one name; only the specific *grand cru* vineyard name is given (not the village in which that vineyard is located). The *grand cru* vineyard name is often preceded by *Le* or *La*.

35 Producers Are Paramount in Burgundy

Who can resist those Discovery Channel documentaries following the hearty souls who nurse fragile creatures like orphaned tiger cubs and maimed fawns to full health?

I was reminded of these shows on a recent trip to Burgundy, where the wine people I met displayed the same attentive, obsessive care in tending to their vineyards. Winemakers spoke of backbreaking days spent pruning their vines of excess grape bunches, an effort to keep vineyard yields down and ultimately make more concentrated, flavorful wine. Chloé de Smet, of the family responsible for the terrific Domaine de l'Arlot in Burgundy's Nuits-St.-Georges, described how during a spring freeze she and her family would spend sleepless nights placing dozens of makeshift coal heaters throughout their vineyards to protect the vines from frost. Winemaker Bernard Morey even spoke of how he used to use small rockets to protect his vineyards from hailstorms—a scheme right out of the Wile E. Coyote playbook.

These extraordinary efforts help explain why, villages and quality rankings aside, producers are of paramount importance in Burgundy. The best producers have a kind of fiery dedication that drives them to find ways to make excellent wine even in off-vintages. Their identity is linked inextricably with their wine; when I asked ace winemaker Simon Bize to describe his wines, he threw up his arms and asked: "How do you describe *yourself?*" Such dedication contrasts with the myriad indifferent Burgundy producers, willing to coast on the reputation of their villages and the scarcity of their wine.

With Burgundy's fragmented ownership of land, where one vineyard often has multiple owners, it is essential to familiarize yourself with which producers keep the faith and which are along for the ride. Think about it: the *grand cru* vineyard Clos de Vougeot, for example, has about eighty different owners. This means that all of its wine has the right to carry the prestigious Clos de Vougeot name, but only some are worth the $70-to-$500 price that this elite designation will fetch. It's like eighty chefs using the same caviar and truffles to make eighty different meals; the good chefs will make masterpieces, the bad ones messes, but they'll all fetch high prices. Knowing the good producers gives you

a fighting chance to steer clear of Burgundy's overpriced duds. Some Burgundy lovers buy on the producer reputation alone. Shortcut 33 lists some of my favorite producers of red Burgundy.

Producer is an intentionally vague term, because in Burgundy there are two types. The first are estate bottlers, or *domaines*, which are small producers that grow their own grapes and make wine in the usual way we see in the United States. The other type are shippers, called *négociants*, typically larger operations that purchase grapes or grape juice from independent growers and then ferment, age, and ship the wine. Sometimes *négociants* buy wine that is already fermented and process it from there; to compete with estate bottlers, some *négociants* also grow grapes themselves. Because they control quality at the source, estate bottlers are generally thought to make more exciting, individualistic wine. While *négociants* have long gotten a bad rap for making less-inspired wine, a number of reputable *négociants*, such as Louis Latour, Joseph Drouhin, and Bouchard Père et Fils, consistently make wine rivaling that of good *domaines*.

While producers are paramount in Burgundy, vintages are also important. With its inland, cool-climate location, Burgundy has frightfully inconsistent weather, seeing more than its fair share of frost, rain, hail, and cloud cover. The meteorological troubles would be a problem for any growing region, but in one whose red wine is based solely on the sensitive and fickle Pinot Noir grape, it means that vintages count more here than in most places. The rule of thumb is that Burgundy sees about three terrific vintages in a decade.

On My Table | **JAY MCINERNEY**, the literary celebrity best known for the 1980s coming-of-age classic *Bright Lights, Big City,* moonlights as a wine columnist for *House and Garden* magazine and is author of the droll, insightful wine book called *Bacchus and Me* (Vintage).

Red Burgundy—Vosne-Romanée, Gevrey-Chambertin, Volnay

d'Angerville, Bertagna, Montille, Lafarge, Domaine Dujac, F. Magnien, Domaine Leroy, Claude Dugat, Dugat-Py, Perot Minot, Méo-Camuzet, J. F. Mugnier, Roumier, Rousseau

White Burgundy—Chablis

Domaine Barat, René and Vincent Dauvissat, Jean Dauvissat, Domaine Laroche, François Raveneau, Savary, Verget—"Steely purity."

Barbaresco

Cereto Cortese, Gaja, Giacosa, Pellisero, La Spinetta, Albino Rocca

Riesling from Austria—"May be the ultimate food wine for the way we eat now."

Alzinger, Brundlmayer, Emerich Knoll, F. X. Pichler, Rudi Pichler, Prager, Hiedler, Hirtzberger, Nigl, Salomon

Zinfandel

Martinelli, Turley, Ridge, Ravenswood, Rafanelli, Renwood, Biale, Neyers, Seghesio, Château Potelle, Hartford Court, Joel Gotti

White Rhône—Condrieu (Viognier)

Yves Cuilleron, Yves Gangloff, Guigal, André Perret, Georges Vernay, René Rostaing

Red Bordeaux

Haut-Brion, La Mission-Haut-Brion, Margaux, Léoville-Barton, Ducru-Beaucaillou, Grand-Puy-Lâcoste, Pichon-Longueville Comtesse de Lalande, Lynch-Bages, Latour, Lafite-Rothschild, Mouton-Rothschild, Cos d'Estournel, Petite Village, Vieux Château Certan, Certan de May, La Conseillante, Cheval Blanc, Faugères, Figeac, Pavie Macquin, Tertre-Rôteboeuf

Southern Rhône—Châteauneuf-du-Pape

Beaucastel, Boisrenard, Henri Bonneau, Clos des Papes, Les Cailloux, Font de Michelle, Texier, Vieux Télégraphe

Burning for Burgundy: Survey Respondents on Red Burgundy

"My first love! Wild, heady wines, and once one has found the right producers, the sky is the limit. There is nothing like the extraordinary, sensual wines of the Côte de Nuits."

—Serena Sutcliffe, head of Sotheby's wine department

"I find great red Burgundy to be the most hedonistic, most ethereal, and most graceful of all wine experiences and as a result the most memorable."

—Geddy Lee, rock musician and collector

"I love the soft and feminine Burgundies because they go so well with the braised winter food I like to cook and eat."

—Mario Batali, celebrity chef

"At its best, red Burgundy has silkier texture and wilder aromatics than anything I know, and it is more food friendly than just about any red wine on the planet. My advice: start with Volnay, the most reliable appellation, and work your way up from village to *premiers crus.*"

—Jay McInerney, novelist and wine writer

"The best are all silk and velvet, and I prefer red wine with most fish dishes."

—Mireille Guiliano, president, Clicquot, Inc.

"There is no greater expression of red in the world when it is done right and from a great vintage. These wines take a lot of time to find themselves and are not flattering in their youth all the time; there are more bad Burgundies out there than any other region as well."

—John Kapon, president and auction director, Acker, Merrall & Condit

36 Beaujolais Nouveau : The Ultimate Starter Red, Fruity and Gulpable

There is an unofficial but vocal fraternity of wine drinkers who have sworn off red wine because of its sometimes bitter taste or its exaggerated reputation for causing headaches (see Shortcut 106). If you have such a Red Objector in your life, the best way to wean him or her off this pigment prejudice is to crack open a bottle of Beaujolais Nouveau, a red that is light and charming enough to win over the staunchest blancophile.

Hailing from the southern part of France's Burgundy region, though it's not thought of as a prestigious red Burgundy, Beaujolais Nouveau is the essence of fruitiness: imagine bright raspberry flavor framed by a zesty backbone of acidity, with none of the bitter tannin that turns off some people. The fruity quality of Gamay, the sole grape responsible for Beaujolais Nouveau, contributes to this vibrancy. So does its *nouveauness*: the wine's grapes are picked, fermented, and bottled all in a matter of weeks, then rushed to the market as France's first wine of the new vintage.

Marketers have seized on the excitement surrounding the wine's early debut, and that's why wine shops and bistros trumpet *"Beaujolais Nouveau est arrivé"* on placards every November. Officially released the third Thursday in November, the wine inspires celebratory tastings and soirées around the world, with some restaurants pouring the first drops of this new wine exactly at the stroke of midnight. You might even consider hosting your own Beaujolais Nouveau party. The wine's fame, easy drinkability, and low price make it the perfect antidote for the chilly days of late autumn. And its light body and lack of tannin allow you to drink it quite chilled.

Despite its popularity, Beaujolais Nouveau should never be mistaken for a wine of breeding or complexity. In fact, some wine snobs dismiss it as no more than happy juice for adults. For most of us, however, its bubblegum ebullience makes it wonderfully *gouleyant,* or "gulpable," but it unfortunately loses its sprightly charm a few months after its November debut. Like a fashionista's no-whites-after-Labor-Day rule, a strict January 1 cutoff date has been imposed on Beaujolais Nouveau by some wine pros, but I've found that the wine usually retains some liveliness through the winter; by late spring its time has passed. For an infusion of Beaujolais exuberance at other times of the year, consider Beaujolais-Villages or the more serious *cru* Beaujolais, covered in Shortcut 51.

On My Table | **PIERRE-HENRY GAGEY**, president of Louis Jadot, leads what is one of Burgundy's finest and largest producers, proving that large *négociants* are capable of making wines rivaling those of smaller domaines.

Beaujolais-Villages
Louis Jadot

Northern Rhône—Côte Rôtie
Guigal

Riesling from Alsace
Trimbach, Hugel, Beyer

Champagne—"As often as possible for an aperitif."
Taittinger, Roederer, Pol Roger

White Burgundy—Puligny-Montrachet
Louis Jadot *premier cru* Les Folatières

Red Burgundy—Gevrey-Chambertin
Louis Jadot Clos Saint Jacques

Vintage port
Taylor, Fonseca

37 Northern Rhône: Where Wine Stops Kidding Around

"**W**e're number three**"** would seem to be the rallying cry for the Rhône Valley, given its somewhat inferior cachet to its sleeker French counterparts, Bordeaux and Burgundy.

What my On My Table surveys found, however, is that the Rhône Valley is actually the favorite region for many insiders. When they dimmed the lights and let their hair down, my survey respondents spoke of wine from the Rhône as "truffles made into wine" (vintner Etienne Hugel), "the greatest red wines in the world" (importer Don Quattlebaum), and reminiscent "of home, the sun, great fruit, spices, sensuality" (Champagne executive Mireille Guiliano).

Perhaps such enthusiasm comes from the fact that when Syrah, the only red grape allowed in the northern Rhône, is grown in challenging soil atop the region's windswept hills, it produces intense wine different from anything else in the world. Wine of the northern Rhône provides a glimpse into wine's most mysteriously dark, brooding side. In finer, more complex bottlings, you may detect things that don't seem like they should be desirable in a beverage, such as tar and leather, but when combined with Syrah's plummy fruit and peppery spice, they make an explosive perfume that penetrates every inch of your body.

Such hedonism comes at a price. Unlike easier-drinking Syrah from other wine regions, such as Australian Shiraz, the finest wines from the northern Rhône can enter the world with punishing tannins. They require patience, sometimes demanding a decade or more to shed their astringency and show their glorious, gripping dark-berry fruit.

If there were an official wine of game meat, wine of the northern Rhône would be it. Its big flavors and heady, almost primal gaminess accentuate the rich, gamy flavors of goose, deer, elk, and other game animals. Lamb, with its strong flavor, is also

"[WINE FROM THE NORTHERN RHÔNE] HAS MYSTERIOUS INNER-MOUTH AROMATICS THAT TRANSPORT YOU TO A SLOWER AND BETTER TIME."

—*Mike Havens,*
winemaker-owner,
Havens Wine Cellars

a perfect choice, as are steak, stews, sausages, and any heavier dish draped in a pepper sauce.

While the northern Rhône also makes some interesting white wine, including Viognier-based Condrieu (see Shortcut 46) and the rich, oily Hermitage Blanc, it is red wine that rules this roost. Here are three main appellations:

HERMITAGE One of the greatest wines of France, Hermitage is the most complex and longest lived of anything coming out of the Rhône. This inky black production hits you between the eyes with plums and blackberries, aromas of cracked black pepper, and firm, pronounced tannins. Many Hermitages, especially finer ones with some bottle age, also offer up the overtones of wild game, earth, minerals, or truffles that make this wine so interesting.

The top of the line in Hermitage is Chave (Shahv), whose densely concentrated and complex charms can set you back more than $100. Also look for Jaboulet (Jah-BOO-leh; famous for its premium La Chapelle bottling), Chapoutier (Sha-POO-tyay), and Delas Frères (Duh-LAH Frehr). Most bottles retail between $50 and $100, with some elite renditions north of that. In good vintages, Hermitage needs a decade or more of bottle age, and prodigious examples have the potential to last for fifty years or more.

CÔTE RÔTIE Like red Hermitage, Côte Rôtie is a special-occasion wine known for its full body, complexity, and tannin. Côte Rôtie translates as "roasted slope," referring to the intense sunlight that bakes the grapes in this hilly place. It is comprised mostly of the Syrah grape, although winemakers sometimes add a bit of the white grape Viognier for aromatic complexity. Speaking of fragrances, some wine pros consider Côte Rôtie the most aromatically exciting of wines, stirring your soul with whiffs of roasted berry fruit, violets and lilacs, along with peppercorns, earth, and even bacon.

Côte Rôtie is a bit more approachable than Hermitage, ready to drink with about five years of bottle age and improving for up to fifteen to twenty years. It rings up in the range of $45 to $80, with some *über*-specimens breaking the $100 mark. The alpha dog of Côte Rôtie is Guigal (Ghee-GAL), a major producer credited with using small oak barrels for aging and other modern winemaking techniques before it was fashionable to do so. Also look for Côte Rôtie from Chapoutier (Shah-POO-tyay), Vidal-Fleury (Vee-dahl Fluh-REE), Jamet (Jah-MEH), and Jaboulet (Jah-BOO-leh).

CROZES-HERMITAGE A kind of Hermitage Jr., with aromas and flavor similar to its more prestigious neighbor but without the richness, complexity, or longevity. This appellation nevertheless makes a straightforward, medium- to full-bodied red, with plummy fruit and fragrant black pepper on the nose and palate. Unlike Hermitage, most Crozes-Hermitage is ready to drink immediately and sells in the $15-to-$25 range. Graillot (Gray-YO) is the benchmark producer, and other reliable names include Chave (Shahv), Albert Belle (Ahl-bair Behl), Jaboulet (Jah-BOO-leh), Chapoutier (Shah-POO-tyay), and Delas Frères (Duh-LAH Frehr).

38 Southern Rhône: Rough-Hewn and Immensely Satisfying

In my living room I have a fluffy sheepskin rug that draws my guests like moths to a flame. Friends take me aside and ask if they can visit with it. They kick off their shoes and rub their feet through it. They roll around on it like catnipping cats. They curl up and fall asleep on it.

This comforting cloud of a rug reminds me of wine from the southern Rhône: it's generally not fancy or expensive, but it is immensely satisfying, especially in the bone-chilling days of winter. Like my jaggedly shaped rug, southern Rhône wine is rough around the edges, with a peppery, smoky rusticity that can be an acquired taste for those used to the smooth, vanilla charms of Merlot. Furthering the sheepskin analogy, they can also have an "animal" quality—flavors of earth, roasted meat, or a funky gaminess that mingles with the essences of blackberries and black cherries.

All this makes for wines of great personality—medium- to full-bodied slingshots of berry and spice coming from grapes that flourish in the region's sunny, olive-and-herbs Mediterranean climate. Indeed, the southern Rhône, located between Lyon in the north and Avignon in the south, is the closest France has to California's sun-soaked climate. Unlike so many Californian wines, however, wine from the southern Rhône often doesn't see a lot of time in new oak, so while it is full-flavored and spicy, it is less likely to have the vanilla character familiar to American taste buds.

Neither will southern Rhône wine have the concentration and power seen in wine in the neighboring north. Whereas northern Rhône reds are based solely on one grape, the mighty Syrah, wine from the southern Rhône can be blended from a cornucopia of grape types. The dominant grape here is Grenache, a supple grape that makes lighter berry-scented wine, with peppery Syrah and Mourvèdre usually playing significant roles, too.

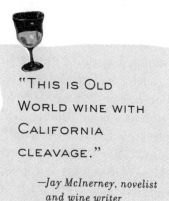

"THIS IS OLD WORLD WINE WITH CALIFORNIA CLEAVAGE."

—*Jay McInerney, novelist and wine writer*

The robust, spicy character of southern Rhône wine cries out for food of the same nature. The gaminess of lamb makes a splendid match, as do rich comfort foods like meat loaf, sausages, hamburgers, and short ribs. *Spice* is the operative word—wherever black pepper and garlic goes, southern Rhône wine will follow along with tail awag. Wine from this region also often has aromas of dried herbs, making it fast friends with rich, herbal sauces.

Although the region produces white wine and rosé (including the extraordinary Tavel), its raison d'être is spicy reds. Here are some of the best:

CHÂTEAUNEUF-DU-PAPE Southern Rhône's most famous wine region, Châteauneuf is the closest the southern Rhône comes to rivaling the complexity and intensity of northern Rhône's Hermitage and Côte Rôtie. While styles vary with the type of grapes used and vineyard location, Châteauneuf at its finest brings together a warm, roasted berry taste with notes of pepper and freshly tilled earth, backed up for a long, lush finish. This wine is so irresistible that it gets its own chapter (Shortcut 54).

CÔTES-DU-RHÔNE The most widely produced wine in the Rhône Valley, Côtes-du-Rhône is hearty, spicy, and unpretentious—a pair of OshKosh overalls to Hermitage's black Bironi three-button. Although it can legally come from anywhere in the Rhône Valley, most Côtes-du-Rhône originates in the flatlands of the southern Rhône, itself a huge expanse of land. Given its variation in geography, and the wine's blend of different grapes, it's difficult to pin down an exact profile for Côtes-du-Rhône. It will often be medium-bodied red with varying degrees of blackberries or raspberries, smoke, pepper, and other spices.

Rarely exceeding $15, Côtes-du-Rhône offers one of the best bangs-for-the-buck in all of wine. This value, combined with its wide availability, is why I call it the "restaurant Rhône"—the Rhône wine to try when you're looking for a low-risk alternative to your usual fallbacks. Guigal (Ghee-GAL) is the benchmark name in Côtes-du-Rhône, joined by major players such as Chapoutier (Shah-POO-tyay) and Château de Beaucastel (Bow-kahs-TEHL). Jaboulet (Jah-BOO-leh) is another mainstay, its vividly named Parallèle "45" consistently delivering an attractively dense package of black cherry and spice. While wine labeled Côtes-du-Rhône-Villages is subject to stricter growing laws and is therefore supposed to be higher in quality, many bottlings of regular Côtes-du-Rhône are just as tasty.

OTHERS Other major southern Rhône designations include Gigondas and Vacqueyras, two villages whose wine was once lumped in with Côtes-du-Rhône-Villages but eventually earned the right to their own appellations. Sturdy and spicy with plenty of the region's characteristic dark berry earthiness, they lie between Côtes-du-Rhône and Châteauneuf-du-Pape in price and complexity. Gigondas, a wine recommended enthusiastically by my survey respondents, usually hovers in the $20 range, while Vacqueyras is a few dollars less. Another name to remember is Côtes du Ventoux, an increasingly popular bargain Rhône in the league of Côtes-du-Rhône. You've probably seen the distinctive "goat label" of the Côtes du Ventoux from La Vieille Ferme (Lah VEE-yah Fehrm), a bold, spicy, classically southern Rhône wine that is a steal at under $10.

CHEAT SHEET

Flavorful, intense, and food friendly, southern Rhône wine offers berry fruit, pepper, and other spices, sometimes mixed with essences of earth, herbs, or game.

LABEL DECODER

Châteauneuf-du-Pape, Gigondas, and Vacqueyras refer to districts within the southern part of France's Rhône Valley. Côtes-du-Rhône, for the most part, also refers to grapes grown in the southern Rhône. Several types of grapes are permitted, with Grenache dominant and Syrah and Mourvèdre also common.

TALK THE TALK

Châteauneuf-du-Pape

	Shah-toe-nuff-dew-PAHP
Côtes-du-Rhône	Coat-doo-RONE
Grenache	Gruh-NAHSH
Mourvèdre	Moohr-VEHDR
Gigondas	Gee-GOHN-dahss
Vacqueyras	Vah-kay-RAHSS
Côtes du Ventoux	COAT doo Von-TOO

MARK'S PICKS

Chapoutier	Shah-POO-tyay
Château de Beaucastel	Bow-kahs-TEHL
Jaboulet	Jah-BOO-leh

FIT FOR FEASTING

Perfect with robust country food like stews (especially cassoulet), sausages, lamb dishes of all kinds; bacon and other smoky fare; dishes with hearty vegetables like zucchini or eggplant; peppery foods; French onion soup and other oniony creations; dishes with olives; aromatic herbs such as rosemary and thyme.

39 Chianti: A Wine Reinvented That Demands Food

> "CHIANTI IS CREATED TO BE AN ACCESSORY TO A MEAL, NOT A MEAL IN ITSELF."
>
> —*Michael Bonaccorsi, the late vintner and master sommelier*

CHEAT SHEET

The prototypical Tuscan wine, Chianti is all about sour berries, savory spice, and its signature swath of acidity, which makes it heroic with food.

LABEL DECODER

Chianti is a district in Italy's Tuscany region. Its primary grape is Sangiovese.

OUTSMART THE TABLE

• The black rooster, or *gallo nero*, adorning the neck of some Chianti Classico bottles is a loose designation of quality created before the current wine laws took effect; many bottles still carry it, though it isn't necessarily a guarantee of good wine.

CONTINUED ▶

The great unanswered question, when Anthony Hopkins's Hannibal Lecter references his pairing of "liver with some fava beans and a nice Chianti" in that famous *Silence of the Lambs* scene, is whether Lecter proves himself a connoisseur or a rube.

The verdict is that Lecter is spot on in his match, as the juicy, tart cherry quality of a good Italian Chianti brings out the best in a slice of gamy liver and earthy fava beans. Yet those unfamiliar with modern Chianti might question why a man of Lecter's refined tastes (however fiendish) would choose a wine once famous for its cheap straw jacket and ubiquity in mom-and-pop joints decorated with levitated salamis and kitschy place mats.

What they don't realize is that the Chianti of today is a far cry from the orange-tinted, harsh plonk whose straw-clad bottle had more utility as a candleholder than as a flavorful wine. In recent decades, winemakers have rescued Chianti from its status as a vinous embarrassment, employing modern winemaking techniques and equipment to make wine that is now the talk of the wine world. Although mediocre, unripe-tasting versions still persist, today there is an abundance of fine Chianti, with basic versions tending to be a bit lighter with cherry-strawberry fruit and a bit of savory spice, while better stuff combines that strawberry perfume with some plumminess, pepper, or earth. But no matter how complex it gets, Chianti remains medium bodied and only moderately tannic, so expect it to contrast significantly with hefty and sometimes gratingly tannic Cabernet Sauvignon.

In no way, however, is Chianti a sipping wine crafted to keep you company by the swimming pool. Its primary grape,

Sangiovese, helps gives the wine a biting acidity that leads to a surprising duality: it is sometimes too edgy to drink by itself but fabulous with food. This otherwise sharp wine positively sings in the presence of oil-based dishes like marinated peppers, olives, and tomato-oriented Italian classics like lasagne and veal parmigiana and tomato-and-mozzarella salad. Like a lion tamer's whip, tart foods neutralize the sour acidity of Chianti, turning it into a purring food friend. Factor in Chianti's not-too-heavy weight and spicy cherry-strawberry fruit, and you have one of the great food-friendly wine types.

When purchasing Chianti, look for the phrase *Chianti Classico*, which means that the wine comes from the hilly, higher-quality Classico part of Tuscany's Chianti district; expect to pay in the $14-to-$20 range. Chianti Classico Riserva is even more prized, denoting that the wine is not only from the central Classico area but has been aged significantly longer in oak barrels and has aromas of smoke and spice to prove it. This top level is generally priced between $20 and $40, a tempting deal when you compare it to the pricier prestige wines of Italy's Piedmont region. There is a raft of excellent Chianti producers large and small, but if you're looking for a dependable starting point, the time-honored blue chips Antinori and Ruffino (you'll recognize the Riserva Ducale's famous gold label) rarely disappoint. But think twice if you plan to give Chianti as a gift to impress; unless he or she is aware of its renaissance, your recipient may assume it is still the checkered tablecloth, Billy-Joel-state-of-mind kind of wine.

• Recent years have seen dozens of American vintners—many of whom have roots themselves in the Old World—experiment with Sangiovese and other historically Italian grapes. While results have often been disappointing, California wineries such as Shafer, Luna, Saddleback, and Pride have produced reliably charming Sangiovese.

TALK THE TALK

Chianti	K'YAHN-tee
Sangiovese	Sahn-joe-VAY-zeh
Ducale	Doo-CAH-leh

MARK'S PICKS

Antinori	Ahn-TEE-no-ree
Castello di Gabbiano	
	Cah-STELL-oh dee Gab-ee-ahn-oh
Castello di Volpaia	Vol-PIE-uh
Cecchi	CHEHK-kee
Fontodi	Fohn-TOE-dee
Frescobaldi	Fres-coh-BALD-ee
Monsanto	Mon-SAHN-toe
Rocca delle Macie	
	ROH-ca deh-leh Mah-CHEE-ay
Ruffino	Roo-FEE-no
San Felice	Sahn Feh-LEE-cheh

FIT FOR FEASTING

A huge range, including tomato-based Italian classics, from chicken cacciatore to baked ziti; gutsy Mediterranean dishes emphasizing oil and/or olives, such as sardines, pesto, and antipasto of all kinds (e.g., marinated peppers, eggplant, sun-dried tomatoes); rabbit; earthy standards such as pasta fagiole and minestrone soup; pizza; dishes flavored with herbs such as savory leaves, thyme, oregano, and mint; Pecorino, Parmigiano-Reggiano, and other dry cheeses; Gorgonzola and other blue-veined cheeses (with richer Chianti).

On My Table | **PIERO ANTINORI** is the legendary owner of Italy's Marchese Antinori, credited with revolutionizing the Italian wine industry and bringing Tuscany international recognition.

Chianti Classico

Felsina, Fonterutoli, Badia a Passignano

Sauvignon Blanc from New Zealand

Cloudy Bay

Bolgheri Superiore [the Italian region that produces many of Italy's Super Tuscans, including Antinori's famed Ornellaia]—"The Italian Médoc."

Cabernet Sauvignon from Napa Valley

Reds from southern Italy

Antinori's Tormaresca [inexpensive blend of Cabernet Sauvignon and Negroamaro, a sturdy red grape popular in the region of Puglia]

Red Bordeaux

Mouton-Rothschild, Château La Lagune, Cos d'Estournel

Champagne

Krug, Pol Roger, Bollinger

40 Brunello Requires Patience, Food, and Serious Financing

Brunello di Montalcino is where Tuscany drops its breezy charm and gets serious. This massive wine eclipses even the Tuscan sun and turns everything to blackberries, chocolate, and leather, delivered on a tannic, two-ton tray.

Tuscany's most celebrated wine, Brunello originates from the grape of the same name, which is actually just a superior strain of Sangiovese, the primary grape of Chianti. Despite being from similar stock, Brunello and Chianti have markedly different personalities, in part because Brunello's hometown of Montalcino is located south of the Chianti zone, which means the grapes get riper, producing heftier wine. By law, Brunello is aged longer than any other Tuscan wine, and, unlike Chianti, which is often blended with other grape types, Brunello stays 100 percent faithful to the intense clutch of Sangiovese. The result is wine that is dark, brooding, syrupy thick, often torturously tannic—a manly man's wine if there ever was one.

Brunello is also a wine inspired by the tortoise, not the hare. The best examples develop at glacial speed, demanding at least a decade to shed their tannic armor and reveal an often stunningly complex mix of blackberry, tar, and chocolate. It's not unusual for a fine Brunello to need at least ten years of cellaring before it is ready to drink; some need double that or longer to reach their peak. Although some producers are experimenting with modern techniques to make their wines more approachable, such as substituting small French oak barrels for traditional Slovenian oak casks, many others remain fiercely wedded to their Old World ways. If there was ever a wine that benefited from breathing, Brunello is it, so consider giving it an hour or more in a decanter before serving.

Brunello requires you to pay to play. If you want to experience Brunello at its best, be ready to venture north of $50 and sometimes

"[BRUNELLO] IS SPECIAL WINE FOR SPECIAL OCCASIONS. DEEP, MUSTY RED WITH A KICK THAT MAKES IT FUN TO MATCH WITH ZIPPY FOOD AS WELL AS GUTSY DISHES FROM SOUTHERN TOSCANA."

—*Mario Batali, celebrity chef*

much higher. Wines of this expense and intensity aren't always easy to find, so don't despair if your favorite wine store carries only a few. Even storied producers sometimes make Brunello that is disappointingly acidic or underripe, so think twice before serving it at your everything-must-be-perfect dinner with the boss. Famous producers include Banfi, a huge owner of vineyards surrounding the medieval hilltop town of Montalcino, and Biondi-Santi, credited with having invented Brunello after isolating the grape over a century ago. An equally impressive pick is Poggio Antico, which I've long admired as much for its elegant wine as for its clean, modern label, boasting a pointy crown that evokes Jughead from the *Archie* comics.

Brunello can be one of the driest wines you'll ever taste, so drinking it without food should be a federal offense. Allow the gastronomic bounty that is Tuscany to transform this edgy prince into an opulent king with Tuscan-style steak and game, pungent mushroom sauces, and aged cheeses.

Brunello's long aging requirements and high price make it an economic necessity for winemakers to offer a more affordable wine that ties up less winery capital and uses fruit not fine enough for Brunello. Hence Rosso di Montalcino, a lighter, fruitier, junior-varsity Brunello released much sooner and far easier to drink when young. Most Brunello producers make a Rosso di Montalcino, typically $15 to $25, in addition to Brunello.

On My Table | **CRISTINA MARIANI-MAY is a family proprietor of Castello Banfi, one of the leading estates of Tuscany and recently named European Winery of the Year by *Wine Enthusiast* magazine.**

Sangiovese [the primary grape of Chianti and Brunello]
Castello Banfi—"Soft in style . . . bright cherry fruit and gentle tannins."

Gavi [a dry white wine from Italy's Piedmont region]
Principessa Gavia—"Crisp, no oak, good acidity; cleaner and less sweet than many popular Pinot Grigios."

Brachetto d'Acqui [Brachetto is an unusual grape from Piedmont's Acqui area]
Banfi Rosa Regale [a sweet sparkling wine]—"A great conversation piece."

Merlot from Chile
Walnut Crest, Concha y Toro—"Lots of forward fruit and soft tannins."

Pinot Noir

Sauvignon Blanc from New Zealand

Late-harvest dessert wine—Moscadello [an Italian variant of the Muscat grape]
Castello Banfi—"Wonderful to sip after a meal with a cookie."

41 Super Tuscans: Big, Rich Rule Breakers

*S*uper Tuscans came to fame in the 1970s when intrepid winemakers decided to use untraditional French grapes like Cabernet Sauvignon, Merlot, and Syrah—then a bold transgression of Italian wine laws that would disqualify these wines from using the famous Chianti name. To add insult to injury, some of these winemakers had the audacity to make their wine outside of the central Chianti hills—in places like Bolgheri, then a marsh-filled backwoods seemingly inhospitable to crafting fine Tuscan wine.

As a kind of oenological dunce cap for their disobedience, these wines were forced to carry the label *vino da tavola*, or "table wine." What wine authorities didn't fathom, however, is how the use of nonsanctioned grapes (blended with the local Sangiovese grape or by themselves) and new locations, coupled with refined techniques like the use of French oak, would produce explosively rich and complex wine. Super Tuscans, as they were called informally, became the darling of connoisseurs, despite—or, given the popularity of anything "banned," *because of*— their lack of an official place name.

Today, though regulations have eased such that some Super Tuscans qualify for status as regular Chianti, many marketing-minded winemakers are in no rush to diminish the renegade appeal of their wines. Indeed, unhindered by place name, vintners were free to dream up fantasy names for their unorthodox creations. The most famous include the legendary *aia*-suffixed Sassicaia (all Cabernet Sauvignon), Ornellaia (primarily Cabernet with some Merlot and Cabernet Franc), and Solaia (primarily Cabernet with some Sangiovese), as well as Tignanello (primarily Sangiovese with some Cabernet), Sammarco (Cabernet and Sangiovese), and Fontalloro (all Sangiovese). You just have to know that these and dozens of others are considered Super Tuscans, because they won't be identified as such on the label.

Some Super Tuscans can improve for decades and, like other

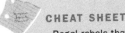

CHEAT SHEET

Regal rebels that they are, Super Tuscans combine the spice and acidity of Chianti with the rich fruit and tannic power of Bordeaux-famed grapes.

OUTSMART THE TABLE

Geography often inspires the fanciful names of Super Tuscans; *Ornellaia* roughly translates as "place of ash trees," while *Sassicaia* means a "place of stones."

ageable reds, are sometimes too bitter in their first five to ten years of life. As you would expect of wines of this longevity and intensity, Super Tuscans tend to be superpricey, with many exceeding $50 a bottle and the most famous hurdling $100 in a good year. The ultimate special-occasional wines, they deserve to be paired with the finest preparations of red meat and other rich creations.

MARK'S PICKS

Fontalloro   *Fon-tahl-LOH-roe*
(from Felsina)
Ornellaia   *Or-nehl-LAH-yah*
(from the producer of the same name)
Sammarco   *Sahm-MAHR-koe*
(from Castello dei Rampolla)
Sassicaia   *Sas-ee-KAH-yah*
(from Marchesi Incisa della Rochetta)
Solaia (from Antinori)   *Soh-LAH-yah*
Tignanello (from Antinori)

Tee-nyah-NEL-loh

FIT FOR FEASTING

Florentine steak and other beef dishes; lamb; game; rich stews; heavy pasta dishes; firm, dry cheeses; Gorgonzola and other blue-veined cheeses.

On My Table | **ERIC OBER** is the former president of both the Food Network and CBS News.

Barolo
Luigi Einaudi—"Great, cozy warmth in winter."

Chianti
Banfi

Super Tuscans
Tignanello—"Years ago, my CBS News colleagues and I finished off the entire two-case supply in Moscow."

Frascati [a dry white wine from Rome that's popular in local trattorias]

Pinot Grigio
"Served at our wedding and still our favorite white wine in the U.S."

42 Barolo and Barbaresco: Heavyweight Superstars with a Mean Streak

Imagine the life of a truffle hound. Under his master's watch, he roams the foggy, autumnal hills of Italy's Piedmont region, snuffling for a scent of white truffle, the rare, uncultivable delicacy Italians call *tartufo bianco*. Patroling forests of willow and oak, trotting past poplar and linden trees, he sniffs the undergrowth, panting, backtracking—stalking any trace of this buried fungus gourmet shops sell for more than $200 an ounce. Then—pay dirt!—the hound yelps and paws the ground, nudging his master to one knobby ball of earthy, pungent, gastronomic gold.

Somewhere along his journey our hound may catch a whiff of the fermenting grapes of two other Piedmontese treasures, the mythic Barolo and Barbaresco. Like truffles, Barolo and Barbaresco can be painfully expensive and an acquired taste. You might even consider them among the least user friendly of wines, because they enter the world with clenched fists of high acid and fierce tannins—austere wines without much fruit to show for themselves. Barbaresco, it should be noted, is generally considered a shade less tannic and rich than Barolo, but the differences are often slight. Only after years of aging, sometimes well over a decade, do the best Barolos and Barbarescos reveal themselves in an explosive bouquet of black cherries, licorice, tar, espresso, cedar, and even truffles, followed by a thick texture and a finish as long as an F-18's vapor trail. When their grapes are extra-ripe, they may also show a bit of sweetness, like cinnamon or kirsch liqueur.

In Piedmont, as in other historic wine regions, a new generation of winemakers is using small French oak barrels and shorter fermentation periods to make Barolo and Barbaresco less tannic and more fruity and approachable. But even these modernists won't turn them into sipping wines, especially in

"OLD BAROLO IS MY ABSOLUTE FAVORITE WINE. WHEN IT IS RIGHT, BAROLO TAKES ME TO A DEEP FOREST IN THE LATE AFTERNOON WITH RAYS OF SUN STREAMING THROUGH THE TREES, GREEN SCENTS WAFTING UP TO MY NOSE AS I WALK."

—*Karen King, wine director of New York's Gramercy Tavern*

CHEAT SHEET

Together with Tuscany's Brunello, Piedmont's Barbaresco and Barolo form a kind of holy trinity of brooding, muscular Italian reds.

LABEL DECODER

Nebbiolo is the grape. Barolo and Barbaresco are districts in the Piedmont region of northwestern Italy.

OUTSMART THE TABLE

Barolo and Barbaresco are often said to smell like "tar and roses."

TALK THE TALK

Barolo	*Bah-ROE-low*
Barbaresco	*Bar-bah-RESS-koe*
Nebbiolo	*Neh-B'YOH-low*

MARK'S PICKS

(both Barolo and Barbaresco unless noted)

Ceretto	*Cheh-RETT-oh*
Pio Cesare (Barolo)	*Pee-oh CHEZZ-eh-ray*
Aldo Conterno (Barolo)	*Kon-TEHR-no*
Gaja	*GAH-yah*
Bruno Giacosa	*Jah-KOE-zah*
Moccagatta (Barbarescco)	
	Mok-kah-GAHT-tah
Prunotto	*Proo-NOH-toe*
Vietti	*VYEHT-tee*

FIT FOR FEASTING

Rich wintertime meat-focused dishes, especially lamb, veal, and beef casseroles; isotto and rich pasta dishes such as tagliatelle in butter sauce; mushrooms, truffles/truffle oil, and other earthy fare; olive oil and butter; mild, firm cheeses; Gorgonzola and other blue-veined cheeses.

their youth. Their grape of origin, Nebbiolo, whose temperamental nature seems tamable only in the hills of Piedmont, is known to produce wines of marked tannin and acidity. For those hooked on the soft, sensual, easy drinkability of wines like Merlot and Shiraz, Barolo and Barbaresco might be an unwelcome excursion.

"Let them drink Merlot," I can hear Piedmontese winemakers stating defiantly, knowing how well their brooding reds match the hearty, carnivore-coddling cuisine of Piedmont. Barolo and Barbaresco beautify the mixed meats of *bollito misto* and the primal heartiness of *osso buco*, as they do any combination of sausages, game, and braised or wine-marinated meats you can muster. Rich fare such as risotto is also tailor-made for these wines, and butter, oil, mushrooms, and sun-dried tomatoes will help tame this savage beast. An hour of breathing in a decanter will also help soften its hard edges.

On the subject of pricing, expect to dole out at least $40 for a bottle of good Barolo or Barbaresco and sometimes much more than that. Bottles marked *riserva* are aged longer at the winery before release.

Angelo Gaja is the closest Piedmont has to a chairman of the board, a restless, uncompromising spirit credited with revolutionizing the Old World ways of Italian wine production. He is most famous for estate-grown, gold-standard Barbarescos and, more recently, opulent Barolos that, though exorbitantly expensive, are worth every penny. Many Piedmontese producers—Gaja included—make both Barolo and Barbaresco.

On My Table | **ALESSANDRO CERETTO** is winemaker and co-owner of Ceretto, one of Italy's most exciting and technologically advanced producers of Barolo.

Barolo
Bricco Rocche Ceretto, Clerico, Sandrone, Roberto Voerzio

Barbaresco
Bricco Asili Ceretto, Sottimano, Moccagatta

Champagne
Salon, Veuve Clicquot, Pol Roger—"I drink it with my girlfriends."

Ribera del Duero (Spain)
Dominio de Atauta

Barbera d'Alba
Vietti, Cascina Chicco, Elio Grasso

Pinot Grigio
Felluga, Girolamo Dorigo, Le Vigne di Zamo

Port
van Zeller, Niepoort—"My favorite wine for meditation."

43 Rioja: The Spanish Classic
That Gives Good Trill

When *I was* first studying the Spanish wine Rioja years ago, I happened to find myself on a long flight seated next to a woman from Madrid. When I asked if she drank Rioja, her face illuminated like a Barcelona boulevard and she declared, "I love R-r-r-rioja," rolling the *r* as if she were Charo's doppelgänger.

While most people don't give the word *Rioja* quite so much (or any) tongue twirl, this wine, which hails from the famous region of the same name, nevertheless deserves a good trill now and then, as it is a source of nostalgia and Spanish pride.

The dominant style of Rioja is a light- to medium-bodied red, often marked by subtle berry-fruit flavors and a lemony tang. (There is also white Rioja, but it's not common enough to discuss here.) Hailing from the region of the same name in north-central Spain, Rioja comprises a number of grapes, the principal one being Tempranillo. This beloved grape contributes to Rioja's lighter body, making it more like Pinot Noir in weight than, say, richer Cabernet Sauvignon. Like lighter styles of Pinot Noir and Chianti, Rioja's lighter body and refreshing tartness make it one of the most versatile red wines for food, perfect for when your table is divided between red and white fans. It is sometimes even light enough to benefit from a slight chill, making it a nifty hammock wine for lazy summer days.

Rioja takes well to oak barrels, a fact that some winemakers perhaps have taken too much to heart. You'll often detect a whiff of vanilla, which comes from Rioja winemakers' longstanding love of sending their juice on an extended vacation in old, strong-scented American oak barrels. Yet when the vacation ends and the wine is released, it is sometimes like an insomniac after a day at the beach: tired and very dry. So be advised that some Rioja will have not the fruity quality of a Pinot Noir or Beaujolais but an ultradry—even leathery or dusty—finish that may be disconcerting to those of us used to ripe, fruit-forward wine.

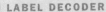
Most Rioja you'll see carries an indication of one of three quality levels that refer to how long wineries have aged the wine in oak and in the bottle before releasing it. Without getting tangled up in precise definitions, just know what they mean about flavor and price:

crianza	lightest, least oaky, and inexpensive
reserva	heavier and more oaky, somewhat more expensive
gran reserva	heaviest, oakiest, priciest, and made only in good years

A new generation of Rioja vintners is offering an alternative to the region's traditionally light and aggressively oaky juice. By employing New World viticultural techniques, including shortening the wine's stay in oak barrels and using the subtler French oak, vintners have been able to craft wines of greater heft and fruit flavor. The best new-style Riojas elbow a place for themselves alongside wines like California Cabernet or red Bordeaux with ripe flavors of plums and currants joined by a healthy but restrained framework of oak. These are wines of power and intensity, closer in style to Spain's other famous red, Ribera del Duero (described below), than to old-school Rioja.

Rioja is pleasing to the price-conscious, with Rioja *crianza* a favorite of those prowling for a cheap but good "house red." Many dependably delightful *crianza* wines can be had for about a ten-spot, including the always pleasurable Conde de Valdemar. Rioja *reservas* run from $15 to $30, and *gran reservas* can cost up to $50 or more.

Ribera del Duero also originates from the north of the country and is somewhat richer and brawnier than the average Rioja. Derived primarily from a close cousin of the Tempranillo grape, it is sometimes blended with Cabernet Sauvignon, Merlot, and other sturdy grapes. Ribera del Duero is responsible for Spain's most famous red, the legendary, oak-lavished Vega Sicilia (especially the Unico bottling, prized around the world), as well as the cult bodegas Dominio de Pingus (Do-MEE-nee-oh deh PEEN-goos) and Pesquera (Pehs-KEH-rah).

A third Spaniard worth knowing is Priorato, an ancient growing region tucked into the mountains southwest of Barcelona. In the last decade, a number of visionary winemakers have transformed Priorato into one of the world's hottest wine names, known for rich, heady, powerful, sometimes savagely tannic juice, and, like the best Ribera del Duero, priced north of $50. The guiding force of Priorato is Alvaro Palacios (Ahl-BEH-row Pah-LAH-thee-oh), whose coveted L'Ermita can sell for as high as $200, although the delicious Les Terrasses is priced more gently at about $25. In that range, also look for Buil & Giné and entry-level bottlings from Mas Igneus. Up-and-comer that it is, Priorato remains a challenge to locate.

 FIT FOR FEASTING

Lighter style: a wide range of lighter meats, pasta, and robust fish dishes; classics like chorizo and tapas.

Heavier style: lamb (a regional favorite), rich poultry, pork, and veal dishes; Spanish Manchego and other dry, firm cheeses; grilled meats and sausage; chili; hamburgers; barbecue.

44 Australian Shiraz: The People-Pleasing "Plush Ripey"

*A*ustralia *is* the world capital for creative language. Who else would call a pub a "rubbity-dub" or a mosquito a "mozzie"?

In this freewheeling linguistic spirit of Bludgers, Brizzies, and Billabongs, I hereby invent my own iconoclastic, Aussie-style term for the country's iconic wine, Shiraz. It is *plush ripey*.

The words should be self-explanatory. Shiraz is rich red wine at its most accessible, juicy and ripe with gobs of oaked-up fruit and typically soft tannins. In Australia's warm climate, Shiraz—which is the same grape as in both American Syrah and the red wines of the northern Rhône—takes on deep, jammy notes of blackcurrants and blackberries, with hints of chocolate and a distinct whiff of vanilla that reflects Australia's love of aggressively scented American oak. Although the grape can make wine evocative of black pepper, as is often the case in America and France, Shiraz's spiciness often comes through a bit sweeter, taking on, for example, notes of cinnamon or cloves. Most are rich and full bodied, though some can be lighter.

In the $15-and-under price range, there isn't a more instantly likable red wine. Making shrewd use of new technologies and cutting-edge equipment, Australians have figured out how to give legions of casual wine drinkers exactly what they want. Like an entry-level Mazda or Stouffer's French bread pizza, your typical $10 Shiraz is affordable, reliable, friendly, and perfectly tuned to mass tastes. Is it any wonder that French winemakers are now more threatened by Australia than any other wine-producing country?

It wouldn't be fair, however, to imply that all Shiraz is predictable or one-dimensional. While you're unlikely to see astonishingly complexity in the lower price range, much of the wine is still delicious. Moreover, Australian vintners have done a masterly job of experimenting with different grape combinations—making affordable yet intriguing wine from

"I'M A BIG FAN OF SHIRAZ . . . GREAT QUALITY AND VALUE."

—*Francis Ford Coppola*

pairing Shiraz with grapes like Grenache, Viognier, and even Cabernet Sauvignon.

Things get really interesting when you loosen your purse strings. In the $20-to-$40 range, and sometimes more than double that, finer versions can show layer upon layer of saturated fruit mixed with vanilla, smoke, espresso, and a velvety finish that lasts longer than you can hold your breath. Much of the best Shiraz comes from grapes grown on older vines, which are plentiful throughout the venerable Barossa and Hunter valleys. One of my favorite sources for old-vine Shiraz is d'Arenberg, whose various offerings are swooningly delicious and dramatically named, like its Dead Arm, Laughing Magpie, and Footbolt vineyard bottlings—the last mercifully under $20. A recent tasting of the Dead Arm had me mumbling the phrase *liquid fudge* over and over.

If you really want to amaze your friends and neighbors, however, find a bottle of *sparkling* Shiraz, which is sometimes available at better wine shops. This rare animal is made by putting Shiraz table wine through the traditional bottle fermentation method used for French Champagne. An acquired taste, it can have a fizzy berry quality that reminds some tasters of a very dry cherry cola.

Australia's most famous wine is Penfolds Grange, known as Grange Hermitage before the winery dropped *Hermitage* to avoid any confusion with the French region of the same name. In terms of prestige, this monumental wine rivals the world's best, including *premier cru* Bordeaux, and often commands at least $200 if you can even find it.

Basic versions of Shiraz are delicious with flavorful everyday fare like pizza, roast chicken, and meats "cooked on the barbie." Upscale Shiraz flatters all kinds of steak, chops, and roasts—with extra pleasure points if grilling or savory-spicy sauces are involved. A supple, sweet-seeming Shiraz also works well with mildly spicy Asian fare, but anything too hot may be unpleasant with an overall dry wine like Shiraz. Some also enjoy spending the remaining drops of a supple Shiraz with a hunk of dark chocolate.

On My Table | **CHESTER OSBOURN** is chief winemaker of d'Arenberg Cellars, one of Australia's leading sources of handcrafted wine.

Southern Rhône—Châteauneuf-du-Pape
Domaine du Vieux Télégraphe, Château Mont-Redon

Priorato and other Spanish reds
Clos Magador, Clos Martinet, [winemaker] Carlos Falco's [Marqués de Griñón wines]

Australian reds—"The biggest and grittiest are the best."
d'Arenberg, Clarendon Hills, Koltz

German Riesling
Egon Müller, [Heymann] Löwenstein

Barolo and Barbaresco

Rosé from Bandol
Domaine Tempier, Château Pradeaux

Northern Rhône—Côte Rôtie
Gilles Barge Cuvée Duplessy, François Villard, Yves Cuilleron, René Rostaing

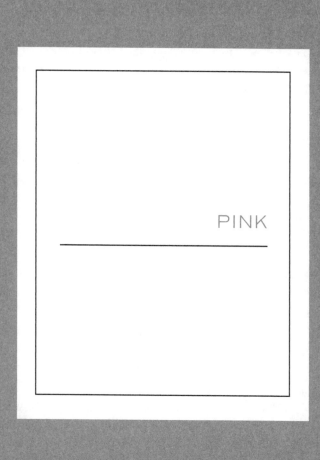

PINK

45 "Real" Rosé: The Mediterranean Summer Favorite

It's the kind of sweltering August afternoon where your 78 rpm world seems to have slowed to 33 rpm. Your shirt sticks to the small of your back, and the air is so heavy it feels like you've woken up, hung over, in the smokers' lounge at Charles de Gaulle.

Now, what sounds better?

1. A jammy room-temperature Cabernet with plenty of smokiness and bitter tannin . . . or
2. A rosé with light berry flavors and a cool, crisp finish

Imagine this scene the next time your friends dismiss rosé as a frivolous pink beverage unfit for discriminating palates. Sure it's pink—or salmon or russet or copper—but don't let its resemblance to the much-maligned white Zinfandel (see Shortcut 20) prevent you from appreciating its miraculous powers of refreshment and food friendliness. It is arguably the most thirst-slaking wine for a hot summer day—just ask the endless supply of sun-ripened Europeans who quaff the stuff like water during summer holidays on the Mediterranean.

Rosé refers to any pink-hued wine that is made when dark grape skins are allowed only brief contact with the juice, thus preventing the wine from becoming fully red. Unlike semisweet white Zinfandel, rosé—the real stuff we're covering here—is made to have less, if any, residual sugar, making it bone dry or perhaps just faintly sweet. Its brief tryst with grape skins gives it a bit

CHEAT SHEET

Liberated of the cloying sweetness that plagues most white Zinfandel, the best rosés have the body and flavor of a light, dry red combined with the refreshing crispness of a white. For an excellent introduction, ask your local wine merchant for a bottle of French Tavel.

LABEL DECODER

Rosé is a style. It can come from any red-wine grape, such as Pinot Noir, Grenache, or Zinfandel.

OUTSMART THE TABLE

• Shippers transporting Tavel in fifteenth-century France used to say they were bringing "*un peu de soleil dans l'eau froide,*" which roughly means "a little sun into the cold water."

• *Vin gris* (literally, "gray wine") is a French term for rosé wine.

more body than white wine, but the affair ends before the wine can have the kind of tannic grip that would prevent it from being served chilled.

As it can be made from any red-wine grape, rosé rears its randy head in every wine region around the world, but Mediterranean Europe has bragging rights on the best stuff. The unofficial headquarters of rosé is France, where it has achieved fame in Tavel (in the Rhône Valley), Bandol (Provence), Anjou (Loire Valley), and Marsannay (Burgundy), among other regions. Bandol's Domaine Tempier, expensive for a rosé at about $25, is always flavorful and charming and considered by many to be rosé at the height of its powers. Most other rosés can be had for less than $15 a bottle.

Other countries have proven that you don't need a beret to make tasty rosé. Some of Spain's larger Rioja producers offer excellent *rosado*. Italy is known for its *rosato*, which is usually light and slightly fizzy, some of the best of which is made from the Barbera grape in Italy's Piedmont region. Finally, some daring American producers, such as California's Bonny Doon Vineyard, are proving that dry and pink need not be mutually exclusive.

Don't be disappointed if your favorite merchant has only one lonely, dusty shelf of rosé wine, as many Americans have yet to overcome their rosé reluctance. No matter: for the price of an average Pinot Noir, you can have two (or three) bottles of rosé's straightforward, summery charm. Grab the youngest bottles you can find and chill them as you would a white. Dry rosé pairs with almost any food, with a special affinity for "pink" meats like ham, pork dishes, and hot dogs, as well as grilled fish, and greasy treats like a nice bag of *pommes frites*.

TALK THE TALK

Rosé	roe-ZAY
Tavel	TAH-vel
Bandol	BAHN-dohl
Anjou	AHN-joo

MARK'S PICKS

French rosé:
Château Routas   *ROU-tahs*
Domaine de Triennes Gris de Triennes
            Gree-duh Tree-EHN
Domaine Tempier   *Tahm-pyay*
Domaines Ott   *Aht*
Mas de Gourgonnier
            Mahs duh Goor-gone-YAY
Vidal-Fleury   *Vee-dahl-Fluh-REE*

Spanish rosé:
Bodegas Muga Rioja Rosado   *MOO-gah*
Cune Rioja Rosado   *Koo-nay*
Marqués de Cáceres Dry Rioja Rosé
            Mar-KESS deh KAH-seh-res

American rosé:
Bonny Doon Vin Gris de Cigare, Joseph Phelps Vin de Mistral Rosé, La Famiglia di Robert Mondavi Rosato Sangiovese, McDowell Grenache Rosé, Solo Rosé.

FIT FOR FEASTING

Almost everything, especially grilled fish (particularly Mediterranean specialties like grilled sardines); tuna Niçoise; tapas; grilled vegetables, ratatouille; mildly spicy food; greasy food like French fries; barbecue and other smoky foods; "pink" fare: pork, ham, hot dogs, shrimp, lobster rolls.

On My Table | **JAMEY WHETSTONE** is the assistant winemaker at Zinfandel mecca Turley Wine Cellars and the sole proprietor of Whetstone Wine Cellars, a boutique winery in Calistoga, California.

Red Burgundy—Chambolle-Musigny, Bonnes Mares, Morey-St.-Denis
Dujac, G. Roumier, Anne Gros, Henri Jayer

Southern Rhône—Châteauneuf-du-Pape or Gigondas
Sobon, Vieux Télégraphe, Marcoux, Solitude, Beaucastel, Boisrenard, Cayron

Southern Rhône—Côtes-du-Rhône-Villages
Domaine Rabasse-Charavin

Pinot Gris from Alsace—"Perfect with spicy tuna."
Zind Humbrecht

Riesling (sweeter styles) from Germany, Austria, or Alsace

Northern Rhône—Cornas [big, full-bodied wine entirely from the Syrah grape]
Thierry Allemand, René Balthazar—"Wild, exotic, *animale.*"

White Rhône
Chave Hermitage Blanc, Beaucastel Vieilles Vignes, Guigal La Dorianne Condrieu

Outsmarting the Basics: Secret Alternatives

We arrive at the part of the book designed to fashion you into the vinous deity among your friends and family. Just when the table is about to settle on yet another Chardonnay or Merlot, you'll come galloping to the rescue and suggest a lesser-known alternative that will bring smiles of surprise to your dining companions. Here we cover wine types that are unfamiliar to casual drinkers but not so obscure that you can't find some of them at wine-passionate restaurants and shops. And because these "secret alternatives" are less popular, many of them are excellent values, waiting to be picked from the vine by someone of your unimpeachable taste. ■

WHITE

_____

46 Instead of Chardonnay, Try Viognier, a Fully Loaded Tropical Fruit Bomb

O*n a recent* visit to Napa Valley's celebrated Joseph Phelps winery, I had a spirited, freewheeling discussion with winemaker Craig Williams, a burly blond former surfer who happens to craft some of the most delicious wine coming out of Napa.

When I asked why, in addition to focusing on familiar varieties like Cabernet, Merlot, and Chardonnay, the winery cultivates the lesser-known Viognier grape, Craig used vivid vernacular befitting someone reared in auto-obsessed southern California.

"It comes fully loaded."

How right he is. Viognier is about as far as you can get from a crisp, herbally scented Sancerre or a light, neutral Pinot Grigio. Like a California Chardonnay, it plays for keeps, offering intense aromas, a full, rich body, and alcohol sometimes pushing a swooning 14 percent. Unlike the archetypal buttery Chardonnay, however, its big personality isn't as dependent on contact with oak barrels. As Williams put it: "We don't need to use new oak or stir the lees [sediment] to create more complexity—Viognier doesn't require add-ons."

When it's well made, then, Viognier is less about buttery vanilla scents and more about tropical fruit aromas so intense that they seem to spell out their own vaporous exclamation point. The scent of apricots, peaches, and flowers (such as honeysuckle or orange blossom) seem to leap from the glass, such that aromatically Viognier can seem like a German Riesling on steroids or the vinous equivalent of a summer walk through a botanic grove. This ambrosia is aided and abetted by the wine's full-bodied, creamy texture, its relatively low acidity, and a finish that seems to go on and on.

"[VIOGNIER] HAS A TROPICAL GARDEN NOSE THAT PUTS YOU IN THE MOOD FOR ROMANCE."

—*Jay McInerney, novelist and wine writer*

If Viognier has a drawback, it's that it is not as food friendly as some lighter, more acidic whites. Though some find that its heady, floral charm overpowers lighter preparations, it is still a good bet with many seafood creations, particularly those with butter, cream, or breading, such as lobster bisque or crab cakes. Pork and ham dishes are also a classic match. With its exotic personality, Viognier has an affinity for the tropical tastes you find in exotic Asian food, such as moderately spiced Thai coconut milk curries, sesame shrimp, satays, and fruit sauces.

In recent years, Viognier has become something of a fashionable favorite for savvy drinkers craving an interesting substitute for Chardonnay. You're going to pay for this trendiness, so expect most bottlings to run from $25 to $40. Saving the day, however, are R.H. Phillips and Pepperwood Grove, both delivering the wine's lush peachiness at under $15. With its low acidity, Viognier generally doesn't have a good track record for longevity, so look for bottles under five years of age.

With all this discussion about American Viognier, it would be negligent to ignore Viognier's homeland—France's Rhône Valley, where small amounts of the grape are sometimes blended with the region's brawny reds to civilize them a bit. The Rhône also makes a white wine based on the Viognier grape that you'll see labeled for its village, Condrieu, a tiny area located on the Rhône River, near the famed red-wine region of Côte Rôtie. With only about thirty thousand cases produced annually, Condrieu is a rare commodity that usually costs $50 or more. At its best, it beguiles you with the best of the grape's tropical aromas and crème brûlée texture. Of growing popularity in wine shops are French bottlings simply labeled *Viognier*, which often cost in the $10-to-20 range because they come from less expensive land outside Condrieu.

CHEAT SHEET

A luscious white if there ever was one, Viognier has Chardonnay's rich and creamy texture, with aromas that transport you inside an exotic grove of apricots, peaches, and flowers.

LABEL DECODER

Viognier is the grape. Condrieu is a region in the northern part of France's Rhône Valley.

TALK THE TALK

Viognier   *Vee-oh-NYAY*
Condrieu   *Coh'n-DREE-uh*

MARK'S PICKS

California:
Under $15—Pepperwood Grove, R.H. Phillips D. H. EXP.
$15 and Over—Arrowood, Hogue, La Jota, Fess Parker, Pepperwood Grove, Joseph Phelps, Pride Mountain, Qupé.

France:
Rhône (Condrieu)—Chapoutier *(Shah-POO-tyay)*, Guigal *(Ghee-GAL)*, Paul Jaboulet *(Jah-BOO-leh)*, Georges Vernay *(Vehr-NAY)*.
Non-Condrieu Viognier—Domaine de Triennes *(Tree-EHN)*, Georges Duboeuf *(Duh-BUFF)*.

FIT FOR FEASTING

Richer seafood such as salmon, mahimahi, Chilean sea bass, and lobster; crab cakes; preparations heavy on butter, olive oil, or cream; lusty pasta dishes; pork and ham dishes; restrainedly spicy Asian dishes incorporating coconut milk, sesame, and other tropical tastes; macadamia nuts, almonds, and other rich nuts.

47 Instead of Chardonnay, Try Zesty Spanish Albariño

Rías Baixas. The uniqueness of its pronunciation—REE-yahs BIKE-sahs—matches the singularity of this Spanish wine region and the wine produced there.

Tucked into the northwestern corner of Spain between France and Portugal, Rías Baixas is a part of Spain's Galicia region, known for its ancient Celtic traditions and a uniquely cool, wet maritime climate. You wouldn't think this rainy region would produce flavorful wine, but that's exactly Albariño: a medium- to full-bodied white with penetrating aromas and a shot of mouthwatering acidity. Albariño's texture is usually big and creamy, but because the wine is rarely fermented in oak barrels, you can't expect the sweet vanilla aromas typical of a New World Chardonnay. The better Albariños I've had seduce you with notes of citrus fruits, peaches, and flowers, sometimes joined by a wet rocks minerality that seems to fit wine from this mysterious seaside locale.

Albariño is now a sensation in the wine world, and many wine-savvy restaurants offer Albariño as a Chardonnay alternative for those in the know. Despite its relative heft for a white wine, its tangy, sometimes even spritzy, acidity makes it a beautiful bedfellow for food, especially heavier seafood dishes, grilled shellfish, and tapas of all kinds. It also makes for a splendid, appetite-priming aperitif.

Most Albariño will set you back only $12 to $20, which makes it a low-risk wine to try out on your friends. The accepted wisdom is that Albariño is best drunk young, so if you have a choice, the younger the Albariño, the better. And don't reach for your diction-

CHEAT SHEET

Spain's best white, Albariño is your midsummer night's dream: an aromatic, creamy white, with spritzy acidity and a mysterious provenance. It is usually medium to full bodied, though lighter, steelier manifestations exist.

LABEL DECODER

Albariño is the grape. Rías Baixas is its region.

OUTSMART THE TABLE

Nicknamed "Wine of the Sea," Albariño's Rías Baixas region straddles the Atlantic coast with an abundance of rolling green hills and eucalyptus forests.

ary if you see *Alvarinho*—this is the Portuguese name for the same grape, one of several grapes used in Portugal's Vinho Verde region. As we cover later, the wine Vinho Verde is prized by bargain hunters looking for a summer refresher, but it is typically lighter and less interesting than Spanish Albariño.

TALK THE TALK

Albariño   *Ahl-bah-REE-n'yoh*
Rías Baixas   *REE-yahs BIKE-sahs*
Vinho Verde   *VEEN-yoh VEHR-day*

MARK'S PICKS

Adega Condes de Albarei, Havens (U.S.), Lagar de Cervera, Lagar de Fornelos, Laxas, Lusco, Martín Códax, Pazo de Barrantes, Valminor.

FIT FOR FEASTING

By itself as an aperitif or with seafood of all kinds, especially Iberian favorites like shellfish, sardines, and grilled octopus; richer preparations of white meat and pasta; marinated mushrooms, garlicky veggies, and other tapas; paella; Caesar salad and other pungent salads; earthy bean dishes.

On My Table | **MIKE HAVENS,** a former college professor, started making Merlot before it was fashionable to do so, and his winery remains one of Napa Valley's leading sources for that varietal, as well as Syrah and other types.

Albariño

Morgadio, Lusco, Pazo de Barrantes—"I will drink these anytime, especially with appetizers or tapas or when cooking."

Riesling from Germany, Alsace, or Austria

Germany: Maximin Grünhauser. Austria: F. X. Pichler, Prager, Hirtzberger, Hirsch, Nigl. Alsace: Marc Temp.

Grüner Veltliner

All of the Austrian producers above and Bründlmayer

Red Bordeaux—St.-Emilion and Pomerol

Pavie, Grand-Mayne, Moulin-St.-Georges, La Dominique, Magdelaine, Tertre-Rôteboeuf, Angelus, Ausone, Cheval Blanc

Northern Rhône—various types

Jasmin Côte Rôtie, Allemand Cornas, Louis Cheze St.-Joseph, Graillot Crozes-Hermitage, Chave Hermitage

Southern Rhône—various types

Château de Saint Cosme Gigondas and Côtes-du-Rhône, Domaine Montirius Vacqueyras, Domaine Fond Croze Côtes-du-Rhône. Minervois: Château Coupe Roses, Domaine de Courbissac, Borie de Maurel.

Languedoc-Roussillon

Château Caladroy, Domaine Gauby, Domaine La Tour Vieille

Sancerre

Domaine Henry Natter, Montagny, Domaine Merlin-Cherrier, Bué, Domaine Matthias Roblin, Maimbray

48 Instead of American Sauvignon Blanc, Try Its Crackly Counterpart from New Zealand

You might be wondering what New Zealand can give you that you can't get from America or France or Italy. Does anybody really pine for a New Zealand prime rib or the latest fashion from Auckland? And if a fix of the rough-riding, outback spirit is what you're after, higher-profile Australia is the logical choice, mate. Yet when it comes to Sauvignon Blanc, think twice before passing over New Zealand. When you order a New Zealand Sauvignon Blanc, the kiwi nation will charm your table with a wine of ripe fruit and mouthwatering tanginess.

Though a relative newcomer among wine-producing nations, New Zealand produces a full range of varietal wines, from rich Chardonnays to increasingly popular Pinot Noirs. Sauvignon Blanc, however, remains the country's showpiece. A New Zealand Sauvignon Blanc has the classic pungent grassiness that makes Sauvignon Blanc so distinctive (see Shortcut 13) but often benefits from something I call the "Crackly Kiwi Factor." New Zealand's intense sunlight ensures that the grapes get quite ripe, imparting the wine with bright aromas of exotic fruits like passion fruit, peach, and nectar. But this ripeness is counterpoised by the region's relatively cool maritime climate, which injects a refreshingly crisp current into the wine. The result is a wine of uncommon purity: you can really appreciate the fruit essences without feeling like your nose is swimming in a tub of Land O Lakes.

Styles of New Zealand Sauvignon Blanc vary, of course, with the winemaker and the viticultural region. Some winemakers, for example, follow the California style of fermenting Sauvignon Blanc in oak barrels, which tones down some of the grape's natural grassiness and acidity. But the predominant method is stainless-steel fermentation, which allows the wine's citrusy

"CLOUDY BAY SAUVIGNON BLANC LAUNCHED OUR PASSION FOR NEW ZEALAND SAUVIGNON BLANC.... IN FACT, WE CARRIED A BOTTLE HOME WITH US TO GIVE OUR WINEMAKER, PLUNKED IT DOWN ON HIS DESK, AND SAID, 'MAKE THAT.'"

—*Lane Giguiere, cofounder, R.H. Phillips Winery*

nature to shine while mingling with seductive aromas of passion fruit and apricots. New Zealand Sauvignon Blanc is like a child who inherits the best qualities of both parents—exotic aromas found in certain Sauvginon Blancs from the New World and the pungency and limy acidity of an Old World Sauvignon Blanc like Sancerre from the Loire Valley (see Shortcut 24).

Many enthusiasts are already familiar with Cloudy Bay, the first New Zealand Sauvignon Blanc to hit big in America. I'm also a fan, but its $30 price tag prevents my regular use of it. Happily, there are a growing number of well-made New Zealand Sauvignon Blancs under $15, including Villa Maria, Brancott, Babich, and Kim Crawford. As with any exotic wine, it isn't always easy to find particular producers of New Zealand Sauvignon Blanc at your local wine store; a trusted merchant can steer you to worthy alternatives.

49 Instead of Sauvignon Blanc, Try Spicy, Nervy Gewürztraminer

I *couldn't take it* anymore. Whenever I had Gewürztraminer with wine-wise friends, someone would invariably say "Smells like lychees."

"What's lychees?" I was afraid to ask, with no clue except vague childhood memories of a New Jersey dive of the same name, catering to gringos with chop suey, duck sauce, and a life-size fiberglass Buddha. So I set out on a mission and trundled down to New York's Chinatown, where I secured one bag of Honda International dried lychees and one can of Wu Chung lychees in syrup.

Back at my place, I spread my specimens on a plate and cracked a bottle of Hugel Gewürztraminer. As I sniffed the lychees, then nosed the wine, it happened—boom!—a startlingly accurate aroma match—one of the most dramatic I've experienced.

Lychees may be its signature aroma, but the famously pungent Gewürztraminer ("Gewürz" to insiders) can show a prism of other scents, from rose water, apricots, and poached pears to ginger, cloves, and allspice. Many have some pepperiness, too, proving truth in advertising, as *gewürz* is the German word for "spicy." You may also detect some minerals or grapefruit, but don't expect Gewürz to be a tongue tingler like Sancerre or Chablis. It has only moderate acidity, which, when coupled with its high alcohol and full body, makes for a rich, spicy white whose texture is mouth filling, sometimes even oily. Such an unusual wine is like steak tartare or New Year's Eve: some can't get enough of it, while others run for the door.

If you're wondering which foods pair best with Gewürz, look to its homeland. Alsatians will confirm that Gewürz is weighty enough to stand up to the richness of foie gras, the nutty earthiness of local Muenster cheese, and the greasiness of pork chops. It is also the traditional wine to have with smoked fish, *choucroute garni* (meats and sausages in sauerkraut), and onion tarts. Gewürz can also deftly perform a cultural about-face, lending its fruity finesse and peppery personality to mildly spicy meals of the Thai, Indian, and Chinese persuasions.

With a personality all its own,
Gewürztraminer is dry and rich, with
signature scents of lychees, rose
water, and a range of other fruits and
spices, all of which derive from the
uniqueness of the grape and its
Alsatian climate.

LABEL DECODER

Gewürztraminer is a grape. Alsace is its
primary region.

TALK THE TALK

Gewürztraminer	*Guh-VURTS-trah-mee-ner*
lychee	*LEE-chee*
choucroute garnis	*shoo-KROOT gahr-nee*
Alsace	*Ahl-ZASS*

MARK'S PICKS

Alsace, France:

Lucien Albrecht	*Lew-SYEN AHI-bresht*
Leon Beyer	*LAY-ohn Beh-yehr*
Albert Boxler	*Ahl-bare Bohks-lehr*
Marcel Deiss	*Dice*
Hugel	*Hew-GELL*
Josmeyer	*JOCE-meyer*
Schlumberger	*Shlum-ber-JAY*
Pierre Sparr	*Pee-air SHPAHR*
Trimbach	*TREEM-bahr*
Zind Humbrecht	*Zeend HOOM-bresht*

Non-Alsace:

U.S:—Chateau Ste. Michelle, Hogue,
Meridian, Navarro.
Italy—Cantina Tramin, Jermann, Pojer &
Sandri (Poe-YEHR eh Sahn-dree).

FIT FOR FEASTING

Excellent as an aperitif or with seafood
of all types (especially smoked salmon);
veal, chicken, and pork dishes (e.g.,
Alsatian pork chops); mildly spicy Asian
food; foie gras; dishes with onions
(onion tarts, onion soup); sauerkraut;
spiced/peppered cheeses, Muenster
cheese (another regional specialty).

Gewürz is a good value, as you can usually find its characteristically long, tapered bottles selling in the range of $12 to $20. Trimbach and Hugel are two names to remember, both making basic-level Gewürz that is widely available and reliably pleasing. Gewürz is cultivated in other parts of the world, such as Germany, the United States, and Italy (where it is sometimes called Traminer), though usually with less success than the Alsatian original. One delightful exception is Italy's Pojer & Sandri Traminer Aromatico, which justifies its name with bright aromas of rose petal and cloves.

Finally, let's not ignore what is perhaps the biggest hurdle to enjoying Gewürztraminer: getting the word out of your mouth. I tell my students to break it into two easily pronounceable parts: guh-VURTS and trah-meener, then combine. Easy, isn't it?

On My Table | **CRAIG WILLIAMS** is the winemaker of Joseph Phelps Vineyards, a Napa Valley institution acclaimed for its Ovation Chardonnay and Insignia Bordeaux-style blend.

Champagne, sparkling wine

J. Lasalle, Paul Bara, Krug, Schramsberg, Veuve Clicquot

Southern Rhône reds—Châteauneuf-du-Pape, Gigondas, Côtes-du-Rhône

Chapoutier, Jaboulet, Vieux Télégraphe, Mont-Redon, La Nerthe, Clos des Papes, Rayas, Beaucastel, Font de Michelle, Domaine Santa Duc, La Vieille Ferme, Château du Trignon

Cabernet Sauvignon from Napa

Alsatian white wines

Hugel, Trimbach, Weinbach, Zind Humbrecht, Deiss

50 Instead of Pinot Grigio, Get Grüner Veltliner for "Insider Cred"

I *think* of Grüner Veltliner as a pro wine, a varsity-level libation, a black-diamond beverage. When I dine with groups of wine insiders, it's almost assured that somebody will order a Grüner. Dependably refreshing, sometimes intriguingly complex, exquisite with food, hard to find, and linguistically exotic (complete with a fear-inducing umlaut over the *u*)—it's tailor-made for the connoisseur weary of the relentless march of Pinot Grigio.

From the moment it touches your tongue, you'll know that Grüner Veltliner is not a butter bath on Chardonnay's palm-lined Easy Street but a plunge into the chilly, glassine waters of the Danube. Though there are fuller-bodied styles, a typical Grüner Veltliner is light to medium bodied with subtle aromas of citrus fruits—white grapefruit in particular—and sometimes green essences (*Grüner* means "green") such as green beans, pureed peas, or even grilled zucchini. Sometimes you'll sniff a bit of peach or melon, too. If there is a common theme among Grüners, it is the faint scent of white pepper and a wet-rocks, minerally aroma similar to the stony tang you get from French Chablis. With little or no oak and a pleasing streak of acidity, all of these factors combine to create not the smokehouse of vanilla and butter you find in many Chardonnays but unadorned, cut-glass purity of fruit.

The most famous white wine from Austria, Grüner Veltliner is pronounced by effecting a toothy Schwarzeneggerian grin and uttering "GROO-ner Felt-LEE-ner." Most of the good stuff originates near the Danube River in the regions Wachau, Kampstal, and Kremstal, so look for one of those locations on the label. Another sign of quality is the name Terry Theise, a wine importer in the Washington, D.C., area who is Grüner's greatest ambassador in the States. But don't worry too much about finding specific producers since even the best merchants typically stock scant amounts of this overlooked wine.

"[GRÜNERS] MATCH FOOD THAT WOULD GO WITH SAUVIGNON BLANC BUT ARE MILDER AND MORE NUANCED THAN MOST SAUVIGNON BLANCS."

—*Larry Stone, master sommelier*

Theise also extols one of Grüner Veltliner's greatest assets: its affinity for vegetables. Rare is wine that pairs well with all types of vegetables, but GV's range of citrusy, green, and other flavors make it compatible with everything in a can of V-8 and then some. When I asked him about it, Theise attributed Grüner's vegetal veneration to the fact that it can have both the "flintiness of a Sauvignon Blanc and the floral notes of a Viognier, giving it very broad versatility." In fact, Theise thinks that Grüner is *the* most flexible dry white wine with food, as suitable with wild-mushroom sauté as it is with a peppery salad. I concur, adding that it even befriends wine terrorists like artichokes and asparagus.

CHEAT SHEET

Beloved by wine professionals, Grüner Veltliner is crisp and food friendly, with subtle citrus and white pepper aromas and hints of green vegetables, pepper, and/or flowers.

LABEL DECODER

Grüner Veltliner is a grape. It comes almost exclusively from Austria.

OUTSMART THE TABLE

Some insiders like to abbreviate Grüner Veltliner as *Grüner*, while others use *GV*. Importer Terry Theise told me that only the nickname *GrüVe* does this special wine justice.

TALK THE TALK

Grüner Veltliner	*GROO-ner Felt-LEE-ner*
Kampstal	*KAMPZ-tahl*
Kremstal	*KREMS-tahl*
Terry Theise	*Theese*
Wachau	*Wahk-AOW*

MARK'S PICKS

Hirsch	
Hirtzberger	
Knoll	*K-nohl*
Nigl	*NEE-gehl*
Schloss	*Shlows*
Weingärtner	*WINE-gart-ner*

FIT FOR FEASTING

By itself as an aperitif and widely versatile with food, especially with a range of vegetables, including bell peppers and peas as well as "problem" veggies like artichokes and asparagus; Caesar salad and other piquantly dressed greens; onion-rich dishes (e.g., onion soup, onion rings); piccata, lime butter, and other citrusy sauces; capers, green olives, sun-dried tomatoes and other marinated treats; lighter white meat and seafood; dishes with fennel; mustard; dishes with herbs (e.g., herbes de Provence, tarragon, chervil, dill).

On My Table | **TERRY THEISE**, owner of Terry Theise Selections, is one of America's top importers of Austrian and German wine and a tireless ambassador for the wines of these underappreciated regions.

Champagne

"Ninety-nine percent from [small-production] growers."

German Riesling

"I like Rieslings between six and fifteen years old . . . always with food . . . most frequently Spätlese quality."

Rieslings from Alsace and Austria

Muscat (dry)

Grüner Veltliner

Red Burgundy

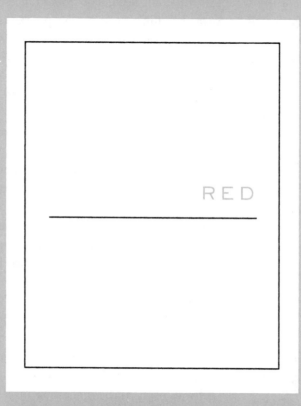

RED

51 Instead of Beaujolais Nouveau, Try the Other, Year-Round Types

For the novice enthusiast, Beaujolais from France may begin and end with Beaujolais Nouveau, the "don't-worry-be-happy" red released every November (see Shortcut 36). But if you look beyond the Ringling Brothers tent that is Beaujolais Nouveau, you'll find other manifestations that range from light and fruity to juice with more structure and staying power. Best of all, these year-round Beaujolais types retain the same juicy charm, easy drinkability, and affordability.

The simpler varieties of year-round Beaujolais are labeled *Beaujolais* and *Beaujolais-Villages*. Both are light, straightforward styles designed to tweak your nose with a refreshing waft of raspberries and cherries. Beaujolais-Villages is said to be a shade more substantial than regular Beaujolais, but the difference is negligible as both are fresh, fruity quaffing wines. These are key when you want to dial up some Beaujolais exuberance after Beaujolais Nouveau season has passed, especially in the summer. They are bargain priced under $10 and will make fast friends with any picnic basket they meet.

Moving to the northern half of France's Beaujolais district, we encounter the jewels in the Beaujolais crown—the *cru* Beaujolais. Mind you, these stones are more cubic zirconium than Harry Winston because no Beaujolais carries the refinement or complexity of a fine Bordeaux or Burgundy. What you do get with many *cru* Beaujolais is a bit less bubblegum buoyancy than regular Beaujolais and a bit more body. If you were reared in suburbia like me, you might also get flashbacks of childhood dirt piles and full-contact games of King of the Mountain, as *cru* Beaujolais sometimes has a bit of earthiness, too.

You won't usually see *cru* Beaujolais by that name on the label but rather by one of the ten *cru* Beaujolais villages from which the grapes come, and each *cru*, or "classified growth,"

"THERE IS NO BETTER EVERYDAY FOOD WINE. SOME, SUCH AS MOULIN-À-VENT, ARE SURPRISINGLY AGEWORTHY AND CHEAP!"

—*Geddy Lee, rock musician and collector*

has its own slightly different personality. Ten villages are a lot to master, especially when the differences in taste are nominal, so start with these four: Moulin-à-Vent, Morgon, Fleurie, and Brouilly. The first two—Moulin-à-Vent and Morgon—tend to be the most complex, substantial, and sometimes even somewhat tannic and are thus sometimes able to improve with age for three to five years; some Moulin-à-Vent wines, the most serious of the *cru* Beaujolais, are said to last even longer than that, in part because they see some aging in oak barrels. In contrast, Fleurie and Brouilly, like most Beaujolais, affect no airs and offer the down-home fruity frivolity we know and love from Beaujolais. Despite residing atop the Beaujolais hierarchy, the *cru* Beaujolais category offers splendid bang-for-the-buck, with most selections tagged under $15.

It is impossible to drink Beaujolais without bumping up against the name Georges Duboeuf. The producer is omnipresent, its familiar floral design adorning virtually every possible type of Beaujolais, along with a flood of T-shirts, pins, and posters reminding consumers of Duboeuf's dominance in the Beaujolais market. Behind the slick marketing, however, owner Georges Duboeuf runs a quality-obsessed operation, rigorously selecting his wine from more than four hundred grape growers. The result is one of the world's great wine values, year after year, whether you're drinking a bouncy Beaujolais Nouveau or a more muscular Moulin-à-Vent.

CHEAT SHEET

A step up from Beaujolais Nouveau, other types of Beaujolais offer year-round availability and often a shade more personality, while retaining the wine's juicy berry pleasure.

LABEL DECODER

Beaujolais is a place. Gamay is the grape. *Cru* Beaujolais refers to one of ten villages in the best part of the Beaujolais region. The ten *cru* Beaujolais are Brouilly, Chénas, Chiroubles, Côte de Brouilly, Fleurie, Juliénas, Morgon, Moulin-à-Vent, Régnié, and St.-Amour.

OUTSMART THE TABLE

The most concentrated of any *cru* Beaujolais, Moulin-à-Vent is named for a three-hundred-year-old windmill that sits in the area's vineyards.

TALK THE TALK

Beaujolais-Villages	*Beau-joh-LAY-Vee-LAHJ*
Moulin-à-Vent	*Moo-LAHN-ah-VAHN*
Morgon	*More-GAWN*
Brouilly	*Brew-YEE*
Fleurie	*Flehr-EE*

MARK'S PICKS

Château de la Chaize	*Shehz*
Drouhin	*Drew-AHN*
Duboeuf	*Duh-BUFF*
Jadot	*Jah-DOE*
Mommessin	*Mon-muh-SAHN*
Michel Tête	*Mee-shell TEHT*

FIT FOR FEASTING

Almost everything, especially casual fare; *pommes frites* and other fried foods; lighter cheeses; tomato-based fare; grilled-vegetable dishes, ratatouille; roast chicken; *coq au vin;* pork dishes; cassoulet; Camembert and other soft cheeses; chèvre and other tangy cheeses.

On My Table | **GEORGES DUBOEUF is the owner of Les Vins Georges Duboeuf, the French wine empire that is virtually synonymous with the region of Beaujolais.**

Northern Rhône—Côte Rôtie
Marcel Guigal

Madiran [a rare, full-bodied red wine from the Pyrenees foothills in the southwest of France]
Alain Brumont

Red Bordeaux—Fronsac
Château les Trois Croix—Leon Family

Irouléguy [rosé and light red wine from the Basque country of far southwestern France, along the Spanish border]
Domaine Brana

Red Burgundy
Domaine Leroy

Beaujolais
"Of course."

White Burgundy—Mâconnais

52 Instead of Cabernet Sauvignon, Try Cabernet Franc (and Chinon)

Cabernet Franc bides its time as one of the lesser grapes in the blend that composes red Bordeaux, but sometimes it emerges as a stand-alone varietal offering a lighter and slightly sassier alternative to Cabernet Sauvignon. "Cab Franc" dials up a Cabernet Sauvignon–like perfume of currant and plum, but it is often less dense than the jam machine that is Cabernet Sauvignon.

Along with its lighter body and higher acidity, Cabernet Franc's sass shines through with a slight hint of herbs or green vegetables. Some detect green peppers, others eucalyptus leaves; for me, green olives are the signal. These aromas, if they're even present, are typically subtle, as they should be; the worst versions of Cabernet Franc take the herby trip too far and seem weedy and unripe.

Cabernet Franc's light and crisp personality makes it an ideal match for food. In fact, some say that food is an all-out necessity with this edgy red. That's good news, because Cabernet Franc will zest up a variety of dishes, and, given its innate greenness, it has a special affinity for dishes with leafy vegetables and herb sauces. Vegetarians, take note!

Despite its growing popularity, Cabernet Franc remains a relatively exotic offering from but a few American wineries. It is more enthusiastically embraced in France's Loire Valley, where it is labeled with the districts of Bourgeuil, Saumur-Champigny, and Chinon. The last, a ubiquity in Parisian bistros, is considered the best and most popular Loire red. As with most cool-climate European wine, Chinon and its brethren are typically less ripe and oaky than American Cabernet Franc. Expect a crisp wine that is light to medium bodied, often with notes

CHEAT SHEET

Terrific with food, Cabernet Franc remakes the Cabernet Sauvignon experience with less tannin and body and often more acidity and an herbal aroma.

LABEL DECODER

Cabernet Franc is a grape. Chinon is an appellation in France's Loire Valley.

OUTSMART THE TABLE

- DNA analysis has revealed Cabernet Franc to be one of the parent grapes (along with Sauvignon Blanc) of Cabernet Sauvignon.
- Cabernet Franc is the dominant grape in Bordeaux's Château Cheval Blanc, one of the world's most celebrated wines.

TALK THE TALK

Chinon   *Shee-NOHN*
Rabelaisian   *Rab-b'leh-shen*

MARK'S PICKS

U.S. *(note that production runs are typically small):*
Benziger, Chappellet, Crocker & Starr, Jarvis, La Jota, Niebaum-Coppola, Pine Ridge, Pride Mountain, Robert Sinskey.

France (Chinon):

Bernard Baudry	*Bare-nar Boe-dree*
Domaine du Colombier	*dew Koe-lon-byay*
Château de la Grille	*lah Gree*
Charles Joguet	*Sharl Zho-geh*
Jean-Maurice Raffault	*Rah-foe*

FIT FOR FEASTING

Vegetables (including grill-friendly types like eggplant and zucchini); dishes with herb sauces (e.g., thyme, saffron, rosemary, sage); tomato-based dishes; chicken, duck, veal, or game birds; beef dishes and steak (with more robust American styles).

of cherries or raspberries and more pronounced herbal aromas.

Attention, sybarites: Chinon was the beloved beverage of François Rabelais, the celebrated French writer of the sixteenth century and native son of the town of Chinon. An unabashed hedonist, Rabelais laced his salty satires with descriptions of Chinon-soaked feasts; thus the term *Rabelaisian*, connoting a kind of coarse and uproarious revelry. He coined an expression that's still common in Chinon today: *"Beauvez toujours, vous ne mourrez jamais,"* which means something like "Drink always and you will never die."

53 Instead of Merlot, Try Argentine Malbec's Blackberry Hedonism

Let's say you're splurging at a big-city steak house. As your tablemates devour the onion bread and whipped butter, you pry open the leather-bound behemoth of a wine list. Therein lies a dizzying array of California Cabernet and French Bordeaux—each one more prestigious and expensive than the next. Is it really necessary, you wonder, to pay north of $60 for a steak-friendly bottle of red?

With any luck, a gently priced savior will be tucked under the heading "Other Wines": Argentine Malbec. Increasingly popular in wine-passionate restaurants, Malbec is the ultimate steakhouse table pleaser, dependable for lush, jammy flavors of blackberries and chocolate, with a minimum of bitter tannin—often at a fraction of the price of American and French blue chips.

For years the grape Malbec kept a low profile, never making much of a splash outside Argentina, its greatest enthusiast, or France, where it is sometimes blended into red Bordeaux or used to make Cahors, the famous "black wine" produced around the city of the same name. In the last decade, however, Argentina has started exporting some incredible bottles of Malbec—wine so rich and flavorful that some experts predict it will eventually achieve Merlotlike popularity in the United States. Until that happens, know that Malbec, like Merlot, is a dark, medium- to full-bodied wine, often with ripe essences of blackberries or sometimes cherries and licorice. It sometimes has a minerally or earthy quality—imagine the smell of summer rain on a gravelly road—that matches the charred, funky character of a juicy porterhouse.

Most of the best Argentine Malbec producers are located in the region of Mendoza, whose high-elevation desert climate is home to world-class wineries such as Catena, Mariposa, and Weinert. Under $15, you'll find the dependably delicious and widely available Altos Las Hormigas, whose explosively fruity nose and velvety texture rarely disappoint; Trapiche and Alamos (a basic bottling from Catena) are two other value Malbecs I love. For slightly pricier Malbec, an excellent producer to watch is Susana Balbo, one of the few female vintners in the high-testosterone world of Argentine winemaking. Her Malbec is packed with ripe berries, and you might detect a pleasing whiff of freshly tilled soil or charred leather; Balbo's Cabernet Sauvignon and Syrah-Bonarda are also reliably excellent. Malbec is becoming an increasingly popular grape in other countries, notably in neighboring Chile and Australia, where it is often blended with Shiraz or Cabernet Sauvignon.

Argentine Malbec is not a wine for the curmudgeonly. After your first glass, its berry-chocolate-smoky bouquet will have cast its spell, leaving you no choice but to sit back, admire the residue of this rich inky potion, and hope that you get to bury your nose in another glass.

54 Instead of Zinfandel, Taste the Mediterranean Sun in Châteauneuf-du-Pape

When the bestseller *A Year in Provence* hit bookshelves, it inspired legions to fantasize about decamping to this glorious land of azure skies, lavender hills, and preprandial pastis. What few realized is that the popes of the fourteenth century were way ahead of the game, making their journey to sun-kissed Avignon a good 670 years before Peter Mayle's account ever seized the popular imagination. Politics, of course, motivated their relocation from Rome to Avignon, but it's hard to imagine that these wine lovers weren't also drawn by this area's prime vineyard land.

Although the popes stayed for only sixty years, that was long enough to sponsor the cultivation of vineyards that would eventually make the best wine of the southern Rhône—Châteauneuf-du-Pape—literally, "new castle of the pope." While it is a wine ideal for those who like red Zinfandel's full body and peppery pull, Châteauneuf is more than a one-grape wine. This vinous lothario entertains the affection of up to fourteen different grape types. Supple, berry-perfumed Grenache is the closest the wine has to a significant other, joined by peppery Syrah and earthy Mourvèdre as very willing mistresses, with most of the other grapes mere dalliances, if they even show at all.

While the exact style of Châteauneuf varies with how much of each grape type a winemaker uses in the final blend, the classic Châteauneuf character is full bodied, with a big hit of ripe berries that almost tastes roasted and an unmistakable edge of pepper, along with minerals and tar. Tasters sometimes also speak of herbs, licorice, and even barnyard aromas. Many of these wines are easy to drink when young, while others have enough tannin to benefit from some years of aging.

Châteauneuf may be located near paradisial Provence, but aspects of its landscape seem closer to what you'd find exploring some mysterious planet. Scattered across the terrain are smooth stones, or *galets*, some of which are as large as softballs. These stones are actually good for the wine, because they collectively act as a gigantic heating pad, trapping in the day's heat and helping

CHEAT SHEET

A product of the southern Rhône's intense sun, mighty wind, and mysteriously stony soil, Châteauneuf-du-Pape is a lusty, full-bodied affair combining ripe roasted berry fruit with pepper and other spices.

LABEL DECODER

Châteauneuf-du-Pape is a village. The wine is a blend of up to fourteen grapes, with Grenache being the most common.

OUTSMART THE TABLE

- Châteauneuf has one of wine's more impressive bottles, usually with a papal coat of arms embossed into its glass.
- Châteauneuf-du-Pape is known as *CDP* in the wine trade.

TALK THE TALK

Châteauneuf-du-Pape
Shah-toe-nuff-dew-PAHP

MARK'S PICKS

Chapoutier	*Shah-poo-TYAY*
Château de Beaucastel	
	Bow-kahs-TEHL
Château Fortia	*FORE-shuh*
Château la Nerthe	*lah NEHRT*
Château Rayas	*Ray-YAHS*
Clos des Papes	*Cloe day POP*
Domaine du Vieux Télégraphe	
	View Tay-lay-GRAHF
Guigal	*Ghee-GAL*
Vieux Donjon	*View Dohn-JHOHN*

FIT FOR FEASTING

Robust fare, especially lamb, steak, and other red meat; stews like cassouolet; olive oil; dishes with Provençal herbs such as rosemary, sage, marjoram; robust vegetable and bean dishes; strong, firm cheeses; Roquefort and other blue-veined cheeses.

the grapes ripen even in the dead of night. Another potential detriment that ends up enhancing the wine is the region's famous mistral, the violent wind that sweeps down the valley. When vineyards are inundated by summer rains, the mistral's arid winds quickly dry the vines and protect them from fungal disease.

If the little bottle of wine depicted on the famous Mediterranean food pyramid stood for a particular wine type, how could it not be Châteauneuf? It not only pairs beautifully with virtually everything considered Mediterranean, but its edginess makes food virtually a necessity. Crusty bread? Check. Robust veggies and bean dishes? Check. Garlic? Check. Olive oil. Double check. Given its ample weight, it is a terrific match with a broad range of grilled meats and stews like cassoulet. Got lamb or pepper sauce or, better yet, lamb *in* pepper sauce? Châteauneuf's peppery, earthy character is just what the *chef de cuisine* ordered.

Châteauneuf used to be a good value, but in recent years prices have crept up, starting at about $25 and sometimes double that or more for finer bottles. While not having quite the reputation for aging as its northern Rhône brethren, at its best it can improve for a good fifteen to twenty years. Among the most famous estates are Domaine du Vieux Télégraphe, named for a telegraph tower in the middle of its vineyards, and Château de Beaucastel, unique in its use of each of the fourteen grapes permitted. Only one grape, Grenache, composes the region's most coveted wine, Château Rayas, almost always a concentrated, succulent effort that easily hurdles $100.

While most Châteauneuf-du-Pape is red, you'll occasionally see Châteauneuf-du-Pape Blanc at auctions, finer shops, and restaurants. Made from a variety of grapes, such as Viognier and Roussanne, this rarity is a rich, full-bodied white, with an exotic floral and honey character. Château de Beaucastel makes one of the best.

On My Table | **FRANÇOIS PERRIN** is the co-owner and winemaker of Château de Beaucastel, one of the Rhône Valley's leading producers of Châteauneuf-du-Pape.

Northern Rhône—Hermitage (red)
Chave

White Burgundy—Montrachet
Leflaive

White Burgundy—Meursault
Lafon

Languedoc-Roussillon
Domaine de Trévallon [full-bodied wine composed of a blend of Syrah and Cabernet Sauvignon]

Red Burgundy—Pommard
Boillot

Riesling from Germany
Grand cru Schlossberg

Cabernet Sauvignon from California
Ridge

55 Instead of Chianti, Try Sexy, Flavorful Primitivo

Before I teach my wine classes, I usually have a pretty good idea of which wines will be crowd pleasers. But last winter I was surprised when I taught a night of Italian reds, including a selection of expensive, complex Barolos, Brunellos, and Chianti Classico Riservas. To my surprise, the darling of the class wasn't any of these blue chips but a $12 bottle with a simple label and a big taste: Primitivo.

My students and I loved this Primitivo for its easy drinkability and warm aromas of plummy fruit and spice. This is what Primitivo, at its best, is about: a medium-bodied red with essences of dried cherries and plums, highlighted by a mouthwatering lemon squirt of acidity but low tannin. I ended up snatching up two cases of the wine (Apollonio Primitivo), and it never failed to seduce the people who drank it.

"PRIMITIVO IS RUSTIC, RAISINY, AND RICH—PERFECT WITH LUSTY TOMATO-BASED HARD-PASTA DISHES WITH LOTS OF STINKY SALTY PECORINO ON TOP."

—*Mario Batali, celebrity chef*

Primitivo was long thought to be an ancestor or sibling of the mostly American-grown grape Zinfandel, but recent DNA testing has shown that they are in fact the same grape. As is often the case between the Old and New Worlds, however, differences in climate and winemaker style produce considerably different wine styles. Italian Primitivo is usually not quite as rich and jammy as American Zinfandel, which has a more oaky, smoky dimension than its Italian counterpart.

Primitivo is made primarily in Puglia, a region located in the sun-drenched heel of Italy's boot and long dismissed as a giant reservoir for bulk wine. Better producers of Primitivo, however, are proving that Puglia can make wines of considerable appeal and flavor, even if they lack the refinement of the juice up north. The real magic comes at the cash register, where your average Primitivo rings up at $12 or less. If I owned a pizza restaurant, I'd serve a free taste of Primitivo to every diner—and I'd probably double the amount of wine sold, given how well the wine matches with the spicy, tangy, charred character of pizza.

If you think about it, the name *Primitivo* fits this rustic, generous wine, its primitive charm offering a refreshing departure from the overintellectualized world of wine appreciation. While invoking Gewürztraminer won't do much to unlock your lover's heart, who can resist the seductive spell of candlelight, soft music, and "Pree-mee-TEE-vo"?

CHEAT SHEET

Sexy, affordable, and aromatic, Primitivo will light your primal fires with soft, spicy fruit and rich, sun-baked flavors.

LABEL DECODER

Primitivo is a grape (the same grape as Zinfandel in California).

OUTSMART THE TABLE

If you like Primitivo, you'll enjoy Salice Salentino, another overachiever from Puglia. Made primarily from the sturdy Negroamaro grape, it resembles Primitivo in its dark color, rich fruit flavors, dependably smooth edges, and affordability. Look for Salice Salentino from producers Taurino (a staple in Italian restaurants) and Cantele.

TALK THE TALK

Primitivo	Pree-mee-TEE-vo
Puglia	POOL-ya

MARK'S PICKS

A-Mano, Apollonio, Calatrasi, Cantele, Cantina del Borgo Reale, Felline, Pervini.

FIT FOR FEASTING

Substantial pasta dishes (e.g., spaghetti bolognese) and southern Italian classics like veal parmigiana and chicken cacciatore; pizza (especially with hardy toppings like pepperoni or sausage); casual meat dishes like hamburger and meat loaf; eggplant and other earthy vegetables; Parmigiano-Reggiano, pecorino, and other dry, firm cheeses.

56 Instead of Beaujolais, Try Dolcetto and Barbera, Piedmont's Fruity Saviors

taly's Piedmont region isn't only about power and pucker. Lurking behind the grandeur of Barolo and Barbaresco are two "second players" of Piedmont—Dolcetto and Barbera—both ready to lick the wounds of those buffeted by the astringency and expense of Piedmont's prestige reds. On the metaphorical highway of Italian wine, Dolcetto and Barbera are the cherry-red VW Beetles zipping past the dark, brooding limousines of Barolo and Barbaresco.

Both Dolcetto and Barbera are straightforward, juicy, light- to medium-weight reds that are almost as integral to the Piedmontese dinner table as salt and pepper. Although they are traditionally simple, everyday quaffers, some winemakers have upped the ante with better grapes, lower yields, and French oak, with results that have brought appreciative nods in the wine world. Generally, however, Dolcetto won't be much more than an upbeat, cherry-cranberry sun splash of a wine, with vibrant acidity and sometimes a moderate grate of tannin. Barbera is also fruity and tangy but often with more plummy or blackcurranty richness and less tannic pucker than its sister Dolcetto, such that it can sometimes be medium to full bodied.

No matter how fruity they are, Dolcetto and Barbera fall outside the smooth, oaky confines of the American comfort zone. Being characteristically rustic Italian wines, they usually have a current of lip-smacking acidity, and Dolcetto in particular is prone to some tannic dryness. The trick is to learn to see such edginess as a gastronomic opportunity, affording a zesty, metaphorical lemon squeeze to light meats, antipasto, and anything with a tomato sauce—spaghetti and meatballs being the classic example. When I'm facing down an Italian-only wine list, with frightfully expensive Barolos and Brunellos and unfamiliar names seemingly from Italy's hin-

CHEAT SHEET

Dolcetto and Barbera are affordable saviors of Italian wine lists. What they lack in complexity they make up for in berry charm, food friendliness, and affordability.

LABEL DECODER

Dolcetto and Barbera are grapes. They are widely grown in the Piedmont region of northwestern Italy.

terland, Dolcetto and Barbera are trusty friends that won't create consternation when the bill arrives.

And on the subject of dinero, Dolcetto and Barbera are typically under $20 in stores, although more ambitious examples can run $25 or more. Dolcetto often comes from vineyards outside the city of Alba or nearby Dogliani, the latter considered the birthplace of Dolcetto, and the wine's official name often includes both the grape and the district—as in Dolcetto d'Alba and Dolcetto di Dogliani. Alba is also a major production zone for Barbera (Barbera d'Alba), as is Asti (Barbera d'Asti), which is said to make a slightly lighter style of Barbera.

In terms of consistency, Dolcetto and Barbera have a mixed record—one bottle can be utterly charming, the next flavorless or unpleasantly tart or bitter. Given its relative scarcity in wine stores, the best advice is to find a merchant with a penchant for Italian *vino* and work with his list.

OUTSMART THE TABLE

Although *Dolcetto* translates as "little sweet one," it is by no means a wine for dessert.

TALK THE TALK

Dolcetto	*Dol-CHET-toe*
Barbera	*Bar-BEAR-ah*
d'Alba	*DAL-ba*
d'Asti	*DHAS-tee*
Dogliani	*Do-LYAH-nee*

MARK'S PICKS (both Dolcetto and Barbera unless noted)

Ceretto	*Cheh-RETT-oh*
Pio Cesare	*Pee-oh CHEZZ-eh-ray*
Michele Chiarlo	
	Mee-KELL-eh Key-AHR-low
Chionetti (Dolcetto)	*Kyo-NEHT-tee*
Coppo	*KOH-poe*
Bruno Giacosa	*Jah-KOE-zah*
Prunotto	*Proo-NOH-toe*
Vietti	*VYEHT-tee*

FIT FOR FEASTING

Very versatile, perfect with pasta of all kinds, especially red-sauce classics (e.g., spaghetti and meatballs); veal and poultry dishes (e.g., chicken marsala); salami, *bresaola* (wafer-thin dried beef), and other antipasti; hearty starches like polenta and risotto; dishes with mushrooms and other earthy fare; rich soups; a range of cheeses, from dry types like Parmigiano-Reggiano to the fresh bite of goat and feta cheese.

Champagne and Sparkling Wine

*O*ne of my greatest pleasures as a wine educator is enlightening people on the daily joys of bubbly. Too often people treat Champagne and sparkling wine like a tuxedo or fine china, saving it only for special occasions. As the coming shortcuts advise, bubbly is an ideal partner for meals and everyday merriment—and your options range from the real Champagne of France to affordable sparklers from regions around the world. ■

57 Only Bubbly from France's Champagne Region Is Truly Champagne

If you wake up one day with a devilish desire to shatter a French winemaker's sangfroid, here's what to do: offer him Champagne and then produce a shiny bottle of Korbel "Champagne," fresh from northern California.

A scowl will emerge faster than you can say bête noire.

This is because in France only bubbly from the Champagne district in northeastern France is allowed to carry the name *Champagne*—anything else can never, ever dream of masquerading as the big C. With the exception of marketing renegades like Korbel, most winemakers outside of France play along and, depending on where they are, differentiate their bubbly as Prosecco (Italy), Cava (Spain), or Sekt (Germany), all of which can be generalized as *sparkling wine*, which is what most U.S. producers call it.

It's hard to blame the French for being so protective when you appreciate the special conditions under which real Champagne is crafted. While Champagne is technically just white wine with bubbles, it's where that wine originates and how the bubbles get there that set Champagne apart. Champagne, the district, is France's most northerly wine region, where the cool climate and chalky soils foster grapes of considerable acidity. French law mandates those grapes be only Chardonnay (a white-wine grape), Pinot Noir (a red-wine grape), or the little-known Pinot Meunier (also a red-wine grape). Every Champagne maker decides how to blend these grapes—or whether to use just one variety, such as Chardonnay—which will ultimately help determine the style of the finished wine (see Shortcut 58).

Champagne is also distinguished by an incredibly labor-intensive production process, one required of all Champagne producers and also emulated around the world by makers of

"I JUST CAN'T IMAGINE LIFE WITHOUT CHAMPAGNE. IT MAKES LIFE HAPPIER, RICHER, AND IS ALWAYS A SPECIAL TREAT . . . A BIT LIKE WATCHING THE SUNSET: NEVER THE SAME YET ALWAYS GREAT."

—*Mireille Guiliano, president, Clicquot, Inc.*

finer bubbly. Called *méthode champenoise* in the Champagne region (and often *traditional method* or *classic method* elsewhere), it requires winemakers to induce a second fermentation in each individual bottle of Champagne. This may not sound like a big deal, but the whole routine involves dozens of steps, including the addition of a special blend of sugar and yeast, aging the wine on its lees (i.e., sediment), and briefly freezing the neck of the bottle to disgorge that sediment. Expensive and time-consuming, all of this personal attention nevertheless creates bubbly of uncommon complexity and finesse—often marked by yeasty, baked-bread aromas and tiny, pinpoint bubbles.

The Champagne most of us encounter is the *NV*, or nonvintage, category, which generally costs between $25 and $45 a bottle. It's NV (or sometimes *MV*, for "multivintage") because the Champagne is blended from grapes harvested over several vintages. This flexibility frees winemakers from relying on the weather conditions of one particular year, enabling them to make a consistent "house style" year after year. That's why you can always count on Taittinger NV to be light bodied and citrusy and on Veuve Clicquot Yellow Label NV to deliver a fuller body with more yeasty aromas. The next chapter lists the general styles of the major Champagne houses.

In years of excellent weather when grapes achieve full ripeness—typically only four or five a decade in the iffy climes of northern France—producers may decide to release *vintage* Champagne—bubbly made solely from grapes of a particular year. Unlike NV champagne, vintage Champagne will display a particular year on the label. Entry-level vintage Champagne runs about $35 to $60 a bottle, while top-level vintage Champagne—ones earning the designation *prestige cuvée* or *tête de cuvée*—starts at about $75 and can run well over $100 a bottle. As we'll cover soon, the great expense of these *prestige cuvées*—including the famous names Dom Pérignon and Roederer Cristal—doesn't necessarily buy you a dramatically *better* taste, though they are generally said to have more complexity and flavor than their nonvintage counterparts; you are arguably paying more for the privilege of consuming a scarce and prestigious commodity, like an Hermès tie or Kobe beef, than for markedly superior taste.

While most of the Champagne we encounter tastes dry, denoted on the label as *brut*, it does come in sweeter styles. If it has just a bit of sweetness, it is labeled, confusingly, *extra dry*. Moët & Chandon's ubiquitous White Star Champagne, for example, is extra dry. For those who crave bubbly with dessert, there are Champagnes that are *sec*, or lightly sweet; *demi-sec*, which is even sweeter; and *doux*, which is very sweet and rarely seen.

On My Table | **CLAUDE TAITTINGER** heads Champagne Taittinger, one of the world's celebrated Champagne houses, established in 1931 by his father, Pierre.

Champagne
Taittinger Brut Réserve

Red Bordeaux—Graves/Pessac-Léognan
Château Olivier—"Every day as a 'table wine' . . . The cost/quality ratio is remarkable."

Pinot Noir from California
Domaine Carneros—"Once or twice a week, as an accompaniment to cheese."

Rosé from Corsica
Domaine Comte Peraldi

Red Bordeaux—St.-Emilion
Cheval Blanc—"For the Christmas and New Year's Eve celebrations."

Tokaji dessert wine
Château Dereszla—"The bouquet is opulent and explodes with honey, pear, and gelée royale."

Malbec from Argentina
Alta Vista—"To go with venison."

58 Judge Champagne by Bubbles and Body

Being asked to distinguish between different bottles of bubbly is like differentiating a crocodile from an alligator: There *must* be a difference, but who knows what it is? And why are you asking me anyway?

Happily, for those in the know, there are two useful ways to discern one Champagne from the next. The first is simply by looking at the bubbles. Before learning about Champagne, I never gave the notion of bubbles a second thought, except perhaps while enduring the inevitable waiters' upsell, "Sparkling or still?" But I discovered that the single most important differentiator in sparkling wine—and especially Champagne—is its bubbles.

Some sparkling wine offers a veritable rush hour of big, sloppy bubbles, like any old glass of Canada Dry. Others don't have much of a bubble at all, just a float of fizzies struggling, but failing, to be more than they can be. The finest Champagnes and sparkling wines, however, are prized for their galaxy of tiny bubbles—millions and millions of pinpoints glimmering their way up the glass, like beads on a string. These bubbles produce what I call a Champagne's "cashmere caress": a blanket of tightly knit bubbles that create a cohesive, creamy texture in your mouth. The bubbles are so fine, so integrated into the underlying wine, that, like the threads of a cashmere scarf, they are noticed not individually but as a smooth, seductive whole.

The other key differentiator for Champagne is body—that is, how heavy it feels in your mouth. As mentioned previously, each Champagne house is, in fact, known for a house style based primarily on how weighty it is. A winemaker in part determines this style by adjusting the proportion of white-wine (Chardonnay) to red-wine grapes (Pinot Noir and sometimes Pinot Meunier) in the final blend. As you'd expect, lighter-style Champagne typically has a higher proportion of Chardonnay, while fuller-style bubbly has more red-wine grapes in the blend. *Blanc de Blancs* on a label means that the wine comes from 100 percent Chardonnay grapes, so you would expect it to be on the delicate side and better with lighter foods. *Blanc de Noirs* champagne, which isn't nearly as common, comes from all red-wine grapes, usually just Pinot Noir.

One style isn't necessarily better—it depends on your personal preference. Expect lighter-style Champagne to have delicate notes of apples and citrus fruits, supported by a wash of tangy acidity and perhaps a hint of yeastiness. Full-bodied Champagne swings for the fences with more intense fruit essences, such as baked apple, while practically spiriting you inside a Pepperidge Farm factory with its toasty, yeasty, nutty flavors. It too should have a nice tingle of acidity, keeping it fresh and exuberant despite its full-bodied power. Here are the hallmark styles of the major Champagne houses, which are best exemplified in their nonvintage (NV) bottlings:

LIGHT BODIED

Billecart-Salmon	*Beel-kahr-Sahl-MOHN*
Nicolas Feuillatte	*Nee-ko-LAH Fuh-YAHT*
Lanson	*Lahn-SOHN*
Laurent-Perrier	*Low-rahn-PEH-hryay*
Perrier-Jouët	*PEH-hryay-Zhew-EHT*
Pommery	*POH-muh-ree*
Taittinger	*Tay-tahn-ZHAY*

MEDIUM BODIED

Charles Heidsieck	*HIDE-sick*
Moët & Chandon	*Moe-EHT ay Shan-don*
Mumm	*Muhm*
Piper-Heidsieck	*PEE-per-HIDE-sick*
Pol Roger	*Pawl Roe-ZHAY*

FULL BODIED

Bollinger	*Bow-lahn-ZHAY*
Gosset	*Go-SEH*
Krug	*Krewg*
Louis Roederer	*Loo-wee Roe-duh-REHR*
Veuve Clicquot	*Vuhv Klee-KOE*

CHEAT SHEET

Distinguish Champagnes of similar quality by their weight—some are produced in a lighter style, while others have a richer, yeastier impact. The best Champagnes, regardless of weight, show a galaxy of tiny, pinpoint bubbles.

OUTSMART THE TABLE

- The ring of bubbles on the surface of fine Champagne is said to form a *collier de perles*, or "pearl necklace."
- Large, ungainly bubbles in Champagne are sometimes called *oeil de crapaud*, or "toad's eyes."

TALK THE TALK

Just as you'd say Jacqueline Bisset (*Biss-EHT*, not *Biss-ay*), the *Moët* of Moët & Chandon is pronounced *Moe-EHT*, not *Moe-AY*, and the *Jouët* of Perrier-Jouët is *Zhew-EHT*, not *Zhew-AY*.

On My Table | **DIDIER DEPOND** is president of Champagne Salon, whose sole product is an ultrarare, ultraexpensive Blanc de Biancs (all-Chardonnay) Champagne.

Champagne
   Laurent-Perrier Ultra Brut and Grand Siècle, Pierre Peters, Delamotte Blanc de Blancs, Salon

Port
   Taylor, Fonseca, Quinta do Vale Dona Maria—"At the swimming pool's edge in the Douro or in front of a fireplace after skiing."

Red Bordeaux
   Branaire-Ducru, Lamarque, Léoville-Las-Cases, Pétrus, Valandraud

White Burgundy
   Domaine Jacques Prieur, Jayer

Jurançon and Madiran [appellations in southwestern France; Jurançon makes primarily dry white wine; Jurançon's neighbor, Madiran, produces mainly rich, sturdy reds]
   Domaine Laplace

Calvados [dry apple brandy from the Normandy region of northern France]

Armagnac [French brandy from the Armagnac region]
   Drouhin Coeur de Lion, Darroze—"Before the Corrida [bullfight] to finish a memorable evening."

59 Superexpensive Champagne: More for the Label Than for the Taste

When the rapper Jay-Z sings about "six bottles of Cris" in his hit "I Just Wanna Love U," is he celebrating the yeasty richness and palate-cleansing acidity of Roederer Cristal?

Doubtful. What, then, explains the enormous popularity of so-called *prestige cuvée* Champagne—as coveted by hip-hop stars and clubbers as it is by wine snobs and even James Bond, who requests a bottle of 1961 Bollinger upon his release from a North Korean prison in *Die Another Day*? Or, as one of my students recently asked, "Is Dom Pérignon really $70 tastier than Veuve Clicquot Yellow Label?"

For most palates, the answer is no. To be sure, French Champagne is made with greater care than most other bubbly, and at the rarefied *prestige cuvée* level, it is lavished with even more personal attention. Winemakers typically use the choicest grapes grown only in years of optimal weather; that's why, with the exception of Krug's legendary Grande Cuvée MV (multi-vintage), Champagne at this level always carries one specific vintage year. *Prestige cuvée* Champagne also receives extra years of bottle aging—up to six years, versus as little as fifteen months for basic-level Champagne—before release to consumers. Winemakers at Krug even ferment the base wine of their Grande Cuvée in oak casks before it gets to its second fermentation, a rare and expensive measure even among top Champagne makers.

All of this extra effort produces Champagne of somewhat greater complexity and flavor, as does the fact that *prestige cuvées*, which people tend to reserve for special occasions, are sometimes kept around for several years before being drunk. (While not everyone agrees with the view that fine Champagne improves with age, I've found that Champagne with ten or more years of bottle age can develop pleasingly rich aromas of hazelnut and

"[I DON'T SERVE]
KRUG CLOS DU
MESNIL OR KRUG
COLLECTION AT HOME
FOR SIMPLE ETHICAL
AND 'DISCIPLINE'
REASONS. . . .
I SIMPLY CANNOT
ALLOW MYSELF TO
TAKE ANY BOTTLE
AWAY FROM A
CUSTOMER."

—*Rémi Krug,
Champagne Krug*

CHEAT SHEET

Although most casual drinkers don't notice a remarkably better taste in *prestige cuvée* Champagne, it remains one of life's great glittering indulgences—both to mark a celebration and as reason for one.

OUTSMART THE TABLE

Krug doesn't make entry-level Champagne—only *prestige cuvées*.

TALK THE TALK

prestige cuvée   coo-VAY

MARK'S PICKS

Bollinger R.D.   *Bow-lahn-ZHAY*
Dom Pérignon   *Donh Pay-ree-NYON*
Krug Clos du Mesnil
     Krewg Klow dew Meh-NEEL
Krug Grande Cuvée
     Krewg Granh Coo-VAY
Moët & Chandon   *Moe-EHT ay Shan-don*
Perrier-Jouët Fleur de Champagne
     PEH-hryay-Zhew-EHT Fluhr duh
          Shahm-PAHN-yuh
Pol Roger Cuvée Sir Winston Churchill
          Pawl Roe-ZHAY Coo-vay
Louis Roederer Cristal   *Krees-TAHL*
Salon Le Mesnil   *Sah-LOHN Luh Meh-NEEL*
Taittinger Comtes de Champagne
     Tay-tahn-ZHAY Kont duh Shahm-PAHN-yuh
Veuve Clicquot   *Vuhv Klee-KOE*
La Grande Dame   *Lah Grahn DAHM*

honey, albeit at the expense of some fruitiness and effervescence.) But even if the added intensity in luxury Champagne compels some wine pros to reminisce about their first "Krug moments" or "D.P. delirium," for most of us the taste difference alone isn't dramatic enough to justify the price difference between a $100+ *prestige cuvée* bottle and its $35 basic-level cousin.

Instead remember what also fuels the high prices commanded by many of the world's finest red and white wine: supply and demand. Although some *prestige cuvées* are made in comparatively large batches—Dom Pérignon, for example, is thought to have an annual production run of more than 100,000 cases—many others are made in smaller batches, an extreme being Krug's Clos du Mesnil, with scarcely 1,000 cases to satiate the world's elite. Amelia Stephan, a representative of Roederer Cristal's U.S. importer, Maisons Marques Domaines, told me that the reason Cristal sees limited marketing is that Roederer "does not make enough to supply the current demand," a fact confirmed by the legions of frustrated restaurant and club owners who beg her office for a more generous allocation.

Perhaps the greatest allure of prestige Champagne transcends taste and even scarcity: its time-honored role as a status symbol. Indeed, no one appreciated the bling-bling value of Champagne more than the Russian upper classes of the nineteenth century. Legend has it that Roederer Cristal came into being when Czar Alexander II commissioned Roederer to make him a special batch of Champagne bottled in clear-cut crystal, so that his guests would be dazzled by the bottle even when it was wrapped in a linen serving cloth. Today, the idea of Champagne lives on as a goal and a symbol, aided by flashy packaging and pop culture's use of it as a marker of prestige and prosperity.

Shallow, you say? Not if we also appreciate that the impracticality and decadence of drinking a glass of something that costs more than a ticket to Paris can be transporting in and of itself. Luxury Champagne dares you to thumb your nose at the numbing banalities of life—the 401K, the endodontist, the in-laws—and focus on what's truly important: the people around you and the mischief yet to make.

On My Table | **RÉMI KRUG** is the fifth generation to run Champagne Krug, the ne plus ultra of luxury Champagne.

Champagne
Krug Grande Cuvée, Krug 1988, Krug Rosé—"No need for me to justify."

Red Bordeaux
Château Margaux, Cheval Blanc, Lafite-Rothschild, Ducru-Beaucaillou, Léoville-Las-Cases, Lynch-Bages, Figeac, Montrose, Domaine de Chevallier, La Conseillante

Sauternes
Château d'Yquem

White Burgundy
Bâtard-Montrachet from Domaine Ramonet or Puligny-Montrachet from Domaine Leflaive

Madeira from the nineteenth century [fortified wine from Portugal's Madeira Island; often has a burned caramel taste]—"Always unique, mysterious, intense: an unforgettable experience!"

Super Tuscans
Tignanello

Vintage port—"Especially with our traditional Stilton cheese at Christmas." Graham

60 Prosecco and Champagne's Other Bubbly Stunt Doubles

> "I LOVE PROSECCO BECAUSE IT IS A GREAT WINE FOR ALL PARTS OF LIFE . . . A SPECIAL OCCASION NEEDS A LITTLE TOAST."
>
> —*Mario Batali, celebrity chef*

When *stalking* bubbles, some connoisseurs lubricate their lips only with Champagne, which, we previously learned, is limited to bubbly produced in France's district of the same name. This is a mistake of monstrous proportions, because beyond Champagne's frosty, chalky soils lies a world of delightful alternatives, with virtually every major wine region sporting its own variations on the bubbly theme. These are the bubbly stunt doubles; like the daredevils who take falls for Tom Cruise and Halle Berry, they are less expensive, a little coarser, but always ready for action. Here are the best of them:

ITALIAN PROSECCO From the grape of the same name, Prosecco is Italian bubbly from the Veneto district of northwestern Italy. Although not known for the delicacy or complexity of fine French Champagne, it has a fresh, citrusy taste that sometimes hints of melon or pears. Prosecco is generally dry (labeled *brut*), though sometimes it will be so delightfully fruity that you'll perceive a touch of sweetness, and occasionally you'll see a mildly sweet version (denoted *extra dry*). Typically under $15 a bottle, this uplifting and summery bubbly so dependably delivers joy I call it *"Prozac*-co." Try Carpenè Malvolti (Kahr-peh-NEH Mahl-VOHL-tee), Mionetto (Mee-oh-NEH-toe), Nino Franco (NEE-noe FRANH-koe), or Zardetto (Zar-DAY-toe).

AMERICAN SPARKLING WINE At best, American sparklers are capable of crossing over to star status, competing with fine Champagne in flavor, intensity, and finesse. Schramsberg's J. Schram and Iron Horse's Late Disgorged Brut are two shining examples. But mostly America—and California in particular—produces tasty, uncomplicated bubbly as refreshing as it is affordable. Originating from grapes that get more sun than their French counterparts, American sparkling wine is more about ripe fruit—aromas of apples, melons, lemons, and the like—than it is about the yeasty, baked-bread clutch of Champagne.

If many of the top California sparkling wine producers sound French, they are. Domaine Chandon is owned by France's Moët & Chandon, Domaine Carneros by Taittinger, Mumm Cuvée Napa by Mumm, and Roederer Estate by Roederer. These are all fine choices and have basic brut NV bottlings in the $18-to-$30 range. Even venerable Veuve Clicquot has a slice of the American pie with Pacific Echo, a name that sounds as if it should be writ in chunky script across an eight-track tape, but nevertheless a delicious value under $15. Another compelling deal is Gruet NV Brut (Grew-AYE), a bottle that looks French, tastes French (well, almost), is owned by French interests, but owes its origin to the improbable locale of New Mexico. Of course, there are also excellent American-owned bubbly producers. Look for Schramsberg (Napa), J Vintage Brut from J Vineyards (Sonoma), Domaine Ste. Michelle (Washington), and my favorite, Iron Horse (Sonoma).

SPANISH CAVA Even if you didn't know its name, you probably already know its look from those coal-black bottles in your supermarket. That's Freixenet (Fresh-shun-NETT) Cordon Negro Cava to be precise. *Cava*, the Spanish name for sparkling wine, delivers bubbles at less than half the price of French Champagne. Though it's made in the traditional bottle-fermentation method like Champagne (and finer American sparklers), it spends less time aging on its lees (i.e., dead yeast cells) than Champagne, which gives it less of a yeasty, baked-bread bouquet and more minerals, earth, or mushrooms. It also comes from little-known Spanish grapes, which helps keep prices down. In addition to the ubiquitous Freixenet, look for the Cristalino Brut, Paul Cheneau Brut Blanc de Blancs, Sumarroca Brut Reserva, and Segura Viudas Aria Brut (Se-GUHR-eh Vee-YOU-duss).

CHEAT SHEET

Beyond Champagne is a range of delicious sparklers at a fraction of Champagne's price.

OUTSMART THE TABLE

• Prosecco is famous as the backbone of the Bellini, the classic Venetian cocktail that mixes Prosecco with peach puree—long a signature drink of Venice's Harry's Bar.
• Most bottles of Prosecco and Cava are so affordable and pleasurable that you should crack open a bottle after a long day or whenever you need a lift. As I urge my students: Stock it like soda.

TALK THE TALK

Prosecco *Pro-SEH-koe*

All are under $10. For an affordable gift with serious bling-bling, track down Segura Viudas Reserva Heredad ($20), a hand-blown bottle tricked out with a silvery metal crest and coaster.

THREE MORE TASTY VALUES UNDER $15 Excellent by the case for parties, weddings, or to have on hand to soothe frayed nerves.

- **Brut Fresco by Chandon Argentina** (Argentina): Showing a hint of sweetness and loads of refreshing fruit, this South American Chandon rivals the offerings of its slightly costlier Californian cousin, Domaine Chandon.
- **Bouvet Brut Signature** (Loire Valley, France): One of the most popular French sparklers outside of the Champagne region, Bouvet (Boo-VEH) pinch hits for the real stuff with pleasing aromas of tart apples and toast.
- **Seaview Brut** (Australia): With fresh apple scents and a clean, creamy texture, it's worth stocking by the case.

On My Table | **HEATHER WILLENS,** a former collegiate all-American tennis champion, is a sales director at New York's Jeroboam Wines, an importer of artisanal wine.

Prosecco
Nino Franco—"So handcrafted, delicate, and fresh that people don't even know the difference between it and Champagne."

German Riesling—especially Kabinett or Spätlese level
J. J. Prüm, Christoffel, Selbach-Oster, H. Dönnhoff, Gunderloch, Robert Weil, Lingenfelder, Müller-Catoir, Fritz Haag

Albariño from Spain
Martín Códax, Pazo de Senorans—"Almonds, flower petals . . . ideal with seafood."

Red Burgundy—Chambolle-Musigny
Roumier, Comte Georges de Vogüé

Tempranillo from Spain [best known for composing Spanish Rioja and Ribera del Duero]—"Earthy . . . you can really taste the land."

Cru **Beaujolais, especially Morgon**

Loire Valley Chenin Blanc—Savennières, Vouvray—dry and sweet wines

61 Eleven Reasons to Drink Bubbly
Throughout Dinner Tonight

If *you really* want to outsmart bubbly, drink it throughout dinner—an option few people even think to exploit. Here are eleven reasons why doing so will make you and your circle the happiest kids on the block:

1. **Frugality:** Often among the less expensive choices on a wine list, bubbly offers excellent value for the money, especially non-Champagne sparklers such as Prosecco, Cava, and American sparkling wine.

2. **Appetite Amplification:** The bubbles and citrusy bite in sparkling wine are virtually Viagra for your appetite.

3. **Food Friendliness:** With its cavalry of grease-piercing bubbles, bubbly befriends everything from creamy pasta dishes to fried foods and pizza (see Shortcut 71).

4. **Lightness:** Sprightly Champagne won't weigh you down like a glass of rich, mouth-filling Cabernet or Merlot.

5. **No Wallop:** Unlike a stiff Tanqueray and tonic and other predinner cocktails, the modest alcohol content in sparkling wine ensures that you won't get too tipsy too fast.

6. **Refreshment:** With its citrusy zing and foamy fun, it's hard to find a better refresher than Champagne and sparkling wine. Is it any wonder that Marilyn Monroe is rumored to have once bathed in 350 bottles of the stuff?

7. **Heroics:** With most people regrettably limiting their bubbly intake to birthdays and ball drops, the door is open for you

"DON'T GO CRAZY DRINKING [CRISTAL]— IT SHOULDN'T BE GUZZLED."

—*Ludacris, rap star and Champagne lover*

to lead your friends to the promised land of regular, through-the-meal bubbly consumption.

8. **Celebration:** Nothing is more festive than an icy bottle of bubbly—from the eruption of the cork and rush of bubbles to the special flute-shaped glasses and shiny ice bucket perched proudly on your table.

9. **Table Envy:** Because of its inherent festivity and rarity at dinner, fellow diners experience irrepressible feelings of table envy. "What are *they* celebrating?" the woman to your right will ask, wishing she were part of the fun.

10. **Chic:** Bubbly lends a degree of jet-setting, front-row-by-the-catwalk chic to any meal. And, no, you don't have to drink it out of a straw, as some fashionistas do, to be *à la mode.*

11. **Seductiveness:** Nothing is better for slipping your beloved's libido into something more comfortable. Like roses and chocolate, Champagne works voodoo on the heart.

OUTSMART THE TABLE

If you ever wondered why "bubbly goes straight to your head," a study by the University of Surrey confirms that bubbly inebriates you faster than non-sparkling wine. Though scientists don't know the exact cause, many believe that the carbon dioxide in the bubbles somehow accelerates the absorption of alcohol into the bloodstream.

On My Table | **LUDACRIS**, the Grammy-nominated rap star from Atlanta, Georgia, has a penchant for fine Champagne and is known for his funky "flow" and sly, debauched lyrics.

Champagne

Roederer Cristal—"I drink it when celebrating. Cris is smooth and one of the best. . . . Nothing accents a celebration like a full glass of Cristal to toast."

Merlot

"I have it with a nice, quiet dinner. Rich and full bodied. It mellows me out, and I also drink it when I already feel mellow."

Pinot Grigio

Dessert Wine

How can we not pity the plight of dessert wine? Neglected by most drinkers, it is like a kindly relative that somehow gets crowded out of the family photo. Many people wrongly dismiss all of it as sickly sweet, better suited for religious rituals than for everyday pleasure. Others relegate it to the same status as the cheese course: a vaguely European extravagance that's too expensive or super-fluous "for normal people." And I sometimes suspect that the world's bed-and-breakfasts secretly connect to the same pipeline of candified booze, which, when offered to guests in grandmotherly crystal, helps to ease the anguish of enduring yet another night of no television and punishingly plenti-ful potpourri.

Happily, it takes only a few drops of the right stuff to transform your perception of dessert wine from an afterthought to a welcome habit. Once you try a few different good ones, you realize that not all of it is cloyingly sweet or expensive—and, when you hit it right, the experience can rise to the level of the sublime. In this section we cover two major categories of dessert wine—late harvest and fortified—focusing on their respective archetypes, Sauternes and port. We also meet the luscious likes of ice wine and other compelling meal enders. ■

62 Rapturously Rotten Sauternes and Other Late-Harvest Wines

Duuring a visit to Harvard Business School in the early 1990s, I sat in on a friend's Decision Analysis class, which happened to be discussing whether the Freemark Abbey winery should make its regular table wine or risk waiting for the right weather conditions to make its expensive dessert wine. The students debated the case study for over an hour. When a class blowhard detailed an elaborate scheme to use a greenhouse to simulate the weather needed for this wine, the professor—who had learned about my interest in wine from my friend—spun around and caught me off guard:

"Well, Mr. Wine Expert, will Larry's idea work?"

I wasn't really sure, but sensing the students' impatience at Larry's long-winded proposal, I offered: "Ahh, ummmh . . . no?"

With that, the class roared appreciatively. I had barely survived my first and only "cold call" at HBS.

My lucky guess was correct because the type of dessert wine being discussed—"late harvest"—can be produced successfully only under special conditions. It is made from grapes picked late in the harvest season so that they are overripe. Finer examples often benefit from the presence of a desirable mold called *botrytis*, or *noble rot*, which shrivels the grapes, concentrates the juice, and ultimately makes wine of an inimitably honeyed, earthy character. The wine is also often aged in oak barrels, giving it an overlay of vanilla-nutty aromas. Late-harvest dessert wine usually comes from white-wine grapes such as Riesling, Gewürztraminer, Sémillon, Sauvignon Blanc, or Chenin Blanc.

The world's most celebrated late-harvest dessert wine is Sauternes, a sweet, honeyed, luscious dessert wine made from botrytis-affected Sémillon and Sauvignon Blanc grapes in France's Bordeaux region. Sauternes will yield the kind of sensory joy that only a week of flotation in a deprivation tank could negate: nectarous, near-narcotic notes of apricots, peaches, and pears combined with vanilla, almonds, or smoke. Is that a pleasing whiff of burned sugar, like a cupful of crème brûlée? Or do you get an earthy, mushroomy edge

Originating from grapes with a higher than normal sugar content, late-harvest dessert wines, at best, offer a heady swirl of tropical fruits and honey, buttressed by a racy vein of acidity.

LABEL DECODER

Sauternes is a district in France's Bordeaux region. Sauvignon Blanc and Sémillon are its primary grapes. Tokaji is a town in Hungary. *Aszú* is the Hungarian name for the botrytis or noble rot that concentrates the grapes. Furmint is Tokaji Aszú's primary grape.

OUTSMART THE TABLE

- Late-harvest wine, like most dessert wines, should be served fully cold.
- In 1986, a bottle of 1784 Château d'Yquem (bearing Thomas Jefferson's initials) sold at a Christie's London auction for $56,588—a world record for dessert wine.

TALK THE TALK

Sauternes	SAW-tairn
Barsac	BAR-sack
Tokaji Aszú	Toh-KAY ah-SOO
Puttonyos	POO-tun-yosh
Beerenauslese	BEER-en-OUSE-lay-seh
Trockenbeerenauslese	
	TROH-ken-BEER-en-OUSE-lay-seh
Sélection de Grains Nobles	
	Say-lek-shawn duh Grahn Noe-bl

courtesy of the botrytis mold? The feel of Sauternes in the mouth is round, voluptuous, and honeylike, meriting an X rating were it not for its clean, counterbalancing current of acidity.

Divinity exacts a high price when its name is Sauternes (or its neighboring district Barsac), so expect to pay at least $30 and multiples of that for the best stuff in the best years. The undisputed high priestess is the eternal, majestic Château d'Yquem. Ranging from about $180 to $400 or more, it is a mainstay of auction houses and patrician gatherings the world over. Not to be morbid, but if you happen to have a friend on death row, Château d'Yquem—an elixir transporting enough for death's door—will say you care enough to send the very best. Closer to earth you find reliably excellent Sauternes in the $30-to-$60 range (and about half that for the widely available 375ml bottles).

A top bottle of Sauternes is wine for the ages, its intense acidity and fruit bestowing on it a life span rivaling that of a Galápagos tortoise. While Sauternes don't *need* age to be delicious, they will gain even more complexity after several years, or decades, of sleep, with some bottles captivating you well past their fortieth birthday.

Many other wine regions produce a late-harvest dessert wine. Several leading U.S. wineries have a late-harvest Riesling, although finding a particular label isn't easy because often only a few hundred cases are made. Don't overlook Tokaji from Hungary, an intense, carameltinged, unctuously textured delight. Tokaji's sweetness and price are indicated on its label by its *Puttonyos* level, a measure of the number of baskets of grapes used during harvest, ranging from 3 to a mind-bogglingly rich 6. It retails in the $35-to-$70 range. Finally, remarkable but exceedingly scarce late-harvest wine is also made in France's Loire Valley (notably, Coteaux du Layon) and Alsace (the rare and wonderful Sélection de Grains Nobles), as well as Germany and Austria (both have a Beerenauslese and Trockenbeerenauslese).

Many connoisseurs like to savor late-harvest dessert wine without any distraction from dessert. If you are going to serve it with dessert, any selection of fresh fruit or moderately sweet desserts will keep things happy. But you need not limit yourself to sweet food. A classic, superindulgent pairing—and one better performed with paramedics at the ready—is that of Sauternes and foie gras, the fattened goose or duck liver. Epicures find that the saltiness of the liver and other high-sodium foods contrasts nicely with the honeyed richness of the wine.

 MARK'S PICKS

Sauternes:

Château Climens	*Klee-MAHNS*
Château Coutet	*Coo-TEE*
Château de Fargues	*Farg*
Château Doisy-Védrines	
	Dwah-ZEE-Veh-DREEN
Château d'Yquem	*Ee-KEM*
Château Guiraud	*Gee-ROE*
Château Lafaurie-Peyraguey	
	Lah-foh-REE-Peh-rah-GEH
Château Rieussec	*Ree-oh-sec*
Château Suduiraut	*Soo-dwee-ROE*

U.S.:

Late-harvest Rieslings from Beringer, Chateau St. Jean, Grgich Hills, Hogue, J. Lohr.

Tokaji Aszú:

Château Pajzos, Domaine Disznókő, the Royal Tokaji Wine Company.

 FIT FOR FEASTING

By itself or with moderately sweet desserts, especially those with citrus flavors (e.g., Key lime pie, lemon tart); crème brûlée; shortbread cookies; biscotti; pound cake or cheesecake; foie gras; Roquefort and other blue-veined cheeses; substantial, salty foods like fried chicken.

63 Coat Your Mouth (and Soul) with Port and Other Fortified Wines

Don't be surprised if the strings of the *Masterpiece Theatre* theme creep to mind when you taste port, because it is a dessert wine as quintessentially English as the queen's accent. Its English connection dates back to the seventeenth-century wars between England and France, which prompted British wine shippers to find an alternative to French wine. They liked what they found in the sun-baked Douro Valley of Portugal, and adding some brandy to the Portuguese wine to stabilize it for the long sea journey back to England, they invented modern-day port.

These days real port from Portugal—always labeled *porto* to distinguish it from the raft of copycat versions around the world—is the most famous kind of "fortified wine"—that is, wine infused with brandy (i.e., neutral grape spirits) sometime during production. With port, brandy is added to the wine during fermentation. This pumps up the wine's alcohol content to about 20 percent and halts the fermentation process, leaving behind the residual sugar that gives port its sweet taste. The wine itself is made from a smorgasbord of little-known grapes.

It is helpful to think of port in terms of two general categories: wood-aged port, which is aged in wooden casks at the winery and thus ready to drink immediately, and vintage port, which requires buyers to age it in the bottle for several years. Here are four styles of port you're likely to see—the first three wood-aged and the last one of the bottled-aged, vintage persuasion:

RUBY PORT At $10 to $15 a bottle, this is the simplest and least expensive style of wood-aged port. Aged in wood for about three years before release, it is a blend of decent-quality grapes from different nonvintage years. Expect a ruby-red color and a straightforward, sweet mix of ripe berry flavors, notes of vanilla, and low levels of tannin. The best rubies are called *vintage character ports*, a confusing name because, unlike real vintage port, they are not made from a particular vintage year. They include the ubiquitous and charming Fonseca Bin 27 (dependably zesty, ripe, and easy to drink), Taylor's 4XX, Graham's Six Grapes, Warre's Heritage, and Cockburn's Special Reserve. Affordable and user friendly, ruby port is good for everyday drinking and by the glass in restaurants.

AGED TAWNY PORT Ranging from $25 to well over $100, depending on the average age of the wines in the blend (as indicated by their *10-, 20-, 30-,* or *40-year* labeling), tawny port offers more subtlety and complexity than ruby port, while remaining eminently easy to drink. Finer versions enrapture you with aromas of caramel, toffee, brown sugar, cedar, and orange peel, wrapped around a core of dried apricots or berries. At their best, they have a silken texture that makes for an endlessly satisfying finish. Aging colors them light brown or tawny; hence their name. English wine authority and port lover Michael Broadbent told me that the best ratio of taste to cost is in ten-year-old and twenty-year-old tawny ports, which achieve an excellent balance between fruit and aged characteristics and sell in the $25-to-$50 range. Tawnies are an excellent introduction to the charms of serious port.

LATE-BOTTLED VINTAGE Unlike the preceding examples, which are blended from several vintages, late-bottled vintage port (or *LBV*) is made from the grapes of a single vintage, typically years of lesser harvest. It is ready to roll when you buy it, having been softened by a few years of barrel aging before release. Retailing in the $15-to-$30 range, it is heavier and richer than aged tawny port—and often not as interesting as that style or vintage port.

VINTAGE PORT Ringing up between $35 and $100 upon release (and more when it's older), vintage port is the varsity league of port—the connoisseur's choice. It is made from the best grapes of a single vintage and only in years when a producer decides harvest conditions are good enough—sometimes only a few times a decade. Vintage port sees a mere two years of aging at the winery, which means it often enters the world with tannins sharp as a dagger, needing at least ten to twenty years to mellow into a drinkable colossus of

The world's most famous fortified wine, port is rich, sweet, high in alcohol, and a civilized way to end a meal or ward off an evening's chill.

LABEL DECODER

Port is named for Oporto, a city in northern Portugal (although its vineyards are located about sixty miles east in the Douro Valley). Port is made from a blend of dozens of unfamiliar grape varieties, the most important of which is Touriga Nacional.

OUTSMART THE TABLE

• Vintage port's glacially slow maturation process has been called a "grim struggle," according to wine writer Matt Kramer.
• British naval tradition requires that one "pass the port"—that is, send a decanter of port clockwise (right to left) around the table.

TALK THE TALK

Douro	DOO-roe
Madeira	Muh-DEAR-uh
Marsala	Mahr-SAH-lah
Muscat de Beaumes de Venise	
Muhs-KAT duh Bohm duh vuh-NEEZ	
Banyuls	Bahn-YULZ

MARK'S PICKS

Top level: Dow's, Fonseca, Graham's Quinta do Noval, Sandeman, Taylor Fladgate.
Very good: Churchill, Cockburn, Croft, Quinta do Vesuvio, Warre's.

FIT FOR FEASTING

By itself as dessert; Stilton cheese, other blue-veined cheeses, and dry, hard cheeses like English Cheddar; salty nuts such as almonds, walnuts, chestnuts, or cashews; figs; a range of desserts, including chocolate creations.

---

a wine. Upon maturity, a fine version will express itself with a panorama of sweet black fruits intermixed with chocolate, earth, licorice, and coffee—an intense, headily concentrated wallop of a wine.

A wine this massive and tannic develops a lot of sediment as it ages, so be prepared to decant it several hours before drinking—both to remove its sediment and to soften its taste through exposure to the air. The best vintage port pushes the envelope of vinous longevity, easily improving for more than fifty years and sometimes hurdling the century mark with aplomb.

Port's higher alcohol content makes it a relatively hardy wine once it's opened. So long as you recork and store the opened bottle in the refrigerator, most types of port—including ruby, aged tawny, and late-bottled vintage—should stay fresh for at least a week and perhaps several weeks, depending on the bottle and how oxidized you like your port to taste. Mature vintage port, on the other hand, is a fragile beast and rarely survives for more than a day or two.

Purists may contend that a nice glass of port is all the decadence they need at dessert time, but many others like to kick up their port pleasure with certain time-honored matches. A classic partner for port is Stilton cheese, its salty taste a pleasing contrast with port's sweet thickness; other blue cheeses as well as dry, hard cheeses like English Cheddar are also a delight. Furthering the sodium theme, you can't go wrong with a nice bowl of salty nuts. On the sweeter side, port can handle a range of desserts. In fact, it is one of the few wines with the flavor intensity to always stand up to chocolate desserts—so bring on the black forest cake or chocolate soufflé.

Unlike most dessert wines, port is not served cold. Treat it as you would a dry, heavy red and serve it at cool room temperature. The one exception is tawny port, which is light enough to bear a moderate chill if you like it that way.

Other fortified dessert wines commonly grouped with port include sweet styles of sherry from Spain

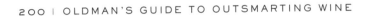

(dark, with a raisiny syrupiness), Madeira from the Portuguese island of the same name (burned caramel taste), and Marsala from Italy (rich, smoky, not just for chicken). France also has some toothsome fortified wines, notably its Muscat de Beaumes de Venise (sweet, medium to full bodied with an intense bouquet of tropical fruit, marmalade, and honey) and the lesser-known but fabulous Banyuls (like a tawny port with notes of black fruits, chocolate, molasses, and spice).

On My Table | **RUPERT SYMINGTON,** the fourth generation of one of port's great families, oversees various Symington properties, which include such port mainstays as Graham's, Dow's, Smith Woodhouse, Warre's, and Quinta do Vesuvio.

Port—tawny
Graham's—"I drink twenty-year-old tawny port, lightly chilled, almost every time I dine at home."

Champagne
Pol Roger

Gigondas
Guigal

Northern Rhône—St.-Joseph [an all-Syrah red that's somewhat lighter and more approachable than Hermitage]
Eric & Joël Durand

Tempranillo
Torres Coronas—"One of the best deals around for everyday drinking."

Sancerre
Pascal Jolivet

Portuguese red wine
Quinta de Roriz's Prazo de Roriz—"A delicious fruity young red that will go with anything."

64 Ice Wine and Others Deliver Liquid Witchcraft

Some dessert wines owe their sweetness not to noble rot or alcoholic fortification but to a trickle of pure, sugar-dense nectar that results from frozen, overripe grapes. This is called *ice wine*—and the original version, German Eiswein, is made in the traditional, labor-intensive, and meteorologically risky method of keeping the grapes on the vine to freeze months after harvest. Fashioned from Riesling and other white-wine grapes, the resulting wine—the precious little of it there is when the weather cooperates—balances luscious sweetness with pure fruit flavors and the lively acidity you expect from a cold-climate region. Many top German and Austrian Riesling producers release a small stash of Eiswein (as do Austrian producers), but expect to pay over $70 and often much more for the chance to sample this nectarous indulgence.

Slightly less rare but equally pricey is Canadian ice wine, also made from grapes naturally frozen on the vine. Comprised mainly of Riesling or a thick-skinned grape named Vidal, Canadian ice wine pushes the envelope with an ambrosial mix of tropical fruits, kept honest by plenty of zingy acidity. The benchmark is Ontario-based Inniskillin, whose acclaimed ice wines start at about $80 and come from various grapes, including an unusual bottling from the red grape Cabernet Franc.

To moderate prices, certain producers circumvent the risk and expense of making naturally frozen wine by freezing the grapes in industrial freezers. While these freezer-frozen versions are not quite as intense as the real deal, they nevertheless deliver pyrotechnic aromatics and flavor at less than half the price. You are probably aware of one of the best and easiest to find: Bonny Doon's Muscat Vin de Glacière (literally, "refrigerator

CHEAT SHEET
Three compelling dessert wines are ice wine, Moscato d'Asti, and Vin Santo.

LABEL DECODER
Ice wine: Comes primarily from Riesling and/or other white-wine grapes.
Moscato d'Asti: Muscat is the grape. Asti is a village in Italy's Piedmont region.
Vin Santo: Trebbiano and Malvasia are the grapes. It comes primarily from Italy's Tuscany region

wine"). Retailing at under $20 for a half bottle, Vin de Glacière is a nectarous mix of passion fruit and peaches, a veritable seduction serum that seems to be on almost every wine list. Look for other American ice wines from this trio of Washington State wineries: Chateau Ste. Michelle, Columbia Crest, and Covey Run.

Moving beyond ice wine, but staying with the Muscat grape, we find Moscato d'Asti, an inexpensive, lightly fizzy wine from Italy's Piedmont region. Its fresh, peachy perfume, restrained sweetness, and low alcohol (5 to 6 percent) are impossible to resist, even after stuffing yourself to the gills with a tray of lasagna. You're probably familiar with its sister wine, Asti (formerly called Asti Spumante, whose infamy derives from all those Martini & Rossi ads during *The Mary Tyler Moore Show* in the seventies, which is more bubbly, sweet, and alcoholic—a world away from the delicacy of Moscato d'Asti. Both retail in the $10-to-$20 range. Serve with lighter desserts like fresh fruit and sorbet.

Another of the delectable *vini dolci* from Italy is Vin Santo—Italian for "holy wine"—a rich, often medium-dry wine originating primarily from Tuscany. By drying out the grapes before fermentation and aging the wine in barrels stored in heated attics, winemakers achieve a wine that combines the taste of dried figs with a nutty-caramel character. It is traditionally the "dipping wine" for biscotti, the small Italian cookies. Be prepared to pay $20 to $60.

TALK THE TALK

Eiswein	ICE-vine
Vin de Glacière	Van duh Glahss-YAIR
Moscato d'Asti	Moss-CAH-toe DAH-stee
Asti Spumante	AH-stee Spoo-MAHN-teh
Vin Santo	Veen SAHN-toe

MARK'S PICKS

German Eiswein:

H. Dönnhoff	DEHN-hohf
Dr. Loosen	LOW-zen
Selbach-Oster	Zell-bok Oh-stir
J. H. & A. Strub	Stroob
Dr. Thanisch	TAH-nish
Robert Weil	Viyl

Canadian ice wine:

Inniskillin, Jackson-Triggs, Konzelmann, Magnotta.

Moscato d'Asti:

Ceretto Santo Stefano
    Cheh-RETT-oh SAHN-toe STEH-fah-noe
Michele Chiarlo Nivole
    Mee-KELL-eh Key-AHR-low
Piazzo   PYAH-zoe
La Spinetta   Lah Spee-NEHT-ah
Vietti   VYEHT-tee

Vin Santo:

Avignonesi	Ah-vee-nyo-NEH-zee
Fontodi	Fohn-TOE-dee
Frescobaldi	Fres-coh-BALD-ee
Isole e Olena	EE-zoe-leh eh Oh-leh-nah
Lungarotti	Loon-gah-ROW-tee

FIT FOR FEASTING

By itself as dessert; with fresh fruit; sorbets; moderately sweet desserts like pound cake, crème brûlée, and shortbread; biscotti; blue-veined cheeses (with richer types).

On My Table | **DONALD ZIRALDO** is cofounder of Ontario's Inniskillin Wines, whose spectactular array of ice wines has brought thrills to wine lovers and international recognition of Canada's viticultural potential.

French Sauternes
Château d'Yquem—"The gold standard for sweet wines."

Super Tuscans
Tignanello

Red Bordeaux—St.-Emilion
Cheval Blanc

Cabernet Sauvignon from Napa
Stag's Leap Cask 23

Amarone [a powerful, heady red made from dehydrated grapes grown in the Valpolicella district of Italy's Veneto region]
Masi

Pinot Grigio

Chianti
Dievole—"[Made by] a young vintner who is passionate."

Special Occasions

Wine rides shotgun with us through life's special moments, inevitably finding its way into celebrations, holidays, and anniversaries. Unfortunately, for many of us wine selection for these occasions is an afterthought, as it is all too easy to fall back on the same tired choices year after year. This section is designed to inspire your vinous creativity and expand your options for a range of occasions. We focus first on two of the most wine-critical holidays— Thanksgiving and St. Valentine's Day—and then consider potential wines for twenty-two other events and experiences, from barbecues and weddings to summertime lollygagging and celebrating an empty nest. ■

65 Thanksgiving Deserves Double-Fisting

Thanksgiving *is* stressful enough without having to endure familial scorn for a poor wine choice. If it's your job to choose the wine this Thanksgiving, your priorities should be (in this order):

1. Smooth family tensions.
2. Please all preferences.
3. Match the wine with the food.

The solution to this seemingly complex challenge is simple: make like the Piano Man and choose bottles of red *and* bottles of white. Such "double-fisting" may at first seem wasteful or decadent to our American sensibilities, but if you think about it, it is entirely appropriate for the occasion. The one holiday honoring plenitude, Thanksgiving is about adding even more to the oversized American plate, a time to free yourself of guilt about consuming belt-busting quantities of food and drink. Like the Pilgrims who embraced their Native American neighbors, it is also, of course, more generally a day of gratitude and bonhomie. What better way to fulfill this spirit of inclusiveness than to cater to both white- and red-wine drinkers?

If you're now convinced of the value of double-fisting, here are some suggestions:

Left Fist (White)

OL' FAITHFUL To please guests hankering for white wine, no eyebrows will rise, of course, if you produce a bottle of California or Australia Chardonnay, sturdy enough to stand up to the rich foods at play. The less wine adventurous the group, the better bet this is. For those willing to assume the added expense, a fine white Burgundy such as Meursault or Puligny-Montrachet will stay within the Chardonnay comfort zone while showing off these wines' uniquely crisp and minerally character.

FOOD-FRIENDLIEST EXOTICA For an even better match with the cranberry-yammy carnival on the table, go for a crisp, slightly sweet Riesling or an exotically spicy Gewürztraminer.

BUBBLE UP Essentially white wine with bubbles, sparkling wine's inherent festivity and palate-cleansing acidity make it an ideal companion for any holiday feast. To match the various flavors of the meal, consider rich-style Champagne such as Bollinger, Louis Roederer, or Veuve Clicquot. If you want to stay American on this holiday, this is the perfect opportunity to try the delicious and affordable charms of American sparkling wine, such as that from Iron Horse, Domaine Chandon, or Mumm Cuvée Napa.

Right Fist (Red)

PATRIOT GAIN Because America is virtually the sole producer of Zinfandel, you can proudly inform your fellow diners that they are drinking a singularly American wine on this uniquely American holiday. The spicy, berry-fruit character of Zinfandel marries well with cranberry sauce, spicy stuffing, and the roasted skin of turkey.

MER-LOVED Like Zinfandel, Merlot has rich berry flavors that fit the meal and the chilly time of the year. And, soft, straightforward Merlot has the kind of mass appeal that will please even your crotchety great-aunt, who probably drinks it with her monthly book club. On an occasion when family tensions can run high, Merlot is the comforting path of least resistance.

FESTIVE FRANCOPHILIA What Beaujolais Nouveau lacks in heft and spiciness it makes up for in impeccable timing. Released just days before Thanksgiving, Beaujolais Nouveau is literally the most *nouveau* wine you can serve at this time of year. The zingy berry flavors in this light, fresh wine will win over your Francophobic relatives, and you can serve it chilled, pleasing the white-wine fans in attendance. Best of all, the money you save by buying this inexpensive wine will justify extra bottles, ensuring that the whole family gets comfortably numb.

On My Table | **MICHAEL BONACCORSI** was the sommelier at Los Angeles's famous Spago restaurant before launching his own winery in Santa Barbara, the Bonaccorsi Wine Company. Tragically, he passed away before this book went to press.

Zinfandel from Sonoma
 Ridge, Rafanelli

Chianti/Sangiovese
 Morellino di Scansano, Fontodi, Felsina, Le Pupille

Barbera—"Dense fruits, low tannin—easy to enjoy."
 Altare, Scavino, Clerico

Southern Rhône—Châteauneuf-du-Pape, Côtes-du-Rhône, Gigondas, Vacqueyras—"Especially for the fall and winter."
 Domaine du Vieux Télégraphe, Domaine Santa Duc, Couroulu

White Burgundy—Puligny, St.-Aubin, Chassagne-Montrachet, Meursault—"Few whites have such a regal character."
 Arnaud Ente, Coche-Dury, Sauzet

66 On Valentine's Day, Say It with Pink Bubbles or with the Label Itself

If all wine, as the Roman poet Ovid once wrote, "makes men more apt for passion," then what wine should you choose on the most passionate of occasions, St. Valentine's Day? Here are five choices—all French, *naturellement*—sure to have you and your lover reaching for the "Do Not Disturb" sign:

ROSÉ CHAMPAGNE No drink says "come hither" quite like rosé (pink) Champagne. Its color blushes with excitement, its bubbles tickle the palate, and its price—steep because of its scarcity—says that you care enough to pour the best. My ace in the hole is the Billecart-Salmon Brut Rosé, a delicate, berry-inflected love potion that's rarely less than $50. If rosé Champagne breaks your budget, consider more affordable rosé sparkling wine from such American producers as Iron Horse, Domaine Chandon, and Roederer Estate.

RED BURGUNDY When it's from a good producer and the right village, red Burgundy can coat your tongue with more velvet than the walls of Mae West's bedroom. A glass of wine from the Burgundian village of Chambolle-Musigny (especially the perfectly named but hard-to-find Les Amoureuses, i.e., "the lovers," *premier cru* vineyard) or Volnay will provide a seductive cherry-raspberry perfume, along with floral notes that evoke violets or—get this—rose petals. As we learned previously, Burgundy is frustratingly scarce, expensive, and inconsistent, but if you're willing to take the risk (which is sexy in itself), consult the picks that follow for excellent Chambolle-Musigny and Volnay producers and Shortcut 34 for more red Burgundy recommendations.

CHÂTEAU CALON-SÉGUR (RED BORDEAUX) Red Bordeaux is already bottled poetry, but if you want to leave no doubt about your amorous designs, the slam-dunk choice is Bordeaux's Château Calon-Ségur, a Médoc third growth from the village of St.-Estèphe. Tailor-made for seduction, this delicious wine features a lover's heart—fat and curvy like a child's drawing—smack in the center of its label. Expect enticing aromas of blackcurrants and plums, sometimes with hints of chocolate and coffee. Unfortunately, this love potion doesn't come cheap: depending on its vintage, recent bottles of Calon-Ségur retail for $30 to $100 or more.

ST.-AMOUR OR FLEURIE (*CRU BEAUJOLAIS*) If the options so far are too expensive, don't fret: the French do love on a budget, too. You'll say it all with St.-Amour, the northernmost of the *cru* Beaujolais villages (see Shortcut 51). Like most wine from Beaujolais, it is irresistibly light and fruity and costs less than $15. If you're not yet ready to utter "amour" to the object of your affections, another well-named choice from Beaujolais is Fleurie. Look for St.-Amour and Fleurie from dependable Beaujolais producers such as Georges Duboeuf, Joseph Drouhin, and Louis Jadot.

TURTLE LOVE Another wine that is affordable and aptly named is Tortoise Creek's Merlot Cabernet Vin d'Oc Les Amoureux from southern France's wallet-friendly Languedoc-Roussillon region. Less than $10, the wine is soft and ripe, with hints of blackcurrant and cedar. Best of all, its festive label depicts two "amoureux" tortoises sharing a creek bed and a bottle of wine. Tortoise Creek also makes an excellent rosé and Syrah-Mourvèdre, both of which carry the Les Amoureux tortoises label.

CHEAT SHEET
Nothing says *amour* like rosé Champagne, red Burgundy, or an aptly titled label.

TALK THE TALK

Chambolle-Musigny	
	Shahm-BOWL Moo-see-NYEE
Les Amoureuses	*Laze Ah-more-ROOZE*
Bouchard	*BOO-shaar*
Comte de Vogüé	*Comt deh VOE-gway*
Duboeuf	*Duh-BUFF*
Faiveley	*FAVE-ah-lee*
Fleurie	*Fluh-REE*
Louis Jadot	*LOO-ee Jah-DOE*
rosé	*row-ZAY*
Volnay	*Vole-nay*
Calon-Ségur	*Cah-lohn-Seh-GOOR*

MARK'S PICKS

Rosé Champagne:
$35 to $50—Lucas Carton, Deutz, Charles Ellner, Nicolas Feuillatte, Moët & Chandon, Bruno Paillard, Piper Heidsieck.
$50 to $100—Billecart-Salmon, Gosset, Pol Roger, Pommery, Taittinger, Veuve Clicquot.
$100 and Over—Perrier-Jouët Fleur de Champagne (decorated with a pattern of white flowers), Taittinger Comtes de Champagne, Veuve Clicquot La Grande Dame.

Red Burgundy:
Volnay—Jean-Marc Boillot, Bouchard Père & Fils, Domaine de la Pousse d'Or, Louis Jadot.
Chambolle-Musigny—Comte Georges de Vogüé, Drouhin, Faiveley, Robert Groffier, G. Roumier.

TEN ADDITIONAL CASANOVA KITS FOR ANY ROMANTIC INTERLUDE

1. Lobster (eaten with the fingers) with Meursault
2. Oysters paired with a fine Chablis
3. Crab-stuffed avocado with a buttery California Chardonnay
4. Any dish incorporating truffles (or the more affordable truffle oil) and Barolo
5. Steamed artichokes and Sancerre
6. Banyuls (a French dessert wine) and dark chocolate
7. Banfi's Rosa Regale Brachetto d'Acqui (a sweet, berry-scented sparkler from Italy)
8. Prozac-co Smoothie: mix Prosecco, vodka, and lemon sorbet together in a blender, serve in a Champagne flute, and top with fresh mint
9. Chaucer's Choice: gently simmer a light red wine with a small amount of honey, nutmeg, and cinnamon (based on the medieval spiced wine called *hippocras*)
10. Cleopatra's Bliss: drink a cold glass of late-harvest dessert wine while reclining in a hot bath of powdered milk

Wines for Twenty-two Other Occasions

BARBECUE/PICNIC/FOURTH OF JULY (inexpensive, fun, pairs well with smoky food)

Beaujolais
Cabernet Sauvignon (simple ones)
Pinot Grigio
Riesling
Rioja (Crianza)
Rosé
Sauvignon Blanc
Shiraz
Zinfandel

PIZZA NIGHT

Chardonnay from the New World
Chianti
Dolcetto and Barbera
Malbec
Primitivo
Prosecco
Shiraz
Zinfandel

SPICY ASIAN FOOD

Beaujolais
Gewürztraminer
Moscato d'Asti
Riesling (off-dry versions)
Rosé
See also Shortcut 69 on spicy food.

EASTER OR CHRISTMAS (ham or lamb)

Aged red Bordeaux
Cabernet Franc/Chinon
Pinot Noir
Rioja (Gran Reserva)
See also Shortcut 65 on Thanksgiving.

PASSOVER/KOSHER

With lighter foods:
Baron Herzog Sauvignon Blanc (California)
Gamla Chardonnay (Israel)
Laurent-Perrier Champagne Brut (France)
Yarden Chardonnay (Israel)
With heavier foods:
Baron Herzog Cabernet Sauvignon or Syrah (California)
Galil Mountain Cabernet Sauvignon (Israel)

Hagafen Cabernet Sauvignon or Pinot Noir (California)
Yarden Cabernet Sauvignon (Israel)

ST. PATRICK'S DAY (corned beef and cabbage)

Beaujolais
Cabernet Franc/Chinon
Dolcetto and Barbera
Gewürztraminer
Pinot Gris from Alsace
Riesling
Also: Vinho Verde (for its green tint)

HALLOWEEN

Alexander Valley Sin Zin (California)
Bonny Doon Cardinal Zin Beastly Old Vines (California)
Bonny Doon Le Cigare Volant ("Flying Saucer") (California)
Cockfighter's Ghost Chardonnay or Shiraz (Australia)
Concha y Toro Casillero del Diablo ("Cellar of the Devil"), various types (Chile)
d'Arenberg Dead Arm Shiraz (Australia)
Devil's Lair Chardonnay or Cabernet Sauvignon (Australia)
Egervin Egri Bikavér ("Bull's Blood") (Hungary)
Leitz Dragonstone Riesling (Germany)
Trevor Jones Wild Witch Shiraz (Australia)
Vampire Vineyards Cabernet Sauvignon or Pinot Noir (Romania)

BIRTHDAY PARTIES AND OTHER SHINDIGS (delicious crowd-pleasers under $20)

Alamos Malbec (Argentina)
Altos Las Hormigas Malbec (Argentina)
d'Arenberg The Footbolt Shiraz (Australia)
Hess Select Chardonnay (California)
Meridian Chardonnay (California)
Paringa Shiraz (Australia)
R.H. Phillips Viognier EXP (California)
Any Prosecco (Italy)

St. Supéry Sauvignon Blanc (California)
Three Thieves Cabernet Sauvignon (1 liter, California)
See also Shortcuts 100 and 101 (Faithful Fifty) and 102.

APPEALING APERITIFS

Albariño
Champagne/sparkling wine (especially the Blanc de Blancs style)
Gewürztraminer
Grüner Veltliner
Moscato d'Asti
Riesling
Sauvignon Blanc/Sancerre/Pouilly-Fumé
Viognier

STEAKHOUSE CLASSICS

Barolo
Cabernet Sauvignon from California
Hermitage
Merlot
Red Bordeaux

STEAKHOUSE VALUES

Cabernet Franc
Cabernet Sauvignon from Chile
Côtes-du-Rhône
Malbec
Petite Sirah
Rioja (Reserva)
Shiraz
Zinfandel

BISTRO STAPLES

Beaujolais
Chinon

Côtes-du-Rhône
Crozes-Hermitage
Mâcon-Villages
Rosé
Sancerre/Pouilly-Fumé

VALUABLE FOR VEGETARIANS (special affinity with vegetables)

Cabernet Franc/Chinon
Dolcetto and Barbera
Grüner Veltliner
Pinot Blanc from Alsace
Pinot Grigio
Prosecco and other inexpensive sparklers
Riesling
Rosé
Sancerre/Pouilly-Fumé

REDS READY FOR FISH

Beaujolais
Chinon
Dolcetto
Pinot Noir
Red Burgundy
Rioja (Crianza)

WINTERTIME HIBERNATION

Chardonnay from the New World
Côtes-du-Rhône
Petite Sirah
Port and other fortified wines
Primitivo
Syrah/Shiraz
Viognier
Zinfandel

OUTSMART THE TABLE

Hungary's most famous red, Egri Bikavér *(EH-gree BIH-kah-vahr)*, or "Bull's Blood from Eger" (listed twice in this section), is a robust wine made from a blend of mostly local grapes. Legend has it that it is named for the Hungarians who defended the fortress of Eger during a sixteenth-century siege by Turkish troops. Before the battle, the vastly outnumbered Hungarians sought courage by guzzling the local wine, which they accidentally spilled all over themselves. When the Turks caught sight of the adversaries splattered with red juice, they supposedly ran for the hills, thinking that the crazy Hungarians had drunk bull's blood.

SUMMERTIME LOLLYGAGGING

Beaujolais-Villages
Grüner Veltliner
Pinot Grigio
Prosecco and other inexpensive sparklers
Riesling
Rioja (Crianza)
Rosé
Sancerre/Pouilly-Fumé
Sauvignon Blanc
Vinho Verde
White Bordeaux

MARRIAGE PROPOSAL

Champagne (Krug, Salon, Roederer Cristal, Dom Pérignon)
Red Bordeaux: a first growth
Red Burgundy: top-level Volnay or Chambolle-Musigny

BACHELOR PARTIES (aka "Guy Pleasers")

The Ball Buster red blend from Tait Wines (Australia)
Cardinal Zin Zinfandel from Bonny Doon (California)
Egervin Egri Bikavér ("Bull's Blood") (Hungary)
Fat Bastard Chardonnay from Thierry and Guy (France)
Gladiator Copertino Riserva or Primitivo (Italy)
Red Zeppelin Syrah from Jory Winery (California)
Screw Kappa Napa Cabernet Sauvignon (California)
Woop Woop Shiraz (Australia)

WEDDINGS (aka "Bride Pleasers")

Budget (great taste, low price, elegant name):
Bouvet (Loire Valley)
Chandon Brut Fresco (Argentina)
Domaine Ste. Michelle Cuvée Brut (Washington State)
Gruet (New Mexico)

Moderate to High End:
Champagne (any NV style from Shortcut 58)
Iron Horse Wedding Cuvée (California)

Dessert:
Champagne or sparkling wine in the *demi-sec* (semisweet) style

SPRUNG-FROM-PRISON WINES (cheap, high alcohol)

Côtes-du-Rhône
Ruby port
Shiraz (inexpensive versions)
Two-Buck Chuck (i.e., any wine from Charles Shaw)
Zinfandel (inexpensive versions)
Also: Ca' del Solo Big House Red and White (their labels depict an old-style prison)

EMPTY-NEST WINES (more expensive, high alcohol)

Cabernet Sauvignon from the New World (top versions)
Chardonnay from the New World (top versions)
Vintage port
Viognier
Zinfandel (top versions)

DEATHBED WINES

Anything from the 1800s (e.g., 1870 Lafite-Rothschild); extra points if it has the initials "Th.J" (for Thomas Jefferson)
Red Bordeaux: Château Pétrus, Château Cheval Blanc, or a first growth; extra points if it's from your birth year
Red Burgundy: any bottle from Domaine de la Romanée-Conti
Sauternes: Château d'Yquem

Food
and Wine

I'm *always* amazed by how otherwise collected people fall to pieces when approaching the pairing of food and wine. They seem to think there's some grand template of correct matches that, if transgressed, will forever brand them gastronomic barbarians. Fueling this fear is the surplus of wine "authorities" who would have us plot food and wine strategy with scientific precision. The shortcuts in this section are designed to convince you that such fuss isn't at all necessary, while at the same time equipping you with a variety of easy-to-implement strategies to bring out the best in both food and wine. ■

67 The Eleven Pleasure Principles
of Food and Wine Pairing

If anything should convince you that precise food and wine matches aren't that important, observe what happens during the dessert course at weddings. Guests happily wash down their wedding cake with sips of celebratory bubbly—even though the combination of dry wine with sweet food is the gustatory equivalent of nails on a chalkboard. But you'll rarely hear guests grouse about it, in part because most of us don't pay that much attention to the interplay of food and wine. And even if we did, the happy fact is that food and wine pairing is like sex or pizza: even when it's bad, it can still be pretty good.

That said, there are time-tested principles designed to bring out the best in food and wine. Following are eleven such pleasure principles. View them not as immutable rules but as informal guidelines that invite experimentation and open new portals to dining pleasure.

1. **Match the Weight:** The central principle of food and wine pairing is simply to serve lighter wines with more delicate foods and heavier wines with richer, more robust fare. The goal is to ensure that neither the wine nor the food obscures the other—so that you can appreciate the flavors in both. The next chapter elaborates on this key point.

2. **Strive for Similarity . . . :** The synergistic benefit of matching similar flavors and textures in food and wine cannot be overstated. This book is filled with dozens of toothsome examples: rich, buttery Chardonnay with equally unctuous lobster and drawn butter; grassy Sauvignon Blanc with herbal sauces; fruity Riesling or Viognier with dishes having fruit sauces or tropical flavors; earthy red Burgundy with earthy foods like mushrooms or lentils; smoky Zinfandel with grilled meats.

3. **. . . or Let Opposites Attract:** Like nuts in chocolate or peanut butter and jelly, sometimes a flavor or textural contrast transports a meal to

new heights. Satisfying contrasts include the acidity of a crisp white with the grease of fried foods or with the creaminess of soft cheese; the saltiness of foie gras or Roquefort cheese with the honied richness of late-harvest dessert wine such as Sauternes; and salty Stilton cheese with sweet-and-thick port.

4. **Sauces Speak Loudly:** A sauce can significantly change the food's compatibility with wine. While a lighter fish like poached sole loves a delicate white, the same fish bathed in a rich, creamy sauce or fried in a thick batter becomes an excellent candidate for a heavier white like Chardonnay or even a lighter red like Pinot Noir.

5. **Crisp Wine Loves Acidity but Detests Sweetness:** As we learned in our discussion of acidity, a crisp, acidic wine, such as Sauvignon Blanc or Chablis, will become less tart in the presence of lemon, tomato sauce, and most other tangy foods. Conversely, as our wedding cake example demonstrates, highly sweet food wreaks havoc on dry, crisp wine, giving the wine a dreadfully sharp taste.

6. **Proteins and Fats Tame Tannic Wine:** Although bitter, tannic wines like Barolo and Cabernet Sauvignon tend to push around most foods, they obediently say "Yes, mistress" in the company of hard cheeses and rich meats. The dry impact of tannin also helps to cleanse your palate of the greases and oils of these foods.

7. **Off-Dry Wine Subdues Spicy Food:** There's nothing like a slightly sweet Riesling to tackle mildly hot Asian food and other spicy cuisines. We expand on this invaluable lesson in Shortcut 69.

8. **Pepper's Positive Punch:** Despite its pungency, pepper is more wine friendly than most people think. A sprinkling of ground pepper on food will sensitize your taste buds and make many wines taste richer and more flavorful.

9. **Be an Indigenist:** Look to a wine region's local cuisine for clues about ideal pairings—locals know best. It's no accident that Primitivo goes so well with gutsy pasta dishes, red Burgundy with *boeuf à la bourguignonne,* and Oregon Pinot Gris with locally sourced salmon.

10. **When in Doubt, Avoid "Prime Time" Wines:** Ironically, some of the best-known wines—Chardonnay, Cabernet Sauvignon, and Merlot—are not always ideal for food because of their weight, high alcohol (which can magnify the hotness in spicy foods), oakiness, and (for the reds) tannin. Better are lighter, crisp, restrainedly oaky wines like Sauvignon Blanc, Pinot Gris, and Riesling on the white side and Pinot Noir, Chianti, Dolcetto, Rioja, and Beaujolais among reds.

11. **Dessert Shouldn't Outsweet a Dessert Wine:** While dessert wine is often best *as* dessert rather than *with* it, it can work alongside dessert so long as it has enough sweetness to stand up to the sweetness in the dessert. So while a sugary-sweet dessert like chocolate cake will dominate a lightly sweet Moscato d'Asti (and make the wine taste thin or even sour), it will meet its match in a fully sweet port.

On My Table | **D A N I E L   B O U L U D** is the celebrity chef and New York–based gastronomic genius behind such renowned restaurants as Daniel, Café Boulud, and db bistro moderne.

Southern Rhône—Châteauneuf-du-Pape
Henri Bonneau Cuvée Spéciale

White Rhône—Hermitage Blanc
Chave—"My favorite for every day."

Northern Rhône—Crozes-Hermitage
Graillot

Red Burgundy
Domaine de l'Arlot

Red Bordeaux
Château Latour

Pinot Noir
Au Bon Climat

Cabernet Sauvignon
Robert Mondavi

68 Match the Weight of the Wine with the Weight of the Food

The maxim "white with white meat and fish, red with red meat" must have been hatched by a fusty, bespectacled disciplinarian with more regard for rules than for the versatility of wine. A more helpful guide for food and wine pairing is this: match the weight, or body, of a wine, with the weight of the food.

The goal is simple: the weight of a wine shouldn't overwhelm its accompanying food and vice versa. If you pair a Pinot Grigio with a plate of lamb chops, good luck tasting your delicately perfumed Pinot Grigio. Similarly, a rich, mouth-filling Cabernet Sauvignon will bully your steamed halibut into gustatory oblivion. Our sturdy chops, then, would meet their match with a hearty Zinfandel or Cabernet, while the halibut would get along famously with our light-bodied Pinot Grigio or Sauvignon Blanc.

The "white with fish, red with meat" law starts to break down when we consider foods of medium weight. Full-bodied whites like a big-style Chardonnay or Viognier flatter fleshy, full-flavored fish like swordfish, tuna, and salmon. But there's no reason you can't also pair lighter reds like Beaujolais and lighter styles of Pinot Noir, Rioja, and Chianti with these dishes. And, while lighter meats like pork, roast chicken, and veal are classic matches with light reds (e.g., light-style Pinot Noir or Chianti), don't hesitate to recruit your full-bodied whites—New World Chardonnay, Viognier, and the like—here.

The Weight of Various Wine Types

Following is an approximation of the body of different wines. Note that each type can vary with individual producer, location, and vintage.

Lighter Whites
Vinho Verde
Pinot Grigio
Alsace (Pinot Blanc)
German Riesling
Sancerre/Pouilly-Fumé
White Burgundy (Mâcon, some Chablis)
Champagne and sparkling wine (varies with the grapes)
Pinot Gris (Oregon, California)
Grüner Veltliner
New World Sauvignon Blanc
Alsace (Pinot Gris, Gewürztraminer, Riesling)
Albariño
White Bordeaux/Graves
White Burgundy (fine Chablis and Côte de Beaune whites)
Viognier
New World Chardonnay
Heavier Whites

LIGHTER

HEAVIER

Lighter Reds
Beaujolais
Rioja (Crianza)
Dolcetto
Red Burgundy
New World Pinot Noir
Chianti (not Riserva)
Côtes-du-Rhône
Barbera
Chinon
Rioja (Reserva and Gran Reserva)
Chianti (Reserva)
New World Cabernet Franc
Red Bordeaux
Merlot
Primitivo
Malbec
Zinfandel
Syrah/Shiraz/many fine Rhônes
Brunello
Super Tuscans
New World Cabernet Sauvignon
Northern Rhône (Hermitage and Côte Rôtie)
Barolo and Barbaresco
Heavier Reds

LIGHTER

HEAVIER

69 Drink a Slightly Sweet White with Spicy Ethnic Food

When my students ask about the best match for fiery Indian food, I invariably think beer. Nothing cools the vindaloo-victimized tongue quite like a frosty mug of Kingfisher. But if it's time for wine, my clear choice is a slightly sweet white wine, preferably a German Riesling.

If sweet wine doesn't seem intuitively matched to spicy food, think about what we drink to cool down chips and spicy salsa: a sugary frozen margarita. Or consider what goes so well with a hot Madras chicken curry: lassi, the sweet Indian yogurt drink. Applying this sweet-and-spicy principle to wine, an off-dry Riesling will take some of the "pow" out of kung pao chicken. Off-dry Riesling is also an excellent choice because it is low in alcohol, and since alcohol tends to magnify the hotness in spicy foods, the less alcohol there is, the better.

Many people find that the delightfully aromatic and irrepressibly fruity Alsatian Gewürztraminer also handles spicy food. Gewürztraminer's lychees-and-ginger character gives it an affinity for similarly spiced Asian foods—though for some, the wine's ample alcohol may heat up aggressively spicy fare.

Spicy food also works with a Moscato d'Asti, the fizzy, low-alcohol Italian wine typically served with dessert but often light enough to refresh a spicy dinner. You might also try an off-dry version of Chenin Blanc, the grape composing Vouvray from France's Loire Valley and varietal wine from California. And a good rosé will always do the trick, its chillability and lack of tannin giving it the wherewithal to soothe the sting from your Szechwan shrimp.

The problem with pairing spicy food with dry, tannic, full-bodied wine is that it exaggerates the wine's natural bitterness. To prove it to yourself, try washing down your Cajun shrimp or green curry chicken with a tannic Cabernet Sauvignon. The hot spices make the dry wine seem harsh, for some even metallic, and the food tastes even hotter.

Because most red wines are dry and fairly alcoholic, I avoid pairing them with spicy food. Some people, however, have luck matching spicy dishes with ripe reds that seem a bit sweet, with low tannin and a restrained degree of alcohol. The eminently chillable Beaujolais, with its sweet, ripe fruit, is a logical choice. Soft, fruity, moderately alcoholic versions of California Pinot Noir and Zinfandel sometimes also have that spice-friendly touch of sweetness.

In the end, remember that the time-tested titan of heat relief is Riesling. But even the most delightful off-dry white won't turn five-alarm flaming orange habanero kimchi into a manageable blaze. For that, crack a tall boy or, when all else fails, swallow your pride and French-kiss an ice cube.

CHEAT SHEET

An off-dry, low-alcohol wine like Riesling is your go-to choice for spicy ethnic food, be it Sichuan, Thai, or Indian, or even the spicy heat of Moroccan, Creole, or Nuevo Latino fare.

On My Table | **CHARLIE TROTTER** is a culinary genius of world renown and owner of Chicago's eponymous temple of gastronomy, named "Best Restaurant in the World for Wine and Food" by *Wine Spectator* magazine.

White and red Burgundy
Coche-Dury, Domaine des Comtes Lafon, Leroy, Dujac, Armand Rousseau, Arnaud Ente

Cabernet Sauvignon
Grace Family, Spottswoode, Diamond Creek, Araujo, Harlan, Quintessa, Sirita, Chappellet, Robert Mondavi—"Tremendous power and seductiveness."

Italian reds from Piedmont and Tuscany
Gaja, Pierro Antinori, Altare, Bruno Giacosa, Isole e Olena

Big Australian reds—"For full-flavored red meats and cheeses."
Penfolds Grange, Henschke, Clarendon Hills, Torbreck, Three Rivers

Spanish reds—"An area to watch! Each year more exciting things are happening and the wines are just getting better."
Alvaro Palacios, Vega Sicilia, Numanthia, Mauro, Pingus, Artadi

Riesling from Germany and Alsace
Fritz Haag, Robert Weil, Josmeyer, Marcel Deiss, Müller-Catoir, Franz Kunstler

Chardonnay from California—"[These] have bright, focused flavors."
Peter Michael, Lewis Cellars, Talbott, Kongsgaard, Hanzell, Gallo, Chateau Montelena, Calera

70 Wine and Cheese: Bedfellows and Power Struggles

Like so many Stones classics penned by Jagger and Richards, the pairing of wine and cheese has achieved a long history of synergistic greatness. But this partnership, like that of the so-called Glimmer Twins, has also been marred by bitterness and unseemly power struggles.

The easiest time for wine and cheese has been in the area of mild, dry cheeses. Firm, relatively mild varieties like Dry Jack or Parmigiano-Reggiano pair well with virtually every wine type. Wash down some dry Cheddar or aged Gouda with a glass of tannic Cabernet or Côte Rôtie and you'll see how the proteins in the cheese make the wine taste smoother. Indeed, my students shout "Olé!" when we drink brawny Ribera del Duero with Spanish Manchego cheese—perhaps the best all-around cheese for wine. Mild, dry cheese also harmonizes with that most delicate of creatures: fine old red Bordeaux or Burgundy, normally problematic because of its fragility. And despite the well-worn myth that red wines are better for cheese, dry cheeses work equally well with white wine, be it a lighter Pinot Grigio, an off-dry Riesling, or a buttered-up California Chardonnay. So, remember: mild, firm cheeses are the closest there is to a universal match with wine.

White wines—especially those of the crisp, tart persuasion like Sancerre or Chablis—are also a splendid match with the chalky acidity in goat cheese. The next time you order goat cheese, or chèvre, you'll spell gustatory happiness in eight letters: S-A-N-C-E-R-R-E. The same holds for fresh cheeses like buffalo mozzarella, which is besotted with the palate-cleansing effect of an acidic white. Lighter, crisp reds—Dolcetto, Pinot Noir, or Beaujolais—are also good bets, as their acidity matches the tanginess in these fresh cheeses without overwhelming them with weight or tannin.

Contrary to party practice, whites and bubbly—not big, bitter reds—are just what the *fromager* ordered with soft, runny cheeses like Brie and Camembert. This is because the mouth-coating quality of these gooey cheeses, together with their moldy rinds, can make a dry red wine taste bitter, at least for some folks. It's better to serve a sprightly glass of Champagne or Sauvignon Blanc to avoid clashing with these cheeses' tongue-bathing butterfat and astringent rinds. The zinginess of a sharp white or a lighter red is an ideal foil to the oozy charms of soft cheese.

Sometimes, however, things get stinky, and you find yourself in the odoriferous company of skull-and-crossbones cheeses like German Limburger, Swiss Appenzeller, and pungent styles of Camembert. Here we call in the big guns: big, powerful reds such as California Cabernet, red Bordeaux, and Italian Barolo. Only these vinous muscle flexers have the requisite tannin and richness to stand up to bacterially gifted stink bombs, whereas most whites would be steamrolled by these nose-numbing bullies.

Blue-veined cheeses like Roquefort and Stilton also need to pick on wine their own size. Not only will a powerful Cabernet, Hermitage, or Barolo stand up to the superpungency of blue cheeses, but it will actually taste better because these strong cheeses tend to tone down its tannic bitterness. The next time a red Bordeaux or Barolo tastes unexpectedly bitter, try a little Roquefort, and you'll see how the cheese eases your perception of the wine's tannin.

At meal's end, another match for blue-veined cheese is sweet, rich dessert wine. Improbable as it seems, sweet, unctuous Sauternes and pungent, salty Roquefort are classic bedfellows, as is port with Stilton. Fans of this match—and they are legion—love the way the textures harmonize (heavy, syrupy wine with rich, creamy cheese), provided that the dessert wine also has enough acidity to cut through the intensity of the cheese. Aficionados also appreciate the opposites-attract flavors of this combination, the sweetness of the wine combining with the savory saltiness of the cheese to create a frisson of gastronomic bliss.

Outsmarting Wine and Cheese

FIRM, MILD CHEESES

Examples: Manchego, Parmigiano-Reggiano, Dry Jack, Cheddar
Best wine matches: everything, including fine old reds

FRESH CHEESES

Examples: goat cheese, buffalo mozzarella, feta
Best wine matches: crisp whites; lighter, crisp reds

GOOEY CHEESES

Examples: Brie, Camembert
Best wine matches: crisp whites; lighter, crisp reds

STINKY CHEESES

Examples: Limburger, Appenzeller, pungent styles of Camembert
Best wine matches: rich, tannic reds

BLUE-VEINED CHEESES

Examples: Roquefort, Maytag Blue, Stilton, Gorgonzola
Best wine matches: rich, tannic reds; sweet dessert wine

71 Bubbly's Best Friends Are Caviar, Sushi, and . . . Popcorn

If *Robin Leach's* famous sign-off were the final word, the best pairing for our "Champagne wishes" would be, of course, "caviar dreams." Salted sturgeon roe is indeed a classic accompaniment to Champagne, in part because the acidity in Champagne lances through the oiliness of caviar, though some purists find that caviar's briny taste makes Champagne taste bitter or fishy. I happen to like the pairing, but I do think its appeal also derives from the thrill of piling luxury upon luxury, the same impulse that causes one to request the penthouse room *with* the Jacuzzi.

Caviar, however, is only the beginning of sparkling wine's long, happy journey with food. So versatile is bubbly that I devote a separate entry urging you to try drinking it throughout a meal (see Shortcut 61). To make the most of your experimentation, remember that you'll keep flavor intensities in balance if you pair lighter foods with lighter styles of bubbly, such as poached trout with light-bodied Taittinger or a bottle that specifically says *Blanc de Blancs*, a more delicate style because it comes from 100 percent white grapes (Chardonnay). Conversely, fuller-bodied sparklers, such as Bollinger or Veuve Clicquot, stand up well to more robust preparations like fattier fish and richer sauces. See Shortcut 58 for a discussion of Champagne styles.

As in all food and wine pairing, there's no need to obsess over achieving a precise match when pairing bubbly with food; it is, after all, traditionally a celebration beverage, to be enjoyed with generosity and mirth. Even so, some time-honored sparkler situations are just too magical to ignore. They are:

AS AN APERITIF If there were only one beverage to negate the day's battles and prime you for the meal ahead, it would be bubbly. Its shimmery appearance, citric snap, and cleansing bubbles wake you up, replenish your soul, and get you drooling for the sustenance ahead. By itself or with hors d'oeuvres, it is *the* liquid prelude.

LIGHTLY SALTY FOODS Sparkling wine also makes an apt aperitif because before dinner we often eat salty nibbles, which, in addition to making you thirsty, tend to tame the crackly acidity in bubbly. Virtually anything edible a bartender slides you—buttered popcorn, salted nuts, tortilla chips, cheese puffs, Parmesan bread sticks, potato chips—teams up beautifully with sparkling wine.

FRIED FOOD Extending the theme of the cardiologically suspect, we arrive at the not-so-sacred altar of fried food. Cook up a batch of your dirtiest, greasiest fried calamari, egg rolls, or French fries, and bubbly will whisk away its greasy baggage like a bellhop at the Four Seasons. You may not want to blow your prized bottle of Cristal on a bucket of KFC, but enlist a frosty bottle of Prosecco or Spanish Cava and your palate will be gratified like nothing else.

CREAMY FOOD Completing the intensive-care troika is—what else—the luscious luxury of creamy food. If it's got a nice "aise"—as in béarnaise, hollandaise, or mayonnaise—a crisp glass of bubbly will machete through the richness and play off the gentle sourness in these artery cloggers. The same goes for a bowl of creamy lobster bisque or risotto.

FOIE GRAS An indulgence in the league of caviar and lobster, the mere presence of foie gras is an excellent justification for cracking a *prestige cuvée*. The creamy texture of fine Champagne is simpatico with the soft, smooth feel of duck or goose liver.

MUSHROOMS Like foie gras, mushrooms have an earthy, meaty personality that pairs well with Champagne and earthier types of sparklers like Spanish Cava. If your wallet can bear it, step up to white truffles, the hauntingly earthy mushroomlike delicacy shaved over pasta.

EGG DISHES If your friends question your prenoon penchant for bubbly, or you have yet to develop one, be advised of the classic match of Champagne with egg dishes. Champagne's yeasty bubbliness flatters a fluffy omelet, a savory frittata, or hollandaise-slathered eggs Benedict.

SEAFOOD OF ALL KINDS All but the grimmest malcontent would fail to see the beauty of pairing a flute of citrusy bubbly with seafood of all kinds, from shellfish like shrimp and oysters to richer fillets of salmon and swordfish.

JAPANESE CUISINE Not a sakè fan? You are hereby advised to cross cultures and try bubbly, which seems to me an even better flavor match with Japanese food, touching on almost every category already mentioned. It incorporates seafood (sushi and sashimi), salty fare (soy sauce), fried food (tempura), cream sauces (sauce with spicy tuna roll), and even egg and mushroom dishes (tamago or mushroom rolls, and so on). What better match for Japanese cuisine, which revolves around fermented food (soy sauce, miso soup, pickled vegetables, the rice vinegar in sushi rice), than Champagne, which itself is twice-fermented and has the yeasty aromas to prove it?

CHEESE As we have covered, sparkling wine does back flips for most kinds of cheese, including fresh, acidic *fromage* like goat cheese and gooey types like Brie and Camembert. Just be careful of the bullying effect of stink bombs like Limburger and blue-veined bandits like Roquefort.

DESSERT An unfortunate inevitability at weddings, dry bubbly clashes with cake and other sweet desserts. If you crave bubbles with your dessert course, look beyond the *brut* (dry) category to semisweet bubbly, often labeled *demi-sec*.

72 Artichokes and Salad Dressing, Infamous Wine Killers

My enthusiasm for wine is matched only by my love of artichokes, which are so dear to me that every year I ship to my New York apartment a crate of giant green beauties from a farm in Castroville, California. But combining these two gustatory passions in the same meal has long terrified wine enthusiasts. This is because artichokes can make a dry wine taste sweeter.

The difference is subtle: an artichoke won't Jekyll-and-Hyde your bottle of Sauvignon Blanc into Hawaiian Punch, but it will make the dry Sauvignon Blanc seem less tart and more fruity. This happens because artichokes naturally contain a compound called *cynarin*, which tends to make everything, including water, taste sweeter. Does this mean you have to steer clear of the mighty 'choke at your next wine meal? Of course not. If you are breaking out a special wine and plan to scrutinize its precise balance of fruit and acidity, you may want to avoid an artichoke's transformative effect. But if you're just knocking back an everyday bottle of wine, an artichoke shouldn't have you running for a spittoon. In fact, if the wine is quite dry and tangy, such as Sauvignon Blanc or Chianti, an artichoke's sweetening effect might make you like the wine better. Grüner Veltliner is another artichoke ally, given its acidity and affinity for green vegetables, described in Shortcut 50.

Like artichokes, salad dressing can take your wine for a stroll on the sweet side. It does this not because of any mysterious chemical, but because of the rule we already covered: acidic food subdues acidic wine. Salad dressing, of course, is among the most sour things we eat, comprised of vinegar, garlic, lemon juice, and other substances that keep the Alka-Seltzer factory fizzing. That's why some connoisseurs never use *Bordeaux* and *balsamic* in the same sentence, and indeed, you may have trouble fully appreciating a delicately balanced

CHEAT SHEET

Choose a tangy, everyday wine with artichokes and salad dressing; these "problem foods" shouldn't be a concern unless you're enjoying ultra-fine wine.

OUTSMART THE TABLE

Joining artichokes in the infamous "problem veggie" category is asparagus, whose unusual taste is said to make some wines taste strangely sweet. Once again, you'll be safe with simple, zingy choices such as Grüner Veltliner, Sancerre, or New Zealand Sauvignon Blanc.

TALK THE TALK

cynarin *sigh-NAR-in*

mature Burgundy with an endive vinaigrette. But no one is going to confiscate your corkscrew if you drink a simple, crisp wine with your dressed-up greens, and you might even find that the tart dressing is the perfect antidote to an overly dry wine. Whether you're having frisée with goat cheese, a Caesar with croutons, or just tossed greens, opt for an uncomplicated, high-acid wine like Prosecco, Sauvignon Blanc, Pinot Grigio, Sancerre, rosé, Beaujolais, or Dolcetto.

On My Table | **FRÉDÉRIC DROUHIN** is a family proprietor of Maison Joseph Drouhin, one of Burgundy's most important growers and *négociants*.

Vintage port
Graham—"Goes wonderfully with a Partagas D4 cigar."

Red Burgundy—Grands Echezeaux
Joseph Drouhin Grands Echezeaux

Alsace dessert wine—Vendanges Tardives/Sélection de Grains Nobles
Gewürztraminer from Hugel

Champagne
Pol Roger, especially *cuvée* Sir Winston Churchill; Roederer

Chianti
Villa Antinori—"In one glass you can taste Italy."

Restaurants

W*e now enter* the nerve center of wine anxiety: the restaurant, with its inflated prices, impenetrable lists, unknowledgeable servers, and public-speaking pressures. Relax: we're going to cover concrete ways of maximizing your wine dollars in restaurants and demystify the tasting ritual. You'll even receive a fail-safe, Mad-Libs-style phrase to order wine without a whiff of embarrassment. We also cover one of my favorite antidotes to overpriced wine lists: BYOB and how to do it gracefully. ■

73 At Restaurants, Avoid the High End and Seek the "Wha?" Wines

Three hundred percent: that's at least how much the average restaurant marks up its wine over the retail price, and some shoot even higher than that. Restaurateurs' reflexive justification is the need to cover costs like glassware, staff wages, and replenishing stock, but most of the wine-drinking public would agree that they are doing themselves and diners a major disservice. Faced with paying $40 or more for a wine they can get at a wine shop for $12, diners end up feeling fleeced or forced to drink wine of considerably lower quality than they would at home. High prices also discourage them from experimenting with new wine types, lowering the overall dining experience and making it less likely they will return.

It is possible, however, to maximize the chance of getting a decent deal if you understand how restaurants price wines. First, don't expect restaurants of the same caliber to price their wines similarly. Prices vary widely among restaurants, depending on the eatery's size, location, and appetite for profit margins. At any restaurant, however, lower-end wines are usually marked up the most—sometimes as much as 500 percent over the wholesale price. So the Pinot Grigio a restaurant sells for $25 probably cost the restaurant only about $5, which means they've pumped up the price 500 percent and pocketed a cool $20 just for popping the cork. But because a similarly high markup on more expensive bottles might scare off diners, a Merlot that cost a restaurant $10 might be only inflated 400 percent to $40, a lower markup to avoid giving diners sticker shock.

Even if it is marked up more gently, the expensive end of a wine list is rarely worth it. Not only are you expected to pay a 15 percent tip and tax on that higher amount, but very expensive bottles in restaurants are sometimes anything but table pleasers. Many of my students—particularly those on expense accounts—report opting for an expensive young red such as

"CUSTOMERS WILL EAT YOU POOR AND DRINK YOU RICH."

—*Restaurant-industry expression*

CHEAT SHEET

In restaurants, be wary of the high end and the "second seat"—and seek out less familiar wine types.

💡 **OUTSMART THE TABLE**

If you're seeking wines for which vintage matters (e.g., a fine Bordeaux or Burgundy), it pays to opt for off-vintages, which are often markedly less expensive and easier to drink when young.

Bordeaux or Barolo, only to find it gum-searingly bitter. The unfortunate fact is that many restaurants sell prestigious bottles that are far too young to be drunk. Even with the requisite maturity, high-end bottles can also alienate your fellow diners with unusual aromas and tastes—such as earthiness or gaminess in certain European wines—that represent a discomfiting change from their usual New World Chardonnay or Merlot. It is safer in restaurants to stay with more moderately priced wine, which won't bankrupt your fellow diners or disappoint them with unfamiliar tastes. And top restaurants with good wine programs tend to include interesting choices on the lower end—selections often ignored by the high rollers who frequent these places.

Even the lower end of the wine list has hazards. Much has been made of what I call the "second seat" of a wine list—that is, the second-cheapest wine that many people select for fear of looking like a skinflint for ordering the cheapest. While it certainly isn't a universal practice, some restaurants sometimes slot an overstocked bottle into the second-cheapest position on the list, mindful that many diners will gravitate to this acceptably thrifty choice. Knowing it will sell swiftly, some restaurateurs mark up that wine more than any other—sometimes making it the worst value on the wine list. While insiders maintain that only a minority of restaurants resort to this ploy, it's good to keep in mind.

Finally, to maximize your wine dollars in restaurants, seek out the "Wha?" wines. By this I mean wines beyond the usual suspects from California (Chardonnay, Merlot, Cabernet Sauvignon) and France (Bordeaux, Burgundy). The more popular a wine is, the more likely you are going to pay extra for that demand—so seek out the wines that make casual drinkers scratch their heads and ask "Wha?" These include less popular basic grapes (Sauvignon Blanc, German Riesling, red Zinfandel) and regional types (Côtes-du-Rhône and Spanish Rioja). Chianti is also a "Wha?" wine—not because its name is unfamiliar but because many are unaware of its reinvention as a quality wine. Also included are most of the "secret alternatives" in this book—wines such as Albariño, New Zealand Sauvignon Blanc, Gewürztraminer, Barbera, Chinon, and the like. As this list demonstrates, names with accents and other foreign flavor are an opportunity for values, because people tend to shy away from the unpronounceable. In contrast, familiar, easily said favorites like Merlot and Chardonnay drop you into the centerfield of the restaurant rip-off zone.

74 The Wine List Reveals Whether a Restaurant Is on Your Side

In conveying how wine friendly a restaurant truly is, a wine list literally speaks volumes. By scanning its organization, clarity, and contents, you'll get clues as to the integrity and energy of the restaurant's wine program. You'll then have a better idea about whether to trust the wine list and the server—and perhaps take chances in choosing a wine you normally wouldn't have. Look for these clues:

Ominous Signs

NO LOW END While wine prices at most restaurants are distressingly inflated, some lists are more deplorable than others. All restaurants, including the fanciest, should have some bottles priced on the low end. This means around $20 at modest eateries and $30 to $35 at pricier establishments.

EXPENSIVE BEAUJOLAIS A good way to gauge the fairness of a wine list is to look at the pricing of a simple bottle of Beaujolais, such as Beaujolais Nouveau or Beaujolais-Villages, if they have it. Retailing at about $8, this wine shouldn't exceed $20 to $30 on a wine list, even at an upscale restaurant. A restaurant selling basic Beaujolais at $35 or more is marking it up well beyond the already inordinate industry standard.

NO VINTAGES A list that fails to supply a wine's vintage—that is, the year on the bottle indicating when the grapes were harvested—reflects a lazy or disorganized wine program. To cite an extreme example, I once found myself at a surreally backward restaurant in Bucharest, Romania, where the list excluded not only the vintage but also the wine's producer. The bottle of "Caburnay" I ordered could have removed paint from a wall.

YELLOW(ED) PAGES A wine list isn't worth much if it isn't updated often to reflect shifting inventory. Good wine lists, like quality menus, are often laser printed so that they can change weekly to reflect shifts in inventory. Leatherbound tomes with yellowed pages, on the other hand, are often out of date—a sign that the restaurant is asleep at the wine wheel.

Hopeful Signs

CREATIVE CHOICES Does the list include the kind of alternative wines featured in this book—gems like Gewürztraminer, Cabernet Franc, Primitivo, Malbec, and the like? If so, someone there must really care about the wine program. On a recent visit to New York's venerable, insomniac-friendly Blue Ribbon restaurant, I had to smile when I read through the vast array of compelling wine choices—it was as if a DJ was trying to impress the patrons with his eclectic and carefully chosen collection of songs.

INTERESTING WINES BY THE GLASS Does the restaurant's creativity extend to its by-the-glass list? Are there only the obligatory Chardonnay and Merlot supplied by the glass, or is there a diversity of offerings, allowing diners to experiment with new wine types? Wine by the glass is a terrific way of expanding your oenological horizons—just make sure the wine is newly opened or has been stored properly so that it is fresh.

SUCCINCT LISTS While a wine list should have plenty of choices, the fifty-page leviathans used by some restaurants are inefficient for the casual drinker looking to choose one bottle in the course of a few minutes. The best lists comprise just a few dozens wines. A separate, unabridged "reserve book" can be kept for incorrigible grape nuts.

WINES RECOMMENDED WITH DISHES Kudos to restaurants with menus recommending different wines with each appetizer and entrée—giving the diner the reassurance of selecting among a few well-vetted choices. Similarly, those fancying a feast should seek restaurants with *menus de dégustation*, or tasting menus, which pair each of many courses with an appropriate wine. Both options point to a passionate and thoughtful wine program, as does the growing prevalence of lists organized by a wine's primary taste, such as "spicy," "smooth," and "fruity."

OUTSMART THE TABLE

- To figure out how much a restaurant paid wholesale for a bottle of wine, look at how much it charges for a glass of that wine; so, if a glass is $8 on the list, there's a good chance that it paid that much for the bottle.
- If you plan to drink several glasses of wine, it's almost always less expensive to enjoy a whole bottle than to order its equivalent by the glass.
- Before your most important restaurant visits, you can completely outsmart wine selection by previewing the list online (many wine-proud restaurants publish at least part of their lists on the Web) or by asking the restaurant to fax its list to you. Then use the various Internet resources recommended in Shortcut 108 to discern which of the wines are winners.

On My Table | **LARRY STONE**, a master sommelier and wine director of San Francisco's Rubicon restaurant, is considered America's unofficial "dean of sommeliers."

Champagne
Veuve Clicquot, Roederer, Delbeck, Krug, Salon

Grüner Veltliner
Prager, Bründlmayer, Hirtzberger, Nigl, Pichler—"Milder and more nuanced than most Sauvignon Blancs."

Spanish "new wave" red wines
Muga, Abadia Retuerta, Moro, Numanthia; anything from Alvaro Palacios, such as L'Eremita, Finca Dofi, and Palacios Remondo; anything imported by Jorge Ordoñez

Riesling from Germany and Austria
Carl von Schubert, Kerpen, J. J. Prüm, Gunderloch, Weil, Prager, Pichler, Hirsch, Diel, Dr. Loosen, Merkelbach, Basserman-Jordan, Schloss Saarstein, Selbach-Oster

Late-harvest botrytised dessert wines
Alois Kracher late-harvest wines from Burgenland in Austria; late-harvest German Riesling from H. Dönnhoff; Sauternes from Raymond-Lafon Sauternes and Yquem; Loire Valley wines such as Pierre Bise Coteaux du Layon, Moulin Touchais Anjou [Coteaux du Layon], Domaine des Baumard Quarts de Chaume, and Huet Vouvray Moelleux and Cuvée Constance; Hungarian Tokaji Aszú from the Royal Tokaji Wine Company

Syrah from Washington State—"A rising-star region."
Three Rivers, McCrea, Cayuse, Columbia David Lake Signature Series

Cabernet Sauvignon
Niebaum-Coppola Rubicon and Cask, Cain Five, Corison, Lewis, Joesph Phelps Insignia, Caymus Napa and Special Selection, Heidi Peterson Barrett's wines [La Sirena, Paradigm, Grace Family, Screaming Eagle, etc.], Pride Mountain, Dalla Valle, Long Meadow Ranch, Sirita

75 Seven Ways You Can Be "Throckmeistered" by a Server

Having taught several wine classes by the time I graduated from college, I had earned the unofficial title of "restaurant wine selector" in my family. To celebrate my graduation, we made our one and only visit to Throckmeister's, a minor-league steak house with a major-league chip on its shoulder. There I ordered a bottle of Robert Mondavi Cabernet Sauvignon, one of the more affordable selections at $35. Our unctuous Bob Barker of a server brought the bottle without presenting it, barely concealing his contempt that a baby-faced ruffian like me had actually ordered the wine. Never mind, I thought, the wine was scrumptious and the food was serviceable, and everyone at the table seemed pleased.

When the bill came, my dad looked at me as if I had deflated the tires of his Volvo. "Ninety-five dollars for wine?"

A hot streak of embarrassment whipped up my spine. There, as the candlelight flickered on the generic equestrian paintings on the walls, I noticed the word *Reserve* etched faintly in the corner of the wine's label. *That scoundrel!* The waiter had brought the Mondavi *Reserve*, which wasn't even on the regular wine list I had ordered from.

Although the waiter corrected his "mistake" and charged us only for the bottle I had ordered, the story serves as a reminder that you have to be on guard when dining out.

In that spirit, the following are seven ways you can get, if you will, *Throckmeistered* by a restaurant's server—so you know to avoid them.

1. **The Upsell:** The greatest sin a server can commit is to push a more expensive wine despite your stated price range or signals to that effect. I was recently at a casual red-sauce Italian joint (hint: it was the subject of a reality show) with a table full of price-sensitive friends. When I asked my server which of three under-$30 wines he recommended with our pasta and meatballs, he dismissed those choices and "strongly advised" a $55

wine—far more extravagant than our budget and food choices. He probably figured I would be too embarrassed to disregard his recommendation—which I promptly did.

2. **Mistreatment of the Young, Unknowledgeable, or Thrifty:** As the Throckmeister's story shows, some servers mistreat diners who don't fit the profile of a "wine connoisseur." Wine service should be the same no matter what you look like or what your order. Once, when my business partner and I dined at a well-known New York restaurant to celebrate a deal, our snippy server took us for neophytes and slyly substituted an inexpensive Chardonnay for the exotic white Burgundy the tasting menu had promised for the second course. When I called him on it, he was so flustered that he left our table and had another server take over.

3. **No Presentation of Wine:** While it might seem unnecessary, a server's presentation of the wine bottle is your chance to verify that he has brought the correct wine. Had my Mr. Throckmeister shown me the bottle of Mondavi Reserve before serving it, the incident would have been averted.

4. **Bad Pacing:** Timing is everything at a meal, and good wine service means that your server supplies the wine list immediately and opens your wine before the first course. On the other hand, servers shouldn't refill your glass before you want more, or top off the glasses of light drinkers who have barely touched their wine.

5. **Careless Temperature Control:** Some servers think nothing of pouring white wine so cold that its flavors are numb. Others will serve a red too warm, rendering its flavors blurred and its taste

OUTSMART THE TABLE

Is it really necessary to include the full cost of the wine in calculating your standard 15 to 20 percent restaurant gratuity—given that a server exerts the same amount of effort in opening a $20 bottle as with a $60 bottle? Assuming that the service was good, the answer is yes—the accepted custom is to tip on the entire bill, including the wine, and not punish your server for a restaurant's unconscionable wine markups. When ordering an extremely expensive bottle, however, many insiders cap the wine tip at a reasonable amount, such as $20 for a bottle in the $100 to $300 range.

overly alcoholic or "hot." You shouldn't hesitate to ask your server to serve a bottle at the temperature you like it. If necessary, ask the server to remove a white wine from its ice bucket or give a red wine a few minutes in the ice.

6. **Bottle Stranding:** All too often servers remove your bottle from the table after pouring a round, only to get busy and forget to refill your glasses promptly. Ask that the bottle be kept on your table or within arm's reach.

7. **Reckless Bubbly Opening:** Nothing is more unsettling than a loaded bottle of bubbly waved in your face as a server struggles to remove the cork. A conscientious server covers the bottle with a protective cloth and gently "puffs" it open in a direction away from your table.

76 Seek Help at Restaurants,
but Be Prepared to Go It Alone

Have *you* heard about the game show appearing at restaurants across the land? You get a few moments to choose from a book of unfamiliar names and then, before a live audience, try to pronounce one of those names to a some-times snarky server. In the process, you pay through the teeth and assume responsibility for your table's libational happiness.

Sound onerous? Selecting wine at restaurants is, for many people. Few things in life demand performance with so little preparation.

Choosing a good bottle need not be traumatic if you keep these two plans in mind:

Plan A: Seeking Help

The best case is a knowledgeable server who can guide you to a good bottle. After all, he should be intimately familiar with the list and which bottles elicit the *oohs* and *ahs* from diners. If your server doesn't seem helpful, ask if there's a sommelier or another server who is.

Before talking with your server, determine if your table has a color pref-erence (white or red) and a price range (low end, midlevel, splurge). You might also determine whether there is a food theme (meat, fish, pasta) and perhaps any other stylistic preferences (e.g., spicy, crisp, nonoaky, low tannin, etc.).

Then, when your server arrives, put these preferences into one simple question. To help you remember how easy this is, I write out this question *Mad Libs* style in the next chapter. If you don't feel comfortable discussing the price range in front of your table—because of a hot date, client dinner, or another reason—simply point to the price range on the wine list. The server should get the point.

Plan B: Going It Alone

If no one seems helpful or you don't get a satisfactory recommendation, be ready to blaze your own trail. If you feel reasonably confident, make a selection based on your feel for the wine list. As we already learned, it's often best to avoid the high end of the list and marquee wine types like California Cabernet and red Bordeaux.

If, however, you feel overwhelmed or risk-averse, consider these fail-safes:

PINOT NOIR I sometimes call it "Pivot Noir" because it so effortlessly pivots between lighter and heavier dishes and pleases fans of both white and red wine. Mouthwateringly crisp and light to medium bodied, often with a touch of sweetness from the wine's natural fruitiness and oak aging, it handles almost any dish except perhaps the heaviest, spiciest meats (e.g., pepper steak) and stinkiest cheeses (e.g., Roquefort). The only downside is its price, which is rarely under $30 at restaurants.

BEAUJOLAIS For a more economical choice, Beaujolais will perform the pivot role with less complexity and weight but plenty of juicy charm. Better wine lists will often have finer Beaujolais, like Moulin-à-Vent, Morgon, Fleurie, and Brouilly.

PROSECCO, CAVA, AND AMERICAN SPARK-LERS An option so overlooked it gets its own chapter (see Shortcut 60), sparkling wine will amplify your appetite, refresh your palate, and give your neighbors a serious case of bottle envy. Best of all, it's often one of the less expensive choices on a list.

CHEAT SHEET
A knowledgeable server or sommelier can steer you to key choices you might never have noticed, but in the absence of wise counsel, be ready to go it alone. You can always fall back on a light red, sparkling wine, and a range of other fail-safes.

OUTSMART THE TABLE
If you're going to splurge on one really good wine at a meal with several bottles, it's often wise to have the best bottle early in the meal. Later on diners don't always have the concentration to appreciate a great wine, distracted as they are with food, conversation, and their own deepening inebriation.

OTHER FAIL-SAFES You'll also play it safe with . . .

Chardonnay: the rich buttery bull's-eye of the American comfort zone

Pinot Grigio: the light, crisp, liquid security blanket that offends nobody

Zinfandel: the lovable tooth-stainer that's often priced less than a Cabernet Sauvignon or Merlot

Shiraz: the instantly likable "plush ripey"

On My Table | **DANIEL JOHNNES** owns Jeroboam Wines, an importer of artisanal wines, and also serves as wine director of New York's famed Montrachet restaurant.

Riesling from Alsace, Germany, and Austria
Alsace: Trimbach, Kientzler, Ostertag, Deiss, Sparr. Austria: Prager, Pichler, Knoll, Nigl, Alzinger. Germany: Gunderloch, Weil, Zilliken, Selbach-Oster, Pfeffingen.

White Burgundy
Mâcon: Lafon, Olivier Merlin, Ferret, Guffens, Thevenet. Côte de Beaune: Roulot, Leflaive, Carillon, Marc Colin, Lamy, Niellon, Ramonet, Bernard Morey. Chablis: Drouhin, William Fèvre, Raveneau, Dauvissat, Louis Michel.

Rosé
Mimo (Italy), Chivite (Spain), Commanderie de Peyrassol (Provence)

Beaujolais
Favorite producers include Château des Jacques, Tête, Duboeuf, Foillard, Vissoux—"My gulping red wine."

Rhône—north and south
Côte Rôtie: Guigal, Clusel-Roch, Jamet, Rostaing. Hermitage: Chave, Delas, Sorrel. Châteauneuf-du-Pape: Beaucastel, Bonneau, Janasse, Pegau, Usseglio.

Red Burgundy
Lafarge, d'Angerville, l'Arlot, Roumier, H. Lignier, Dujac, Trapet, Grivot, Mugnier

"Don't Worry, It's on the Company"

Avoiding marquee wines is sound advice when you are footing the bill, but an expense account changes the rules of the game. You can't go wrong selecting any of these treats often seen in the middle to high end of wine lists:

BUBBLY AND WHITE

Beringer Private Reserve Chardonnay (California)
Bollinger Champagne Brut (Champagne)
Cakebread Chardonnay (California)
Chalone Chardonnay (California)
Cloudy Bay Sauvignon Blanc (New Zealand)
Livio Felluga Pinot Grigio (Italy)
Grgich Hills Chardonnay (California)
Louis Latour Puligny-Montrachet (France)
Robert Mondavi Fumé Blanc (California)
Veuve Clicquot Yellow Label Brut (Champagne)

RED

Antinori Chianti Classico Riserva (Italy)
Au Bon Climat Pinot Noir (California)
Banfi Chianti Classico Riserva (France)
d'Arenberg Laughing Magpie Shiraz (Australia)
David Bruce Pinot Noir (California)
Duckhorn Merlot (California)
Château Gruaud-Larose (Bordeaux)
E. Guigal Châteauneuf-du-Pape (France)
Hess Collection Cabernet Sauvignon (California)
Robert Mondavi Reserve Pinot Noir (California)
Joseph Phelps Cabernet Sauvignon (California)
Ridge Zinfandel (California)
Ruffino Chianti Classico Riserva Ducale Gold Label (Italy)
Stag's Leap Wine Cellars Cabernet Sauvignon (California)
Swanson Merlot (California)

77 Order Wine with This One Simple Phrase

If *your server/sommelier* seems potentially helpful, just utter *this one simple phrase:*

"Can you recommend a   red/white . . .
_____

color

in the $25/$40/   **OR**   like these
etc. range."   [point to prices on wine list]."
_____   _____

price (discretion unimportant)   *price (discretion important—e.g.,*
                                          hot date, client dinner)

If you have other preferences and/or have identified food themes at the table:

"And, if possible, a wine for   fish/pasta/red meat/etc. . . . .
_____

food themes

OUTSMART THE TABLE
Another way to smoke out interesting
selections is to ask your server what
wine the chef drinks when he or she is
off-duty.

that is   crisp/oaky/spicy/earthy/etc."
_____

other preferences

Seven Ways to Outsmart Wine with Business Meals

1. **Seek a "Business Honest" Price:** Unless the table intends to splurge, aim for a wine priced in the midrange, erring on the side of frugality. Your choice should convey a fiscally responsible, "business honest" sensibility—not so expensive that it casts you as a cash-torching Gatsby, but not so cheap that it risks insulting your guests.

2. **Prepare to Point:** To keep pricing discreet when ordering, remember that you can always point the server to the price range you're looking for ("I was looking for something like this . . .") rather than talk dollars in front of the table.

3. **Pinot Noir:** Pinot Noir, the juicy berry kiss, is always a good overall bet, pleasing the plethora of red-wine fans while light enough to keep blancophiles pacified.

4. **Don't Forget the Fail-safes:** Business meals aren't the best time for experimentation, so it's fine to fall back on fail-safes like Chardonnay, Zinfandel, and Shiraz. If you're feeling more adventurous, try Côtes-du-Rhône on the lower end and Châteauneuf-du-Pape in the midrange. And if an expense account is in play, consider one of the blue chips from the "Don't Worry, It's on the Company" list on page 252.

5. **Forge Ahead:** While it's always helpful to consider table preferences, don't stall the ordering process by waiting for consensus—you may never get it.

6. **Sneak a Peek:** As advised previously, you can often preview a restaurant's wine list by Internet or fax. Cross-reference these wines with the online databases listed in Shortcut 108 and you'll know exactly what to expect.

7. **Defer to the Alpha Dog:** When there's a connoisseur or an executive significantly senior to you at the table, it's wise to offer him the mantle of wine selection, as it conveys your trust in his judgment and takes you off the hook.

On My Table | **KAREN KING** is wine director of New York's Gramercy Tavern and a multiple James Beard Award winner.

Sancerre
André Neveu, Jolivet

Grüner Veltliner
Prager, Rudi, F. X. Pichler, Nigl, Bründlmayer

Riesling from Germany
Selbach-Oster, Strub, Dönnhoff

Southern Rhône—Côtes-du-Rhône—"The more funky-barnyard aromas, the better."
Château Rayas La Pialade, Domaine Grands Bois, Janasse

Chianti
Rodano, Felsina, Fontodi

Barolo—"The older, the better."
Bartolo Mascarello, Giacomo Conterno, Giuseppe Mascarello, Aldo Conterno, Abbona

Madeira—"[Its history, longevity, and volcanic vineyards] bring to mind the notion of an elixir."
Barbeito, Blandy, Leacock

78 Don't Sniff the Cork

One of my favorite wine books, a dusty French guide from 1927 called *The Art of Drinking,* contains an illustration of a tuxedoed wine enthusiast cradling a cork underneath his pointy nose and sniffing as if his life depended on it. The caption reads *Sentir le Bouchon* ("Smell the Cork").

It is wrong.

There's not much to be gained by smelling—or squeezing, for that matter—the cork. When a waiter presents the cork to you, there's only one thing to do: nothing. Just put it aside.

Some say that feeling a cork for dryness can indicate whether excessive amounts of oxygen have crept into the bottle and spoiled the wine, but you'll smell and taste that soon enough anyway, as discussed in the next shortcut.

Inspecting a cork for the stamp of its winery used to be a way of ensuring its authenticity, but that was hundreds of years ago, when wine bottles didn't have labels. Unless you're drinking a very old and rare wine, there's no need to scrutinize the cork.

Of course, you're bound to run into old-fashioned types—perhaps a longtime wine collector or even a sommelier—who still give their corks a good Eskimo kiss. Let them have their fun, but realize that the vast majority of wine experts see no value in doing this.

CHEAT SHEET
Just say no to cork inhalation!

TALK THE TALK
sommelier   *sum-ell-YAY*

79 You Probably Don't Need
to Send That Bottle Back

In theory, once you've determined that your server has brought the bottle you ordered and you've gotten a good whiff of the wine, the rest of the wine ritual allows you to be a tableside Emperor Nero or Roger Ebert, giving some wines a triumphant thumbs-up and others a cathartic thumbs-down.

In practice, however, you're expected to be more like my sixth-grade social studies teacher, the always charitable Mrs. Bowser, who gave passing marks to all but the most egregious offenders.

This is because there are really just two times when a bottle needs to be sent back. The first is when the wine has become oxidized—sometimes called "cooked"—because of exposure to excessive heat or a bad cork seal. Oxidized wine has a flat, prunelike smell, like that opened bottle of wine you forgot to throw away last New Year's Eve.

The other, more common justification for returning a wine is when it has become "corked," which is simply when the wine has taken on the musty smell of damp newspaper or rotten wood because of a contaminated cork. This is something that can happen to any kind of wine, no matter how fine it is or how carefully the bottle is stored. It happens during cork production when mold in the natural cork combines with the chemicals used to clean that cork, afflicting the wine with a malodorous compound called trichloranisole, or *TCA* to wine buffs. I estimate that about one in twenty bottles, or approximately 5 percent of wine, is afflicted with cork taint; some wine pros put that number at 10 percent or higher.

The key is not to confuse a wine that tastes different than you expected—perhaps because it's unusually tart or tannic—with one that has truly gone bad. If you haven't had your share of fine old Burgundy, for example, the curious baconlike gaminess you smell in that ultraexpensive bottle of Le Chambertin is by no means cause to send it back.

If a wine tastes disappointingly different to you but doesn't have the telltale signs of spoilage, let it sit a bit in your glass or try it with food, and it will often taste better, or at least tolerable. You might also try tasting the wine in a new glass, because if your glass contains a trace of residual detergent or was washed alongside a row of anchovy-crusted plates, your wine will suffer accordingly.

If you believe the wine has spoiled and deserves to be returned, it's best to avoid direct confrontation. "You know, I think this wine is corked . . . could you take a sniff or taste and tell me what you think?" is usually all it takes to get the bottle replaced. If your server seems extra cheerful when he snatches it back, it may be because he truly believes the customer is always right, or, quite possibly, he's elated at the nightcap you've just donated to the wait staff.

On My Table | **SIRIO MACCIONI,** a native of Tuscany, is the brains and passion behind Le Cirque 2000, New York's mecca of gastronomy and high society.

Chardonnay
Al Poggio, Castello di Ama [Italian Chardonnay], Newton

Super Tuscans
Antinori's Tignanello and Solaia—"[The latter] is one of the greatest wines ever for me."

Cabernet Sauvignon
Spring Mountain Reserve

Red Burgundy—Chambolle-Musigny

80 If You BYOB, Call Ahead, Order a Courtesy Round, and Give Your Server a Taste

For those of us who collect wine but are culinarily challenged, there are few opportunities to pair our prized bottles with professionally prepared food. That's why restaurateurs who encourage patrons to bring their own wine, whether due to a lack of liquor license or to compassion for hapless cooks like me, are humanitarians of the highest order.

How and when you can bring your own bottle (BYOB) is often a source of confusion for consumers because restaurants are wildly divergent in their policies. Some will treat your bottle like one of their own, serving it to you with professionalism and good cheer, in return for your paying a corkage fee. A few enterprising eateries even hold special wine nights where they waive the corkage fee. Unfortunately, other establishments will consider your bottle an affront to the unspoken expectation that you're coming for *their* food and *their* (heavily marked-up) wine. To them, BYOB is tacky and unnecessary, like taking a flute to the symphony or shampoo to a hair salon. In some places, the practice is even prohibited by state or local laws.

Not to worry. Here are some easy guidelines to ensure angst-free BYOB:

1. **Call:** Ring up the restaurant in advance to inquire about the appropriateness of bringing your own stash and the amount of the corkage fee. If you wish to bring a bottle requiring decanting, you might arrange it during this call. Always note the name of the person with whom you speak, in case there's a conflict later on.

2. **Contemplate:** Decide whether the corkage fee seems reasonable to you. I use $25 as a dividing line when I take wine to relatively upscale restaurants in expensive cities like New York, Chicago, and Los Angeles. A fee of $10 or $15 is the sign of a truly BYOB-friendly establishment, but I'm sometimes willing to pay as much as $25 if the restaurant is first-class and has its own excellent wine list. To me, any-

thing over $25 seems punitive, as if the restaurant is sending the message "We won't stop you, but you're going to pay a premium for it."

3. **Select Carefully:** If you're willing to pay the corkage, remember that you should never bring a bottle that the restaurant already offers on its wine list. If there's any doubt, call ahead to ensure your bottle is clear. Unless you're taking wine to a restaurant with no liquor license, reserve BYOB for bottles that are rare, old, or special in some other way.

4. **Order a Courtesy Round:** Before your wine is opened, it's good karma to order a round of cocktails or bubbly as an aperitif. Or if you plan to drink several bottles, consider ordering the first bottle off the wine list and drinking your bottle next. Sometimes a server will drop the corkage fee if you also order a bottle from the list.

5. **Share:** In the spirit of generosity, consider giving a taste to your server (or the sommelier or chef). Most waiters will be overjoyed to get a sample of the exotic juice they have been serving you. Your largesse may also inspire your server to waive the corkage fee.

6. **Tip:** While the gratuity, of course, is a personal decision, I usually tip on the value of the bottle I've brought. A server or sommelier who does a good job of handling your wine deserves a reward for his or her efforts.

Handling
and Serving

W*ine is one* of those things in life that should come with an instruction book but doesn't. How is the casual enthusiast supposed to know the ideal temperature to serve wine? Or how to get the most out of a corkscrew—and the best ones to use? And why didn't anyone tell us to add water to our ice buckets or not pop open a bottle of bubbly as if it were a roman candle? Let this section be your user's manual for the facets of handling wine you never learned. ■

81 The Best Corkscrew Is the Waiter's Friend, but You Must Choke the Lever

Anger, bargaining, denial, depression, acceptance . . .

These are not only famous steps of coping with death, but also the emotions a winemaker experiences when a clueless college student botches the opening of one of his best bottles.

Or at least it was when I was helping a distinguished vintner open his wine before a meeting of the Stanford Wine Circle, a club I ran in college. In the nervous rush of cranking out corks, I unceremoniously snapped the cork of one of his $80 bottles of reserve Cabernet Sauvignon.

He cringed, scowled, and then flashed me a watch-the-master look as he grabbed another bottle. As he struggled to open it, *he* broke a cork. So much for the wisdom of experience.

What both of us failed to do—which would have saved both corks (and a goodly amount of scowling) is something I call *choking the lever*. When you use a "waiter's friend"—which is the simple pocketknife-with-a-lever-arm gizmo favored by many pros—you must remember to wrap one hand around the neck of the bottle so your hand covers the lever as the cork comes out. This keeps the lever steady and allows you to pull the cork out with one (relatively) smooth motion.

What makes the waiter's friend my corkscrew of choice is its simplicity and portability, as well as its nifty little blade for cutting the wine's foil wrapper (just don't pack it in your carry-on if you want to keep it). Just be sure to insert the screw (also called a *worm* or *helix*) deep into the cork and then hinge the metal lever on the grooved lip on the bottle before lifting the cork out. The waiter's friend ranges in price from a basic $5 supermarket version to over $100 for a sexy, wood-carved Laguiole from France. I've had great success with the Boomerang model, which has a foil cutter built into its handle and sells for about $7.

A close second in usefulness is the deceptively effective Screwpull, which looks like a big plastic clothespin with a long worm in the center. After clamping

Simple to use, inexpensive, and portable, the waiter's friend is the best style of corkscrew on the market. A basic plastic Screwpull is also very effective.

OUTSMART THE TABLE

- If the cork breaks as you pull it out, the most vital thing to remember is to reinsert the worm fully into the remaining fragment, and to do so at an angle (rather than perpendicularly) to avoid nudging it into the wine. As you extract the fragment, push it against the bottle to ensure that it stays securely on the worm. Don't fret if cork pieces crumble into the wine—you can spoon out larger remnants or strain the wine with a paper coffee filter.

- Whether you remove the foil capsule on a bottle's neck is at your discretion; traditionalists keep it on, but cut off the capsule below the neck's grooved lip to prevent any foil from touching the wine as it pours. You can cut the foil with a small knife or a simple foil cutter sold at most houseware and liquor stores.

- Don't scoff at synthetics: despite their pedestrian appearance, plastic stoppers are increasingly winning over wineries and consumers alike for their ability to eliminate the scourge of cork taint. Though it's too early to declare their effectiveness with ageworthy wine, all signs indicate a vast improvement over using tree bark (i.e., natural cork). Screw tops also appear to be superior closures (Plumpjack's $150 Cabernet Reserve being the paradigmatic example), but it remains to be seen if consumers will warm to the idea of twisting open their favorite *grand crus* as they would a bottle of Mad Dog 20/20.

its two plastic legs around the bottle, you simply twist the handle again and again until the cork magically slides up the worm. There's no pulling or pushing involved. A basic model costs about $20 and comes in several colors. Don't confuse the basic plastic Screwpull with the fancy Screwpull Lever Model and similar devices. Costing anywhere from $80 to twice that amount, these gunlike gizmos clamp on to the bottle top and extract the cork with one quick pull of the lever. While they make an impressive gift, they are truly useful only for those who frequently open large numbers of bottles.

Finally, you've probably seen the two-pronged cork extractor, a big name for a simple little loop handle with two metal blades. The goal here is to insert the blades all the way down the sides of the cork, and then twist the cork up and out. Because it has no worm to bore through the cork, it's useful for extracting fragile old corks that are wedged tightly into the bottle. Perhaps I lack the requisite coordination for this device, but I find it tricky to use—and virtually useless with loose-fitting corks. Although its nickname is "Ah-So" for its supposed ease of use, unless I'm dealing with an old, fragile cork, I give this option an "Ah, No."

Another gadget to avoid is probably already familiar to you: the wing-type corkscrew, named for the two levers on the side of its base. As you turn the worm into the cork, the levers lift up—which is why some French call it a *de Gaulle*, after the former French president who liked to end his speeches with arms raised high. The fatal flaw of this corkscrew, however, is that its worm is usually too small and thick, making the device cumbersome and prone to break corks.

On My Table | **STEPHEN MUTKOSKI** is a professor of hotel administration and the creator of Cornell University's renowned "Intro to Wine" course, which attracts more than eight hundred students each semester.

Riesling
Finger Lakes, New York: Hermann Wiemer; Mosel-Saar-Ruwer: Carl von Schubert, Selbach-Oster, Dr. Loosen.

Red Burgundy
Daniel Rion, Méo-Camuzet, Bruno Claire, Sylvain Cathiard, Nicolas Potel

Pinot Noir from California
Au Bon Climat, Talley, Wild Horse, Ramsay

Red Bordeaux—"I look for the values in the fourth and fifth growths like Talbot, Camensac, Lynch-Bages, Cantemerle, and also in the *cru bourgeois* category."

Various wines from Italy—"Probably every third bottle of wine I open is one from Italy."
Ceretto, Mastroberardino, Castello Banfi, Aldo Conterno, Castello di Volpaia, Masi, Zenato

Champagne and other bubbly
Laurent-Perrier, Pol Roger, Moët & Chandon—"When friends are visiting"—otherwise, Prosecco, Crémant, or a local Finger Lakes sparkler

Sauvignon Blanc from New Zealand
Glazebrook, Giesen, Kim Crawford

Port—"To sip by the fireplace."
Fonseca, Dow's, Sandeman

82 Serving Wine: Quantities, Order, and the Unexpected

The Quantities

"WHEN YOU ASK A FRIEND TO DINE, GIVE HIM YOUR BEST WINE! WHEN YOU ASK TWO, THE SECOND BEST WILL DO!"

—Henry Wadsworth Longfellow, nineteenth-century poet

½: As full as your glass should be, so that you have plenty of room to swirl your wine.

1: The number of bottles you should plan per guest during a full evening of entertaining, unless the majority of the guests will not be drinking. Running out of wine is *the* cardinal sin of entertaining. If other types of alcohol are available, you can reduce the quantity of wine accordingly.

5: The approximate number of servings in every standard-size (750ml) bottle of wine.

100: The approximate number of calories in a 5-ounce glass of wine, with reds having a few more calories than whites. Richer, more alcoholic dessert wine can have 150 calories or more per glass.

The Order

When more than one wine type is involved, it's best to go from a wine of lower intensity to one with more power, as we don't want the lingering effects of a big wine to overpower the impression of a delicate one served subsequently. So, serving order is generally:

COLOR: White ──→ red
before

WEIGHT: Light ──→ heavy
before

FLAVOR: Dry ──→ sweet
before

The Unexpected

MOLD Mold that is visible when you remove a wine's foil capsule is not cause for consternation. It is a natural by-product of storing the wine in humid conditions and will not affect the wine adversely. Simply wipe it off and remove the cork as normal.

CRYSTALS The purple or white crystals on the bottom of the cork or floating as a cluster in the wine are benign. They are simply a crystalline deposit of tartaric acid (like the cream of tartar used in cooking), which can form when a wine has been stored at an unusually cold temperature or when the wine leaves the winery without sufficient cold stabilization, a process that removes excess tartaric acid.

83 You Can Serve Some Reds Quite Chilled: The Cross-Dressers

The waiter screwed up," said my know-it-all friend after receiving his very chilled glass of Beaujolais. "Red wine isn't supposed to be chilled."

What my friend didn't know is that some reds tend to taste better when served quite chilled.

To be sure, few people like their red wines served glacially cold; low temperatures can harshen the perception of tannin, making a rich, tannic red taste even more gum-numbingly astringent. Think of what happens to extra-strong tea, which contains ample tannin, when you put it on ice: it gets bitter. Drinking a red wine ice cold will also inhibit its flavors, making its fruit seem, in wine parlance, "closed down" or "tight." In contrast, whites are more fridge friendly because they aren't tannic and often have simpler flavors. So while a well-chilled white such as Riesling or Pinot Grigio will taste crisp and refreshing, a cold Cabernet or Shiraz can show an excess of tannic bitterness and muted flavor. (Of course, serving a white ice cold can also numb its flavors—something to avoid when drinking a fine white whose nuances you seek to appreciate.)

What surprises many people, however, is that most reds can benefit from a slight chill; as the next chapter explains, a bit of coolness—three to five minutes in an ice bucket or fifteen minutes in a refrigerator—can focus a red wine's flavors and reduce the perception of its alcohol. In fact, a subset of reds benefits from an even chillier reception—at least ten minutes in an ice bucket or up to an hour in the refrigerator. The classic case is Beaujolais, the light, berry-fruit, feel-good elixir from France. Nothing is more refreshing than knocking back a few glasses of well-chilled Beaujolais-Villages at a picnic or barbecue.

Other red wine types benefit from extra chilling if you happen to have a lighter-style version. A light-style Pinot Noir, for example, has the delicate berry essences and low tannin that welcome a nice amount of chilling. But you might not want to inject as much chill into a fuller-style Pinot Noir, such as a *grand cru* Pommard from Burgundy, whose noticeable tannins and acidity might become too pronounced with extra chilling. Similarly, while a light-bodied Rioja Crianza can take a nice chill, you might want to go easier on the more hefty and powerful Rioja Reserva or Gran Reserva. While price is often an indicator, it is not always obvious if a particular wine is a lighter or heavier style; when in doubt, query your server or wine merchant.

The common theme among all very chillable reds is they are light bodied, have low or no tannins, and aren't so nuanced or expensive that you have to worry about masking their flavors. Think of them as the wine equivalent of cross-dressers: light and fresh, they are white wines masquerading as reds.

CHEAT SHEET
While it's ultimately up to your personal taste, the reds I call the *very chillable cross-dressers* can benefit from at least ten minutes in an ice bucket or an hour in the refrigerator.

Very Chillable Cross-Dressers

Beaujolais Nouveau and Beaujolais-Villages

Light versions of the following:

Dolcetto and Barbera
Cru Beaujolais
Pinot Noir
Chianti
Rioja Crianza
Chinon

84 Drink Whites a Bit Warmer, Reds a Bit Cooler

How about a nice glass of warm Coke? A cup of lukewarm tea? And may I bring you a nicely chilled bowl of *soupe à l'oignon gratinée*?

More than we even realize, a liquid's temperature plays a critical role in its smell and taste—and whether we end up liking it. This explains why some wine folks obsess over the serving temperature of wine, viewing a wine's temperature like a socialite appraising the lighting inside her favorite lunch spot—careful modulation is needed to ensure optimal appearances.

The good news is that unless you're a wine pro, there's no need to give this subject too much thought. Your personal tastes should ultimately determine how you drink wine; if all white wine tastes better to you ice cold, so be it. But you might want to know that many wine aficionados feel that white wine often tastes better a little warmer and red wine a shade cooler.

Most of us are used to drinking white wine as we would a Heineken—pull it from the refrigerator, fumble it open, and drink up. When a simple quaffer like Pinot Grigio is involved, this is the ideal way to do it, especially in the broil of summer, lazing about a picnic table or swimming pool. But when you are drinking a finer white—say a pricey California Chardonnay or French Condrieu—in a setting where you really want to appreciate its subtleties, you might allow a cold white to warm up for fifteen minutes or so before serving. As eating a frozen banana or candy bar demonstrates, coldness numbs our perception of flavor. A slightly warmer temperature therefore unleashes a fine white wine's aromas and flavors. It also subdues the wine's acidity, which is less noticeable at warmer temperatures.

When it comes to red wine, most of us keep it on a rack and drink it at room temperature. Because coldness will make a tannic wine like Cabernet Sauvignon taste even more bitter, it is indeed wise not to want to make your red wine ice cold. Instead of coldness, however, sometimes a red wine benefits

"FIGHT BACK WITH ALL YOUR STRENGTH AND COURAGE AGAINST AMERICAN SOMMELIERS WHO INSIST ON SERVING WHITE WINE HOT."

—*Alan Richman, wine and food writer, on the tendency of some wine pros to take this chapter's lesson too far*

from a bit of *coolness*. This is because a warm red sometimes has the scent and taste of alcohol—called "hot," as we've learned previously—and a slight chill tends to make this coarse alcoholic sensation less noticeable.

A bit of chilling also tends to "focus" a red wine—that is, it delineates the aromas and flavors of the wine, allowing you to appreciate the subtleties and balance that get diminished at the 68 to 72 degrees most people keep their homes. This chillier temperature is consistent with how wine was traditionally meant to be drunk, where, in the drafty manor houses of nineteenth-century Europe, room temperature was more like 60 degrees. Therefore, many reds benefit from fifteen minutes in a refrigerator or three to five minutes in an ice bucket—just long enough to give the wine some focus without accentuating its tannins. If you're enjoying a particularly light and tannin-free red such as Beaujolais or light-style Pinot Noir—the kind I deem a very chillable cross-dresser (see Shortcut 83)—you can chill it for an hour or more in the refrigerator or for at least ten minutes in an ice bucket.

Treat Champagne and other bubbly like simple whites and serve them cold. Not only does the cold help retain bubbles upon opening, but many people find that the bubbly texture of sparkling wine shows best under cold conditions. Some like bubbly a bit warmer to accentuate its aromas and flavors, particularly for a high-end or mature bottling known for its complexity. Coldness also suits most types of dessert wine because it emphasizes the wine's acidity, which is the essential counterbalance to a dessert wine's sweetness. Like a fine bottle of white or bubbly, lighter-bodied dessert wines of great complexity, such as a fine Sauternes, are sometimes more interesting when removed from the refrigerator fifteen minutes before serving. Dark, heavy dessert wines—vintage and ruby port being the prime examples—should be treated as heavy reds—give them only a slight chill to focus their flavors.

CHEAT SHEET

Fifteen minutes before serving, try removing your fine whites from the refrigerator and inserting your reds. Your whites will gain nuance in aroma and flavor, with less pronounced acidity, while your reds will seem more focused and less overtly alcoholic.

OUTSMART THE TABLE

At restaurants, don't hesitate to ask your server to forgo an ice bucket for your whites and employ a few minutes of bucket time for your reds. Be sure your server keeps your bubbly cold in a Champagne bucket throughout the meal.

Serving Temperature Chart

Use this as a starting point, then adjust to your own taste.

Whites	DESIRED TEMPERATURE	FRIDGE TIME	OR	ICE BUCKET TIME
Simple, "picnic" whites	fully chilled (fridge temp)	2 hrs.		20 mins.
Fine whites	a bit warmer (than fridge temp)	defridge 15 mins. before serving		
Reds				
Most reds	a bit cooler (than room temp)	15 mins.		3 to 5 mins.
Cross-dressers (i.e., very light reds)	much cooler (than room temp)	1 hr.		10 mins.
Other				
Bubbly	fully chilled (fridge temp)	2 hrs.		20 mins.
Rosé/blush	fully chilled (fridge temp)	2 hrs.		20 mins.
Most dessert wine (not port)	fully chilled (fridge temp)	2 hrs.		20 mins.

85 Chill Wine with a Bucket, Ice, and—Don't Forget!—Cold Water

Unlike *Snickers* bars, wine isn't better frozen.

This I learned the hard way, repeatedly, after rushing to chill a bottle of wine by sticking it in the freezer. Without fail, "freezer amnesia" soon sets in, and an hour later I'd discover my now cryogenic bottle biding its time alongside my year-old Häagen-Dazs container and other neglected artifacts.

If you can remember to rescue your wine in time, then twenty minutes in the freezer will get a bottle sufficiently cold, perhaps too much so if you like your wine only moderately chilled. To avoid any chance of freezer burn, you can always just stick the bottle in the refrigerator, which usually takes at least two hours to instill a complete chill.

The surest method of cooling down your wine, however, doesn't involve electrical appliances of any kind. Just take an ice bucket, the deeper the better, fill it about two-thirds full with ice, and insert the bottle well into the ice. But don't forget this extra, often-overlooked step: pour a good amount of cold water into the bucket. The water fills the air pockets between the ice and cools the wine faster.

To fully chill a bottle of white, bubbly, or dessert wine, allow about twenty minutes in the bucket—though you might give a fine white wine less time, to avoid numbing its precious flavors. A light, quaffable red like Beaujolais can benefit from about ten minutes in an ice bucket, and heartier reds can taste more focused and less "hot" with up to five minutes of chill time.

CHEAT SHEET

Don't forget to add cold water to your ice bucket—the best way to chill wine.

OUTSMART THE TABLE

If your ice bucket is not deep enough to immerse the bottle completely, chill the bottle neck-first for ten minutes, then flip it over and cool the bottom.

On My Table | **NEIL DEGRASSE TYSON**, the youngest-ever director of New York's Hayden Planetarium, is an avid wine collector and a monthly essayist for *Natural History* magazine and has received the singular honor of being named "sexiest astrophysicist alive" by *People* magazine.

Rioja

Southern Rhône—Côtes-du-Rhône

Zinfandel—"Big alcoholic ones from California's Amador County. Even the bad ones are interesting."

Chardonnnay
Talbott, Kistler, Kendall-Jackson—"Very consistent year to year."

Conundrum from Caymus Vineyards [an unusual white that blends Chardonnay, Sauvignon Blanc, Sémillon, Viognier, and Muscat]—"It has everything I get in expensive white Bordeaux, but it has a touch of American sweetness to it—so I match it with Thai food."

White Bordeaux

Sauternes—"It's almost hard to find a bad one."

Red Bordeaux
Château Haut-Marbuzet

Port—"[Fonseca's] Bin 27 comes through for me every time at only about $12 a bottle."

86 Decant Wine to Soften a Youngster or Clean an Elder

In the wine world, decanting is a bit like taking vitamins: some swear by it, others do it on special occasions, and a third group deems it a waste of time. I'm here to tell you that decanting—pouring wine from its bottle into another container, typically a large glass carafe, or decanter—is useful in three situations.

First, decanting can soften a young red wine with bitter tannins, such as gum-puckering Italian Barolo or Cabernet Sauvignon. Many people find that an astringent red can become less bitter, and sometimes more aromatic and flavorful, with an hour or more of exposure to air. Think of decanting for aeration like an NHL penalty box: after sitting out for a period of time, the wine will behave better.

Such aeration—or "breathing"—is best accomplished where the largest possible surface area of wine comes in contact with the air. That's why pouring the wine into a large glass decanter, or oversized wine glasses, is far preferable to simply uncorking a bottle, which doesn't allow enough air through its thin neck.

To accelerate the aeration process, some people like to use two decanters, pouring the wine back and forth between the vessels for a few minutes. While this will do even more to soften a red wine's tannic edges, no amount of effort will transform a tannic brute into a gentle, velvety prince.

The second situation that calls for decanting is when you want to remove sediment from red wine. After about ten years or more of bottle age, deeply colored, brawny types of red wine—Cabernet Sauvignon, Hermitage, Barolo, vintage port—tend to "throw sediment"—that is, their color pigments and tannins solidify and appear in the wine as clumpy deposits. While this gunk is perfectly harmless, most people find it about as texturally pleasant as sandy spinach, so the goal is to separate it from the wine. To decant for sediment, you need only:

The act of decanting—pouring wine
from its bottle into a large carafe—is
useful to soften a young, tannic red;
to remove the sediment of an older,
ageable red; or, if you're so inclined,
as a courtly way to build anticipation
before drinking.

OUTSMART THE TABLE

To enjoy the last drops of a bottle of
wine decanted for sediment, pour the
last half inch or so through a coffee
filter.

MARK'S PICKS

Decanters come in a spectrum of
shapes, sizes, and prices; many have
a traditional carafe or laboratory-
beaker shape, while others have
curves evocative of ducks, balloons,
and diamonds. Decanters.com provides
a handy overview of major decanter
types. Here are three excellent brands:

Riedel: Famous for its assortment of
top-of-the-line crystal decanters, most
priced between $100 and $300.

Spiegelau: Like its glasses, Spiegelau
offers near-Riedel-like quality at a
fraction of the price, with many
decanters less than $50.

Ravenscroft: Another excellent value
in decanters—sturdily made, interesting shapes in the $30-to-$50 range.
(I've enjoyed my Ravenscroft Excalibur
decanter, a large, elegant $40
showstopper with a swanlike neck.)

1. Stand a bottle up, preferably for a day or more, so that the sediment settles to the bottom.

2. Get yourself a decanter, typically a large glass or crystal flask, but it can be any clean container suitable for liquids. In a pinch, I've used a flower vase and an empty water jug. See Mark's Picks for decanter recommendations.

3. Find a light source, such as a small flashlight or a candle. Open the bottle, then pour your wine slowly and continuously into the decanter. Do this over (or slightly in front of) the light source, so that it illuminates the neck of the bottle, giving you a clear view of the wine flow.

4. Stop pouring when you see the sediment enter the neck of the bottle.

Take extra care in decanting for the sediment of a fragile wine. The lighter the variety and the older the wine, the more you run the risk of stripping the wine of its delicate aromas and flavors. Whereas a dark, brawny, tannic Barolo with ten years of bottle age may not be in much danger of losing its charm after decanting, a faded-out, delicately perfumed red Burgundy of the same age may already be knocking on death's door. Like a sunset, its glory may last only a few minutes in the open air. You should thus be prepared to start drinking a fragile wine soon after it is decanted, or ditch the decanter and live with the gunk.

The final case for decanting is more about enhancing your experience than about improving the wine. When times call for "turning the knob to 11," in the parlance of *This Is Spinal Tap*, your decanter might just do the trick. In this age that spurns handwritten notes and homemade cuisine, there's nothing like a bit of Old World ritual to make a celebration or seduction even more special. You fetch the decanter. Maybe you also light a candle. You pour the wine ever so slowly, admiring its glimmering greatness. Your guests look on with appreciation and awe, impressed with your old-fashioned *savoir faire.* You pour the wine, and it tastes even better because you built the anticipation with what can be called, if you will, a kind of gastronomic foreplay.

Often Decanted for Sediment When Mature

Fine types of . . .

California Cabernet
Red Bordeaux
Barolo and Barbaresco
Brunello and Super Tuscans
Northern Rhône (Hermitage, Côte Rôtie)
Vintage port

87 Use Wine Glasses Like Forrest Gump: Thin, Big, and Simple

There are literally thousands of kinds of wine glasses on the market, but to choose well, you need only remember Forrest Gump: thin, big, and simple.

Thin: While there's nothing technically wrong with drinking from a thick glass, most people prefer a glass that has a thin rim, or lip. A thin lip focuses your attention where it should be: on the wine, not the glass. I once taught at a restaurant that used only stubby, thick-lipped glasses. They made you feel as if you were sipping from Fred Flintstone's mug—or drinking more glass than wine.

Big: To better your chances of swirling without spilling, use wine glasses that are at least 12 ounces and have a wide bowl to collect the wine's vapors. Exactly how large you go is a matter of personal preference, though some find that glasses pushing 24 ounces are cumbersome.

Simple: Your glassware should be simple on several fronts. It should have a simple design, with no gratuitous etchings or colors that will prevent seeing the wine clearly. You should also strive for simplicity with regard to variety; for most people, one all-purpose glass is enough. Some glass makers sell differently shaped glasses for different wine types—one size for red Bordeaux, another for red Burgundy, for example—but I haven't found that these variations make a dramatic difference in how the wine tastes. The one exception is Champagne, which is best in a thin, flute-shaped glass to prolong the life of its bubbles. Finally, because it's so easy to break wine glasses, especially during a long night of wine revelry, it's wise to do most of your imbibing in glasses that are simply priced.

WHAT TO BUY The casual wine enthusiast won't go wrong with a few sets of simple, roomy wine glasses purchased at a home goods store like Bed

Bath & Beyond, Williams-Sonoma, or Crate & Barrel. Crate & Barrel's 18-ounce Nora Goblet and 22-ounce Elite Chardonnay glass have both proven trusty, all-purpose companions throughout the years, and at about $6 to $9 a glass, ones that are painlessly replaceable.

While I recommend doing your everyday drinking in low-cost glassware, you may want to consider keeping a set of expensive glassware on hand for special occasions. Austrian-based Riedel Crystal, long the gold standard in stemware, offers several quality levels of glasses (the more expensive being handmade and comprised of finer grades of crystal) and a multiplicity of shapes within those categories. There is virtually unanimous agreement among my wine-passionate friends that Riedel's machine-blown Vinum series is the perfect choice, providing Riedel's legendary quality at a price far less than the company's expensive, handcrafted Sommelier series.

While there's seemingly a different Vinum glass shape for every day of the year, I've been very satisfied with just the 13-ounce Riedel Vinum Chianti Classico/Zinfandel glass ($90 to $120 for a set of six), which, despite its name, works beautifully for both red and white wine. If you desire a larger glass, the Riedel Vinum Bordeaux glass ($100 to $150 for a set of six) is a fine choice, its large, less-tapered bowl holding a generous 21.5 ounces of wine.

More affordable alternatives to Riedel are the German-made Spiegelau glasses, which provide a similarly high standard of quality at a better price.

If you do invest in high-end glasses, be sure to avoid washing them in your dishwasher, where they are more likely to be scratched, break, or suffer a flavor-marring coating of detergent.

CHEAT SHEET

The best wine glasses are large, thin, undecorated, and, for most situations, inexpensive.

TALK THE TALK

Riedel   *REE-dill*
Spiegelau   *Spee-gill-LAU*

MARK'S PICKS

Under $10/glass: Riedel Overture series, Spiegelau Authentis series, Stoelzle-Oberglas Vinea series, various entry-level offerings at home-goods stores.
$10 to $30/glass: Riedel's midranged Vinum series, Spiegelau Vino Grand series.
Over $35/glass: Riedel Sommelier series.

On My Table | **WADE WOLFE** is the general manager of Hogue Cellars, one of Washington State's largest wineries and a beacon for the price-conscious.

Zinfandel and other red wines from California's Amador and El Dorado counties (e.g., Granite Springs, Sierra Vista Winery, Madrona, Latcham Vineyards)

Rosé
   Sangiovese rosé, Eberle Syrah rosé

Dry whites from the Pacific Northwest
   Washington State: Hogue Cellars, Barnard Griffin Winery, Washington Hills Cellars, Thurston Wolfe Winery. Oregon: Adelsheim, Duck Pond Cellars, Eola Hills Wine Cellars, King Estate, Rex Hill Vineyards.

Cabernet Sauvignon (including blends)
   DeLille Cellars, Bookwalter Winery, Chateau Ste. Michelle, Barnard Griffin Winery, Kiona Vineyards Winery, Quilceda Creek Vintners, Wineglass Cellars, Woodward Canyon Winery, especially Nelms Road label

Sparkling wine from California
   Domaine Chandon, Roederer Estate

88 Use a "Towel and Twist" to Puff—Not Pop—Open a Bottle of Bubbly

What is it about opening a bottle of bubbly that channels the savage beast? Some see a minihowitzer in every Champagne bottle, forever aiming its cork at the nearest chandelier. Others want to shake and spray their bottles as if they have a weepy George Steinbrenner in their midst. Still others like to play Sunday samurai and behead their Champagne bottles with a large knife, an ancient custom the French call *sabrer la bouteille.* And what of all those boat christeners—Ted Knight's wife in *Caddyshack* being the most memorable—who beat their bottles across a boat's bow, saying "I christen thee . . ."

It's time to mute the mayhem and open bubbly with the safety and style that this supernal beverage deserves.

1. **Chill:** Chill the bottle until ice cold, as coldness minimizes the pressure in the bottle.

2. **Protect:** You never know when a cork may fly before its time, so always point the bottle in a safe direction and keep a thumb over the cork during the entire opening process.

3. **Strip:** Peel the foil and unwrap the wire cage covering the cork, sliding it off with your thumb still at the ready.

4. **Cover:** If a towel or cloth napkin is available, slip it over the bottle's neck. The towel will help you grip the cork and catch it in the event of a premature eruption.

5. **Turn:** Holding the bottle at a slight angle, grip the cork firmly through the towel. Then, with your other hand, turn the base of the bottle slowly

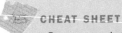
in one direction. As they turn the bottle, some people like to turn the cork in the opposite direction. This also works, but I find that turning just the bottle, not the cork, helps you keep the firmest grip on the cork.

6. **Puff:** Your cork will "puff" open, saving you bubbles and a midnight visit to the emergency room.

On My Table | **MIREILLE GUILIANO** is president of Clicquot, Inc., the New York–based marketing arm of Veuve Clicquot.

Champagne
Veuve Clicquot, Roederer, Krug, Paul Bara, Egly-Ouriet [the last two are small-production "grower" Champagnes]

Red Burgundy—"The best are all silk and velvet."
Comte Georges de Vogüé, Bouchard Père et Fils, Lafon, Dujac, Arnoux, Roumier, Domaine de la Romanée-Conti

White Burgundy—Meursault, Puligny-Montrachet, Chassagne-Montrachet, Chablis
Coche-Dury, Bouchard Père et Fils, William Fèvre

Rhône—north and south
Jaboulet, Chapoutier, Guigal, La Nerthe, Tardieu-Laurent

Red Bordeaux—Pomerol and St.-Emilion
Trotanoy, L'Evangile, Bon Pasteur, Cheval Blanc

Sauvignon Blanc from New Zealand
Cloudy Bay

Merlot from California
Duckhorn, Newton unfiltered

Storage and
Vintage

The *mythology* of the wine cellar looms large in the popular imagination. What other beverage merits its own room in people's houses? We now tackle the often misunderstood subject of wine storage and when and why you'd even want to "lay down" wine for a period of time. But first we cover a topic for anyone who has ever winced at pouring leftover wine down a drain: how to lengthen the life of opened wine. ∎

89 Leftover Wines Are Like Houseguests: Most Lose Their Charm After a Day or So

Having a friend spend the night in your home can make for a cozy and convivial evening. But for most of us there's only so long you can share your dental floss or aerate the Aerobed. Before long, the good feelings fade and your guest is about as welcome as cracker crumbs in a newly made bed.

So it is with opened wine. While oxygen starts working its mischief on wine the moment the cork comes out, you probably won't notice a major decline during the day you open it. A tannic, astringent red wine, in fact, may actually "breathe" or improve in the first hours of air exposure, losing a bit of its bitterness. The general rule for opened wines, provided they are recorked and refrigerated, is that they will taste almost as good as new up to a day, perhaps two, after being opened. A very simple wine—such as that $6.99 Chardonnay from your local 7-Eleven—may even taste acceptable up to a week after its debut. The less complexity a wine has at the start, the less there is for time to steal.

How can you tell if an opened bottle of wine has worn out its welcome? You'll wonder who eighty-sixed the tongue-teasing tingle in your Sauvignon Blanc, what happened to the berry perfume in your Pinot Noir, or why your once fruity Chardonnay now tastes mostly like wood. Fear not: wine doesn't go bad in the way six-day-old chicken chow mein devolves into a digestive war zone; drinking it won't earn you a prayer session at the porcelain altar. Instead, opened wine becomes dull and one-dimensional, "flat" in winespeak, because it loses its unique aromas and flavors.

Exactly how long a wine will stay fresh depends on its particular grape type(s) and style and, of course, your own taste. Wines with high levels of acidity, Sauvignon Blanc and Alsatian Riesling for example, tend to keep it together a little longer. As one would expect, sweet wines with high alcohol content are also longer-lived; port and sherry, for example, being fortified with brandy, are hardier and sometimes able to survive a week or more.

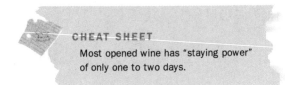
If you're serious about prolonging the life of an open bottle, consider some of the techniques and gadgets described in the next chapter. Just remember that it's better—gastronomically and karmically—to drink all of your wine the day you open it, hangovers notwithstanding. If necessary, use any leftovers as an excuse to fire up an impromptu sangria soirée or *coq au vin* cookoff!

On My Table | **DOMINIC SYMINGTON** is one of the key figures in port production, overseeing his family's portfolio of renowned port companies, including the likes of Dow's and Warre's.

Red Bordeaux
Mouton-Rothschild, Lynch-Bages, Beychevelle, Ducru-Beaucaillou, Pontet-Canet

Northern Rhône
Jaboulet, Guigal, Chapoutier

Champagne
Pol Roger, Laurent-Perrier

Portuguese red wines
Chryseia in conjunction with Bruno Prats and Quinta de Roriz by my family and João van Zeller; also Quinta do Vale Meão, Quinta do Crasto, Herdade do Esporão Alentejo Reserva—"Reminiscent of the Rhône style—spicy, warm, and with great aging potential."

Late-harvest dessert wines and ice wine
Sauternes: Rieussec, Alsace Vendange Tardive, Egon Müller Riesling Eisewein Scharzhofberger—"My mouth waters even thinking about the 1983."

Vintage port

Aged tawny port
"If I had to be stranded on a desert island, I would try to make sure I had a pipe [port barrel] of tawny port . . . sublime, nutty, with a hint of caramel and orange peel flavors."

90 Lengthening the Life of Leftover Wine

admit it: I own a pump that few people know about. (No, it's not a "girth grower" hawked in the back of gentlemen's magazines, although if I did, I'd probably keep that a secret too.) The pump I have is the Vacuvin, an inexpensive plastic pump that fits atop a specially made rubber stopper that you insert into an opened wine bottle. Pump the lever several times, and it creates a partial vacuum in the bottle. (While Vacuvin is the best-known pump, other companies make similar devices, such as the Rabbit Lever Vacuum Pump.)

Does this rigmarole really extend the life of opened wine? The answer is yes . . . but. In my experience, vacuum pumps can add at least an extra day or two of drinkability to opened wine, but they aren't going to make a dramatic difference or resurrect a wine from the Underworld of Oxidized Wine. The mere act of uncorking a bottle introduces enough oxygen into the wine that a wine begins to lose its freshness from the moment it parts with its cork. Still, I always keep my pump and a few plastic stoppers on hand to give any leftover wine a brief reprieve from its inevitable decline. Be sure to pump up as soon as possible after you open the bottle.

If gadgets aren't your thing, there are simpler ways of prolonging the life of your wine. One is to do what you probably do already: quickly recork the wine and store it in the refrigerator. The trick is to refrigerate red wines too, which may seem peculiar, since most red wines don't normally see time in the icebox. Remember to allot about an hour to bring the wine up in temperature; less if you pour the cold wine directly into glasses. But it's worth it: as any mortician or cryogenicist can confirm, cold temperatures slow down biological deterioration of all kinds. Be sure to refrigerate any bottles you stopper and pump too.

Another technique is to pour leftover wine into half bottles, recork, and refrigerate. Wine tends to last a little longer in smaller bottles because there's less oxygen between the top of the wine and the cork. You can purchase small bottles at houseware stores, or you can save the bottles and corks from half

CHEAT SHEET

Always recork and refrigerate leftover wine; use pumps to eke out a few extra days of life.

OUTSMART THE TABLE

To quickly bring a refrigerated red back to drinking temperature, soak the bottle in a bucket of warm water (70°F) for about ten minutes.

MARK'S PICKS

Vacuum pumps (e.g., Vacuvin Wine Saver—about $10 for a basic model); extra vacuum stoppers (about $4); metal Champagne stopper (about $8).

bottles you consume. At the risk of profaning wine's aristocratic mystique, you can even use that plastic Evian water bottle you bought at the gym—just scrub it down, screw the top tightly, and hide it if company unexpectedly drops by.

Finally, if you are reckless enough ever to have any leftover Champagne, be advised that there are stoppers made specifically for sparkling wine. Available at most wine shops and houseware stores, Champagne stoppers typically have a clam shell shape and metal arms that clamp snugly atop a Champagne bottle. These devices will increase your bubbly's staying power by at least a day or two.

91 Don't Sweat Storage Under Six Months

After the fifth or so nasty bottle, my family started doubting the intentions of my dad's friends.

Every year various friends would give him a few bottles of wine as Christmas gifts, which he would promptly store in the basement of our New Jersey home—thinking, like most people, that a wine's proper place was in a "cellar." When my parents went to drink those bottles a year or two later, the wine was, almost without fail, redolent of something you'd pour on a salad.

"Some friends you have, Dad! Nothing but the *best* for you!"

In truth, however, his friends' malevolence wasn't to blame but our marginally insulated basement and the seasonal extremes of New Jersey. Unbeknown to us at the time, the temperature shift between frigid Jersey winters and sweltering summers would expand and contract the wines' corks, allowing oxygen to seep in and oxidize the wine. And if that didn't ruin the wine, the dog days of August would surely cook the flavor out of it.

These two pitfalls—temperature fluctuations and sustained high heat—are all you have to worry about for the vast majority of wine. Some people get hung up on things like precise temperature and humidity levels—but those concerns are only for the tiny elite of wines meriting long-term storage, as covered in the next chapter. Because most wine doesn't improve with age and gets drunk within a few months, you need only protect it from yo-yoing between temperature extremes or from weeks of excessive heat (which begins at about 72°F, the point where chemical reactions really start to roll).

What this means is that, contrary to popular thinking, wine that you want to store for near-term consumption won't "go bad" if it stays in the typical home environment of 68°F to 72°F. The wine may mature faster in this relatively warm air, and may thus lose a bit of fruitiness after several months or a year, but this degradation won't be noticeable in the wines meant for short-term consumption. In fact, the scores of everyday bottles I've kept in a cool, dark cupboard of my apartment always taste fine even after a year or two.

Speaking of cupboards, you'll maximize the chance of avoiding fluctuations and excessive heat by opting for storage conditions that are cool, dark,

OUTSMART THE TABLE

In general, rich, tannic red wine can endure harsher conditions than lighter reds, whites, and sparkling wine.

and flat. This means storing wine in a closet, under the bed, in an insulated basement, or even in an unused fireplace—anywhere it is steadily cool and dark. Avoid proximity to heaters, ovens, refrigerator vents, ultraviolet light, or sunlight—anywhere light or heat can push the temperature into the hot zone. Even though they are cool and dark, refrigerators are not a good place to keep unopened wine for more than a week. The frigid temperature tends to flatten the taste of the wine, and the dry air eventually dries out the cork. Moreover, the motor of the refrigerator imposes harmful vibrations.

It's also always a good idea to store your wine horizontally, as most wine racks do, ensuring that the cork stays in contact with wine and avoids drying out and eventually letting air in. You should also keep your wine from pungent odors such as stored food or household chemicals (which can slowly infiltrate the wine) and sustained vibrations (which, like direct light or heat, can prematurely oxidize the wine).

92 When Storing Ageworthy Wine Over Six Months, Cellar It at 55°F

I *recently* toured the famous wine cellar of New York's '21' Club restaurant to see how its wine cellar compares to my own. The results:

'21' CLUB Seventeen thousand bottles stored in an underground, three-chambered Prohibition-era vault outfitted with a secret entrance.

MARK A couple of cases of collectible wine housed in one guitar-amp-sized storage unit emitting a slight electric "buzz."

Okay, maybe '21' has me beat—but the point is that not everyone needs a subterranean vault to store ageworthy wine.

As we've already learned, most of the wine we buy doesn't get better with age and will be no worse for the wear being stored for the short term in a cool, dark corner of your home. But collectible wine—the finest red Bordeaux, California Cabernet, and other rare specimens mentioned in the next chapter—will need special handling if you plan to store it for longer than about six months. This is because we want ageable wine to mature slowly, gradually achieving complexity and fine texture like a beautiful patina on old silver. Wine kept at steady room temperature won't necessarily die a sudden death, but without temperature control, it will mature too quickly and be denied the finer nuances that slowly aged wine can achieve.

Centuries of experience have shown that the optimal temperature for aging wine is around 55°F—cool enough to prevent premature aging but not so cold that it retards a wine's maturation. Long-term storage also requires a sufficient amount of humidity, which keeps corks from drying out, preventing oxidization and evaporation.

The following are three major ways you can achieve temperature and humidity control needed for the long-term storage of ageable wine:

WINE STORAGE UNITS These are the plug-in, stand-alone coolers that vary in appearance from simple, Ramada Inn–style minifridges to under-the-counter wine grottos to oak-paneled armoires with stained-glass doors. They differ mechanically from a standard refrigerator in that they keep wine at "cellar temperature" (52°F to 58°F), at ideal humidity (at least 70 percent), and with a minimum of vibration.

Having owned three such units, I think they are a good option for those living with limited space or likely to move residences every few years or who have second homes. The downsides are that they occupy a lot of room, run up your electric bill, and—most frustratingly—never seem to hold enough bottles once you have the collector's itch. Wine magazines and wine accessory catalogs are filled with ads for wine coolers of various sizes and styles, ranging from $500 for a simple fifty-bottle unit to several thousand dollars for an impress-the-in-laws cabinet holding several hundred bottles. Top brands include Vinothèque, Marvel, and Eurocave. Be wary of the wine fridges found at home supply stores; they often lack the requisite humidity control needed for long-term storage.

CUSTOM CELLARS If you have room to spare and a collection topping about a thousand bottles (or plan to have one), consider creating your own cellar. Some collectors adapt a walk-in closet or a room in their basement, while others build such an enclosure from scratch. Either way, the room has to be well insulated and, unless it naturally varies between about 52°F and 58°F, it will require a temperature and humidity control unit. You will also need to outfit it with proper racking, a hygrometer (which measures humidity as well as temperature), and, if there's room, perhaps a small table at which you can bask in the glow of your liquid assets and whisper to yourself, "I *am* the master of my own domain." Your favorite wine merchant can refer you to various consultants and builders available to assist in cellar design and construction.

REFRIGERATED WAREHOUSES A final option for those with large collections is professional wine storage. Many cities have temperature-controlled warehouses where you pay to store your wine on an annual or monthly basis. Rates vary with the city and amount of wine being stored; one major New York warehouse charges $750 per year for a locker that holds 54 wooden cases (i.e., 648 normal-sized bottles). The disadvantage of wine lockers is, of course, the inconvenience of having your wine off-site. But, as one friend pointed out, such inaccessibility carries the benefit of at least partially concealing a growing wine obsession from one's spouse.

93 Precious Little Wine Improves with Age

In my first year of law school, a group of wine-loving classmates invited me to a special wine dinner in which each of eight guests was to contribute a mature bottle to the elaborate meal the hosts cooked. No problem, I thought. I'll take along one of the bottles of 1970 Gruaud-Larose I had picked up at my first wine auction a few years before.

When I arrived, everyone was duly impressed with this magnificent old bottle and the small "Acquired at Sotheby's" brag-tag affixed to its back. But when we opened and poured it, it had the appearance of volcanic mud and the fragrance of well-worn wrestling shoes.

"We'll keep it on the table in a decanter; perhaps it will improve," the hosts offered graciously as they poured the other guests' wines. The rest of the night my wine adorned the table like a beaker of brown venom—a sad reminder of what could have been.

Embarrassed at the time, I now chalk up this oxidized bottle (happily, the only one of the case) to the exciting unpredictability of old wine—you never know exactly how such wine will evolve, even if it has been stored with care.

This uncertainty begs the question of what even constitutes ageable wine. Despite the common conception that aging is a good thing for any wine, only about 2 percent of the world's wine becomes more pleasurable and interesting with bottle years—most of it red wine. The wines comprising this minuscule group of ageable reds have one commonality: noticeable levels of tannin that gradually diminish over the years, leaving a greater range of aromas and flavors in their wake. They also tend to have ample acidity and flavor concentration. Among these ageable reds are famously long-lived wines like the best red Bordeaux, Hermitage, and Barolo; a longer list follows.

The even tinier percentage of ageworthy white wines includes those with high amounts of acidity like top renditions of white Burgundy and German Riesling. This acidity acts like tannin in red wine, slowly diminishing to reveal a compelling array of secondary aromas and flavors in the wine. Whereas some reds require aging because they are so bitter in their youth, such as the finest red Bordeaux in the best years, aging white wine is not done for necessity but simply to achieve greater complexity in the wine.

Even if you have a traditionally ageable wine type, the million-dollar question confounding and titillating connoisseurs everywhere is when to drink a bottle of maturing wine. There are no easy answers, since much depends on the wine's vintage and producer, as well as how that particular wine develops in the bottle. Tasters are looking for that time when a wine's tannins and acids have softened and secondary aromas—such as mushrooms, earth, and leather in red wine or nuts or dried fruits in white wine—have emerged. Reassuringly, such optimal maturity is almost never a fleeting, IPO-style peak, but often a gradual arc than can last for years.

To gauge the ageworthiness of a wine, start with its grape type. For example, wine from the tannic, thick-skinned Cabernet Sauvignon grape takes longer to come around than that from the more fragile Pinot Noir grape. So while the finest Cabernet-dominated red Bordeaux needs to be laid down for fifteen years or more before reaching ideal maturity, an ageable Pinot Noir–based red Burgundy might show its best stuff in only eight years. The vintage year, as we'll soon cover, will also give you an indication of the extent to which a wine is built to last, as will the track record of its producer. It is helpful to consult the tasting notes of major wine critics like Robert Parker, Steven Tanzer, Hugh Johnson, and the editors of *Wine Spectator* magazine, all of whom stake their professional reputations on making general predictions as to when to drink or hold particular bottles of wine.

The best judge of a wine's readiness to drink, however, remains your own palate, and that is why it is valuable to buy several bottles of an ageable wine, so that you

CHEAT SHEET

While the vast majority of wines are meant for immediate consumption, a small number will change for the better with years of bottle age.

OUTSMART THE TABLE

- If you're really at a loss as to a wine's ageability, follow my "seven-down" rule: if it's red, expensive, and made from a tannic grape, it can't hurt to lay the bottle down for at least seven years.
- Just because a wine is on the market doesn't mean its ready to drink. Because many expensive, ageable bottles are often bitterly tannic in their youth, they ironically are the least likely to give you immediate pleasure.
- As I've learned the hard way, when opening an old bottle with guests, always have a backup bottle ready in case your featured bottle disappoints.

FIT FOR FEASTING

Highly seasoned food can overwhelm a delicate, old wine, so plan your menu accordingly. Hard, mild cheese is always a safe partner for mature wine.

can taste how it develops over the years. But remember this incontrovertible fact: many serious collectors, forgetful of the treasures they have amassed or fearful of committing "infanticide" by drinking a wine too early, end up waiting too long to enjoy their wine. By the time they open a bottle, the wine is already limping into senility with faded, fruitless flavor. If you're going to err, do so by trying wine on its early side. Seize the day by seizing your glass.

Ageable Wine (Mostly the Finest Versions in the Best Years)

RED

Red Bordeaux
California Cabernet Sauvignon
Northern Rhône (Hermitage and Côte Rôtie)
Red Burgundy
Châteauneuf-du-Pape
Brunello
Barolo and Barbaresco
Super Tuscans
Other proven agers: Penfolds Grange (Australian Shiraz), Vega Sicilia (Spanish Ribera del Duero)

WHITE

White Burgundy (Chablis, Puligny-Montrachet, Chassagne-Montrachet, Meursault, Corton-Charlemagne)
German Riesling
Alsatian Riesling
Gewürztraminer
White Bordeaux
Vintage Champagne (especially high-acid Blanc de Blancs)

DESSERT

Vintage port
Sauternes and other fine late-harvest styles

94   Vintage Matters Less Than You Think

Some years ago, I created for my wine classes a chart of vintages of the world's ageable wines, a little square smaller than a credit card and laminated so that it could be surreptitiously fingered out of one's wallet, like a cheat sheet in algebra class. Students begged me for extra charts. Friends hounded me for them. I ended up running to Kinko's several more times just to satisfy this unexpected demand.

But I never made those charts again, mostly because *I* barely used them myself. What seemed like a neat idea—a secret weapon to be used on hot dates and business dinners to divine the perfect bottle of wine—served as little more than decoration for my wallet. This is because I rarely purchased the kind of wine where vintage mattered that much—and when I did, there was usually a knowledgeable salesperson or sommelier around to guide me in the right direction. Such are the realities of vintage, a sometimes important but largely unneeded complication to casual wine enjoyment.

Vintage, of course, is the year printed on a wine label, which indicates the year in which a wine's grapes were harvested. What it really reflects, though, are the weather conditions of that particular year. A good vintage typically has a lot of dry, sunny days and cool nights so that the grapes ripen nicely on the vine and achieve balanced levels of acidity. A bad or off-vintage is the inverse: copious cloud cover and rain and/or frost during the spring planting season and/or rains before harvest in the fall. The funny thing about vintages is that they are sometimes no easier to predict than a horse race: a mediocre growing season can be saved by a few weeks of perfect weather right before harvest, and months of banner conditions can be annihilated by torrential rains at harvest time.

The good news for consumers today is that winemakers can outsmart Mother Nature like never before. Advances in technology have helped wineries compensate for the effects of ill weather, maximizing the flavor of their wine even when the grapes aren't ideal. Also, some wineries have the luxury of blending wine from vineyards in different locations, so if one vineyard under-performs, another can pick up its slack. And the most skillful winemakers will

OUTSMART THE TABLE

• Producers in France's Champagne region and in Portugal's Oporto region (where the dessert wine port originates) "declare a vintage" only in years of excellent weather, so by definition *vintage* Champagne and *vintage* port come only from the best years.
• For the connoisseur in your life, a special (but likely expensive) gift is a bottle of fine wine from that person's birth year.

do whatever it takes to save face in disappointing vintages, such as selecting only a minuscule portion of the grape harvest for fermentation.

The upshot is that vintage just doesn't matter as much as it once did. This is particularly true in New World regions like California, Chile, and Australia, where the weather is so dependably sunny that there is relatively little year-to-year variation. Things get a little dicier in the sun-challenged climes of Europe. Anyone who has spent time in Bordeaux, Burgundy, Germany, or northern Italy can attest to the mercurial nature of the weather there. Because these regions are more vintage sensitive, you may want to be more careful when purchasing wine from years reputed to have been meteorologically challenged. Even so, few vintages are complete washouts, and never forget that the best producers find ways of compensating for nature's shortcomings.

If there is one time when vintage considerations are essential, it is when you are focusing on the tiny amount of ageworthy wine on the market. Here a top vintage will tell you that your $100 bottle of Californian Cabernet or red Bordeaux likely has the requisite tannin and flavor concentration to improve over the years, making it a good candidate to lay down for some time. A lesser vintage doesn't necessarily mean that the wine will taste bad, just that the wine will probably be lighter and less concentrated, lacking the structure to gain complexity over the years. It is ironically this difference that makes the best recent vintages of certain prestige wines an undesirable choice in restaurants, because they are often not ready to drink. So while an obscenely expensive Bordeaux from a ballyhooed vintage may sear your gums with bitter tannin, a similar wine from a lesser vintage has the dual advantage of being half the price and softer and more approachable—thus better for immediate pleasure.

Unless you're prepping to be a contestant on a wine version of *Jeopardy!*, there's no need to *memorize* vintages. Most collectors eventually commit a handful of top years to memory, but with the easy availability of good wine advice both online and in shops, it's not necessary to do so. Vintage charts appear everywhere, but they have their limitations since no one rating can take into account the climatic variations *within* a particular region, and even if they did, initial assessments sometimes prove inaccurate down the line. In any case, always seek several opinions and don't rely too much on any one assessment, since there are plentiful exceptions to the tenuous rule of vintage.

Purchasing

If Charles Dickens had written about two of my least favorite characters of wine retail, he would have called them Mr. Cragglescruel and Ms. Nothing-know.

Mr. Cragglescruel presides over his cramped store like some hoary beast guarding his lair. With bloodshot Archie Bunker eyes, he answers questions with a snide impatience and recommends bottles with a "take it or leave" arrogance. Across town, Ms. Nothingknow assumes her usual position behind the cash register, her mind filled with things like inventory, profit margin, and nabbing shoplifters. When asked if she has a Grüner Veltliner, her face registers puzzlement as she points to the back to the shop, where there's no Grüner but a sea of warm bottles baking under the fluorescent light.

This section is designed to help you avoid the Cragglescruels and Nothingknows of wine retail. We consider what to look for in a good wine merchant but also cover strategies to find excellent wine in the absence of helpful assistance, including more than a hundred bargain picks in my "Faithful Fifty" lists. Finally, because so many give the gift of wine, we cover a range of compelling options for both the casual drinker and the vinously obsessed. ∎

95 Six Signals a Merchant Has "the Love"

They're called *shelf talkers*, but most of them deserve to be called *shelf hawkers*.

I'm talking about the little signs on wine store shelves. If they're even present, they may be little more than canned marketed copy from the wineries themselves, about as trustworthy as a streetwalker's proposition—"Come on, baby, take me home. I love you long time." Occasionally, however, you find a shop that writes its own shelf talkers, with personal, passionate descriptions of what makes a wine special, recommended food matches, and helpful facts about the winery or winemaker.

Custom signs like these reflect a merchant's real enthusiasm for wine—a signal that you are in one of the special breed of wine shops that take their job seriously. Here are five more indications of an enlightened wine shop—one in business not just for profit but also "for the love":

VARIETY While no merchant can stock everything, better ones will supply plenty of options beyond the usual suspects like Chardonnay and Merlot, including less commercially popular types like Prosecco, Riesling, Alsatian Pinot Gris, and Cabernet Franc. Top wine shops also typically have a special section devoted to rare, collectable wines, sometimes relegated to a special chamber not unlike the "adult section" of a video store.

NEWSLETTERS Good wine shops often send or e-mail a free newsletter to clients. The most useful newsletters aren't just sales catalogs but are also stocked with insights about wine regions, industry trends, and good values. California's K&L Wine Merchants, for example, has a monthly newsletter that includes chatty sidebars written by its knowledgeable staffers.

FREE TASTINGS Where the law permits, better shops hold tastings to expose customers to new wine types. This is a risk-free way to sample wines you haven't had before, but don't feel obligated to buy any of the wine if you don't want to.

CAREFUL HANDLING Like a good pet store, a conscientious wine merchant handles the inventory with loving care. As you would with a puppy's nose, feel the bottles to make sure they are cool—or at least aren't baking next to a radiator or sweltering in direct sunlight. If they are, there's a good chance that the wine is on the road to ruin, if it isn't there already. Also, make sure most of the bottles are stored horizontally so their corks stay in contact with the wine and don't dry out.

REASONABLE PRICING The best wine shops won't necessarily be the cheapest, but then again, they shouldn't gouge consumers either. What many people don't realize is that the price for one particular wine can vary dramatically from store to store—a fact easily confirmed by a quick Internet search. Not only will a fair retailer charge reasonable prices; it will also have a range of attractive options at all price points. It will also give breaks to those who buy in volume, such as a 10 to 15 percent discount on purchases of cases.

On My Table | **PETER GRANOFF** co-owns San Francisco's Ferry Plaza Wine Merchant and pioneered e-commerce for wine when he launched Virtual Vineyards, which later became wine.com.

Riesling from Germany and Austria
Fritz Haag, Weins-Prüm, Künstler, Gunderloch, Mantlerhof, Nigl, Donabaum

Sauvignon Blanc
New Zealand: Neudorf, Huia. California: Honig. Loire: Vacheron. South Africa: Mulderbosch, Buitenverwachting.

Pinot Gris from Oregon
Ponzi, Elk Cove

Pinot Noir from California, New Zealand, and Oregon
Walter Hansel, Highfield Estate, Huia, Olivet Lane, Bonaccorsi

Southern Rhône—Côte-du-Rhône—"Meaty reds at moderate prices."
Domaine de l'Oratoire, Domaine de Renjarde

Champagne—"Any good wine from the region."

96 Seven Ways to Outsmart Wine Purchasing

While *nothing* beats a high-quality wine shop and caring merchant, the plain truth is that you'll often have to fend for yourself when buying wine. The following are seven more strategies to help you navigate the wilds of wine purchasing:

DON'T ASSUME EXPENSIVE IS ALWAYS BETTER Spending more can increase your odds of getting good wine, but quality isn't always keyed to price. Pricing reflects a winery's production costs, such as the cost of grapes, winery equipment (especially oak barrels), labor wages, the time a wine is allowed to age in a winery, and the cost of all that fancy packaging. The price is also often linked to heavy marketing costs like those big shiny ads in *Wine Spectator* and PR people. Also, as Burgundy lovers are reminded with painful regularity, the powerful forces of scarcity drive people to pay whatever it takes to have what others can't get. Finally, critical acclaim and a winery's own reputation inflate prices beyond the intrinsic quality of the wine.

VALUE LIES WITH THE "WHA?" WINES As is true in restaurants, the best values in wine shops are what I call the "Wha?" wines—less familiar types like Sauvignon Blanc, German Riesling, Zinfandel, Albariño, Gewürztraminer, Barbera, Chinon, and the like (see Shortcut 73). Because they're less known by consumers, you'll avoid the comfort premium retailers charge for knee-jerk favorites like Chardonnay, Merlot, and Cabernet Sauvignon.

LOOK BEYOND WINE MERCHANTS While personal attention and storage conditions aren't always their forte, supermarkets and discount warehouses can offer some of the best deals around, assuming the local laws allow them to sell alcohol. It's become almost chic to buy your everyday wine at the likes of Costco, Target, Wal-Mart, Sam's Club, and Trader Joe's, the last of which is home to the phenomenally popular Charles Shaw wines (nicknamed "Two-Buck Chuck") that sell for under $4 a bottle. (The verdict on Two-Buck

Chuck: not particularly interesting, but if the price weans more people off sugary jug wines, it is a success.) And, as I describe in Shortcut 99, these stores sometimes offer good deals on premium wines too.

DON'T OVERLOOK THE OLD RELIABLES While they don't carry the buzz of new-generation and boutique wineries, many larger, time-tested wineries continue to offer high quality at fair prices. Old-guard wineries like Beringer, Beaulieu, Robert Mondavi, Gallo (the high-quality Gallo of Sonoma), St. Supéry, and Chateau St. Jean are sometimes overlooked by consumers—and the reasonable prices of their basic-level offerings positively reflect this neglect.

BUY SINGLE BOTTLES *AND* CASES Once, when I was buying a case of California Cabernet Sauvignon, a wine retailer admonished me against getting a full case of the same wine: "Why would you ever buy that much of the same wine? There are too many good wines out there."

He was right in that most of us don't try enough new wine—part of the joy of wine is discovering new producers and styles. But there is also much to be gained by buying wine by the case. Not only do many stores offer a 10 percent to 15 percent discount for case purchases (including "mixed cases" of different wines), but it's always rewarding to have a stash of wine available for casual dinners at home, unexpected company, and last-minute gifts. And if you've already tasted the wine and love it, why not multiply your pleasure? It's like what my mom always says about clothes: if you find something that really fits you well, get more of it, because you may never see it again.

USE TECHNOLOGY Your computer and phone are powerful tools for locating good values and tracking down wine. A Web search of local wine shops will help you find the best prices—which, again, can

OUTSMART THE TABLE
Bargain hunters and "Wha?" wine seekers will appreciate the emergence of Best Cellars, a retail chain focusing on affordable, small-production wines. Upping the ante on consumer friendliness, these stores organize their wine not by grape or region but by eight taste categories, such as "fizzy," "juicy," and "smooth." See www.bestcellars.com.

differ significantly from merchant to merchant. To get an even broader view of pricing, or to find a rare bottle, visit a site called Wine-Searcher.com. Its ingenious database allows you to enter in the producer, name, and year of wine and then returns links to wine shops around the world that stock the wine, listed by price.

Another way of sourcing a bottle is to call its distributor or importer, who should be able to give you a list of the wine shops in your area that are likely to stock the wine. Contact information is usually on the back label of the bottle—if it isn't, or if you don't remember it, you can contact the winery or search the Internet for the contact information of the distributor or importer.

IMPORTERS AND MORE Speaking of importers, keep an eye out for wines from the portfolio of a specialist importer, as discussed in Shortcut 98. And when all else fails, you'll likely be rewarded by choosing a wine from one of my "Faithful Fifty" lists (Shortcuts 100 and 101; see also Shortcut 102).

97 Eight Label Buzzwords to Know

Free range—for years this menu term mystified me. Is a chicken "free range" because it is cooked on an open grill? Or is it from a "range" of poultry sources? Or is it foul found roaming free—like a wild stallion on a prairie meadow?

It was years before I learned that a free-range bird is simply one that has had access to the outdoors, a fate presumably more humane than being cooped up, as it were, in a crowded factory.

Wine labels have their own confusing buzzwords. Here is the scoop on some common ones:

VARIETAL Wine labeled with the name of the grape, as opposed to the name of the region. Chardonnay, Cabernet Sauvignon, and Merlot are examples of varietal wines. Wine from the New World—e.g., the United States, Australia, Chile, New Zealand—is usually labeled by varietal.

APPELLATION The name of an offically defined growing region. The world's model for such legally protected place-names is France's *Appellation d'Origine Contrôlée* system (abbreviated *AOC* or *AC*). AOC laws impose quality standards on a wine from a specific area (e.g., allowable geographic boundaries, grape types, and alcohol levels) that it must meet in order to earn status as a controlled appellation wine and cite this fact in small letters on its label. An AOC can be an entire area, like Bordeaux, or a specific area therein, such as the region Médoc or the subregion Margaux. Other well-known appellation systems are Italy's *Denominazione di Origine Controllata (DOC)* and Spain's *Denominación de Origen (DO)*. European producers tend to label their wines by appellation, using a place-name rather than the grape variety.

RESERVE This term usually designates an estate's finer wine, but because it has no legal meaning in America, this isn't always the case. Kendall-Jackson's Vintner's Reserve Chardonnay, for example, is a basic-level wine. In Italy and Spain, however, the terms (*riserva* and *reserva*, respectively) indicate that a wine has conformed to specific aging requirements and other qualifications.

OLD VINES (or *Vieilles Vignes, Vigne Vecchie, or VV*) Although there's no legal definition here either, it usually signifies wine from vines that have decades of age, often forty years or more. Vines this old produce fewer grapes, and those grapes are usually more concentrated, ultimately yielding wine that is more likely to have intense flavors. Examples include the Cline Ancient Vines Zinfandel and Pascal Bouchard's Chablis Vieilles Vignes.

UNFILTERED This designation tells you the wine has not undergone filtration, a process performed after fermentation to give wine a clear appearance and remove extraneous particles. Many winemakers believe that filtration strips a wine of some of its character, so avoiding it may make the wine more aromatic and flavorful.

ESTATE BOTTLED A general sign of quality, indicating that the grapes have been grown, vinified, and bottled on the grounds of a wine estate. This means the producer has been able to control the entire process of creating the wine, as opposed to using grapes from an outside source. French wine labels designate estate bottling as *Mis en Bouteille au Château* ("bottled at the château").

MERITAGE An invented term (*merit + heritage*) and registered trademark that refers to wine made from a blend of grapes rather than one particular grape type. An industry consortium, the Meritage Association, imposes several conditions before it will officially recognize a wine as Meritage, such as that it be made from at least two Bordeaux grape types, such as Cabernet and Merlot for red Meritage, or Sauvignon Blanc and Sémillon for white Meritage. Joseph Phelps's Insignia and Opus One are examples of wine licensed to carry the Meritage designation.

CUVÉE Although it has other definitions, overall *cuvée* generally means a specific blend or lot of wine, such as Cuvée Natalie, a delicious blend of Sauvignon Blanc and Riesling from Santa Barbara's Brander Vineyards.

98 Importer Names—Secret Seals of Approval on the Back Label

Imagine if you had an incredibly picky and knowledgeable mother choosing wines for you. Visiting the vintners herself, she'd shake her head disapprovingly, raise a skeptical eyebrow, and launch into a laundry list of demands:

- *"I want the best wines you can make—quality is more important than quantity."*
- *"I hope you don't filter your wines, because it will strip them of flavor."*
- *"I'm going to have these wines sent to me in temperature-controlled containers, so they won't be damaged by heat along the way."*

"I LIKE ANYTHING THAT JORGE ORDOÑEZ HAS SELECTED. HE IS AN AMAZING IMPORTER WHO HAS FIRED UP THE MODERNIZATION OF MANY SMALL WINERIES IN SPAIN."

—Larry Stone, master sommelier

This is more or less what a great wine importer does—traveling the world to ferret out the best-quality wine for his portfolio—and, in effect, serving as your fussy mother of wine selection. Their effect on wine quality cannot be overstated—as they have the ability to influence producers to make wine of the highest integrity and then export it with the utmost of care. And producers listen: nobody messes with Mom.

Appearing on the back label of imported wine bottles, an importer's name is one of the great clues to a good wine, though few casual drinkers even know to look for it. The name of a high-quality importer acts like a seal of approval—a sign that a fastidious expert has secured the best possible wines under the best possible conditions.

While many large corporations do a fine job of importing wine, it is an elite cadre of artisanal importers that truly serve as quality markers for consumers. Some of these importers deal exclusively with the wines of one country, while others have a broader portfolio. Most carry wines at a range of price points, from $12 miracles to $90 masterpieces. Don't despair if you don't see certain

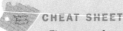

importers' wines regularly on shelves and in restaurants—many distribute only to certain regions and deal with wines made in tiny quantities.

Here are thirteen specialist importers at the top of their game:

Eric Solomon/European Cellars (North Carolina): A virtuoso in sourcing treasures from Italy, France, and Spain, he has an impressive track record for finding incredible bargains from fledging wineries of France's Rhône Valley and Spain.

Grateful Palate/Dan Philips (California): Imports a range of plum Australian wines, as well as gourmet bacon and coffee.

Jeroboam Wines/Daniel Johnnes (New York): Ferrets out treasures from France, including Burgundy, Rhône, and the Loire. Also check out the excellent picks in *Daniel Johnnes's Top 100 Wines* (Penguin).

Jorge Ordoñez/Fine Estates from Spain (Massachusetts): A master of Spanish wines, also with a knack for sourcing affordable selections. The Ordoñez name was cited enthusiastically by several of my survey respondents.

Kermit Lynch (California): A longtime importer of French wines, including unknown gems from the Languedoc-Roussillon, Alsace, the Rhône, and even Corsica. Lynch is a trailblazing figure who has inspired a generation of importers with his crusade for wine quality and proper shipping conditions. His beautifully written *Adventures on the Wine Route* (North Point) is one of the most inspiring wine books on the market.

Kysela Père et Fils (Virginia): Covers several countries, with a strong focus on France's Burgundy and the south of France.

New Castle Imports/Don Quattlebaum (South Carolina): A master of French wines, with deep coverage of Burgundy and the Rhône Valley.

Robert Kacher (Washington, D.C.): An ace importer of French wine, including the Rhône, Loire, Burgundy, and Champagne.

Rudi Wiest/Cellars International (California): Handles a deep selection of German wine, whose silhouetted wine-glass logo has been a mark of quality since the 1970s.

Terry Theise Estate Selections (Maryland/Washington, D.C.): A man obsessed with identifying the finest wine from Austria and Germany, as well as artisanal "grower" Champagne.

Vin Divino (Chicago): A golden name for French, Italian, and Austrian wines.

Vine Connections (California): A small but important champion of excellent wines from Argentina.

Winebow/Leonard LoCascio (New York): A key player in fine Italian wine, with a gift for sourcing high-quality, backwater estates of southern Italy.

On My Table | **KERMIT LYNCH** is a Berkeley, California, importer, merchant, and author whose name is synonymous with artisanal wine of the highest caliber.

Rosé
Tempier, Fontsainte, Mas Champart

Southern Rhône—Gigondas—"What can I say? I own it. I make it the way I like it."
Les Pallières

Northern Rhône—Cornas
Clape, Verset, Allemand

Northern Rhône—St.-Joseph—"Delicious Syrah in a seductive style—serious and easy at the same time."
Chave

White Burgundy—"My favorite white wine region since I began drinking wine."
Coche-Dury (Meursault), Raveneau (Chablis), Roulot (Meursault), F. Jobard (Meursault), Dauvissat (Chablis)

Savennières [from France's Loire Valley, known for white wine from the Chenin Blanc grape]
Château d'Epiré

Dolcetto—"Delicious, versatile reds so easy to love."
Aldo Marenco

99 Costco Offers a Do-It-Yourself
Treasure Hunt

Well past the fifty-five-pound sacks of Purina Dog Chow, beyond the 188-dose jugs of sugar-orange Metamucil, and a safe distance from the forty-count Depends "Extra Absorption" Underwear, I found my booty: a stash of 2000 Château Mouton-Rothschild at $267.99 a bottle. This was, believe it or not, a relative bargain compared to the $400 to $500 demanded by upscale wine merchants.

This wasn't some drunken reverie inspired by an overdose of daytime TV commercials, but a recent visit to the Costco Warehouse in Wayne, New Jersey. If you haven't heard, Costco—long known for its rock-bottom prices for bulk consumer goods like Charmin and Slim Jims—has emerged as America's eight-hundred-pound gorilla of retail wine sales. In 2003 it was projected to sell $620 million worth of wine, up from $130 million in 1998. It offers wine in any state in which it can obtain a license to do so, and as this book went to press, it had wine in about 280 stores out of 330 nationwide.

The good news for wine enthusiasts is that Costco has a lot more than wine in a box. At any given Costco you'll find heavy hitters like Dominus Cabernet and Bertani Amarone sharing the bin with everyday gems like Hess Select Cabernet and Ravenswood Zinfandel. Costco doesn't stock just token quantities of auction-level wines like Dom Pérignon and first-growth Bordeaux; it is the nation's largest seller of them. Best of all, it works the same too-good-to-be-true pricing voodoo on wine that it does with Tootise Rolls. While many wine shops mark up wine 50 percent or more over cost, Costco caps its markup at 14 percent, with many wines going for well below that. On my recent visit, Veuve Clicquot Yellow Label NV was $31.99, a $3 to $6 savings over various U.S. retailers I checked. The 1999 Ruffino Ducale Chanti Classico was $17.99, a $3 to $10 savings. If you buy by the case, the difference really hits home.

But with only 150 to 200 different wines in each outlet, you can't always locate particular brands or several types of one style. Unabashedly a ware-

house, Costco doesn't have roving wine experts ready to guide you in your wine purchases, a fact that fine wine merchants eagerly emphasize. Some merchants also stress that Costco's wines aren't kept under exactingly cool conditions to prevent them from aging prematurely or spoiling over time. True, but stock rotates so quickly that storage isn't an issue. Finally, some say that it ruins the romance of wine to buy amid the glare of fluorescent lights and Kitty Litter. If you can overlook the spartan aesthetics, however, Costco lets you avoid inflated wine prices and plow your savings into something truly romantic—like an extra bottle of wine for those really late nights.

100 The Faithful Fifty Whites: Fifty Best Buys Under $15

When *family* and friends hit me up for the best values in white wine, I send them this list, which has been shaped and edited lovingly over a decade of teaching, buying, and relentlessly quizzing my wine friends. These are whites that are consistently delicious, widely available, and usually priced under $15.

Mark's Faithful Fifty Whites

"NEVER BE ASHAMED TO TRY A 'CHEAP' ($12–$25) BOTTLE IN A RESTAURANT. I HAVE FOUND MANY GREAT WINES THAT ARE UNDER THE RADAR SCREEN."

—*Greg Norman, pro golfer and winery owner*

Argiolas Vermentino (Italy)
Babich Sauvignon Blanc (New Zealand)
Beaulieu Vineyard Coastal Chardonnay (California)
Bogle Sauvignon Blanc (California)
Brancott Sauvignon Blanc (New Zealand)
Buena Vista Sauvignon Blanc (California)
Ca' del Solo (Bonny Doon) Big House White (California)
Casa Lapostolle Sauvignon Blanc (Chile)
Chateau Ste. Michelle Pinot Gris (Washington State)
Chateau Ste. Michelle Riesling (Washington State)
Chateau Ste. Michelle Sémillon (Washington State)
Chéreau Carré Muscadet (France)
Martín Códax Albariño (Spain)
Columbia Crest Chardonnay (Washington State)
Columbia Crest Sémillon-Chardonnay (Washington State)

OUTSMART THE TABLE

Some of the best wine deals are found far off the beaten track. Keep these options in mind:

Stellenbosch *(Stel-un-BOOSH):* The "wine farms" in South Africa's beautiful Stellenbosch region are increasingly a source for value, especially its zesty, grassy, unoaked New Zealand–style Sauvignon Blanc, which usually stays within the $15 zone.

Muscadet *(Moose-cah-DAY):* Bracingly crisp and priced under $10, this old standard from France's Loire Valley is a perennial favorite for summertime seafood feasts.

Vinho Verde *(VEEN-yoh VEHR-day):* Costing as little as $3 a bottle, this lemony crisp Portuguese favorite is ideal for summer fish fests or, with its slight green tinge, St. Patrick's Day.

Kim Crawford Chardonnay Unoaked (New Zealand)

Kim Crawford Sauvignon Blanc (New Zealand)

Gallo of Sonoma Chardonnay (California)

Geyser Peak Sauvignon Blanc (California)

Hess Select Chardonnay (California)

Hogue Fumé Blanc (Washington State)

Hogue Riesling (Washington State)

Hugel Gentil (France)

Louis Jadot Mâcon-Villages and Mâcon Blanc (France)

Louis Jadot St.-Aubin (France)

Kenwood Sauvignon Blanc (California)

La Crema Chardonnay (California)

Leitz Dragonstone Riesling (Germany)

Lindemans Bin 65 Chardonnay (Australia)

Luna Pinot Grigio (California)

Meridian Chardonnay (California)

Robert Mondavi Fumé Blanc (California)

Robert Mondavi Private Selection Chardonnay (California)

Oxford Landing Chardonnay (Australia)

Penfolds Koonunga Hill Chardonnay (Australia)

Pepperwood Grove Chardonnay (California)

Pepperwood Grove Viognier (California)

Ponzi Pinot Gris (Oregon)

R.H. Phillips Chardonnay (California)

R.H. Phillips Sauvignon Blanc (California)

R.H. Phillips Viognier EXP (California)

Rosemount Chardonnay (Australia)

St. Supéry Sauvignon Blanc (California)

Georg Albrecht Schneider Kabinett (Germany)

Strub Niersteiner Riesling Kabinett (Germany)

Trimbach Gewürztraminer (France)

Trimbach Riesling (France)

Trimbach Tokay–Pinot Gris (France)

Villa Maria Sauvignon Blanc (New Zealand)

Zaca Mesa Chardonnay (California)

On My Table | **LANE GIGUIERE** is cofounder and brand manager of California's R.H. Phillips, a source of some of the best values in wine.

Sauvignon Blanc from New Zealand
　　Kim Crawford, Spy Valley, Lawson's Dry Hills

Tempranillo from Spain
　　Rioja: Roda, Remelluri. Ribera del Duero: Condado de Haza.

Gewürztraminer from Alsace—"This is a summertime, kick-your-feet-up-and-watch-the-grill kind of wine."
　　Hugel, Trimbach, Zind Humbrecht

Pinot Noir—California and Oregon
　　Williams Selyem, Domaine Drouhin

Sancerre—"Lemony, steely, slightly herbal, with a crisp, clean finish."
　　Henri Bourgeois, Pascal Jolivet

Chianti—"A crowd-pleasing red for dinner parties when you aren't sure what wine everyone will like."
　　Antinori, Badia a Coltibuono, San Felice

Chinon—"A full-flavored red with berry fruit and spice . . . my new favorite since traveling in the Loire Valley last summer."

101 The Faithful Fifty Reds:
Fifty Best Buys Under $15

Because a majority of wine drinkers love red wine, and *everyone* loves a good deal, it's no surprise that the question I'm asked most often is "What are the good, cheap reds?"

Here is my carefully crafted list of the Faithful Fifty Reds—fifty wines that get top marks for taste, affordability, and availability.

Mark's Faithful Fifty Reds

Alamos Malbec (Argentina)
Altos Las Hormigas Malbec (Argentina)
A-Mano Primitivo (Italy)
Apollonio Copertino (Italy)
Apollonio Primitivo (Italy)
Argiolas Perdera (Italy)
Banfi Centine (Italy)
Black Opal Shiraz (Australia)
Wolf Blass Shiraz–Cabernet Sauvignon (Australia)
Bogle Petite Sirah (California)
Ca' del Solo (Bonny Doon) Big House Red
   (California)
Castaño Hécula or Monastrell (Spain)
Castell del Remei Gotim Bru (Spain)
Chateau Ste. Michelle Cabernet Sauvignon
   Columbia Valley (Washington State)

Chateau Ste. Michelle Merlot (Washington State)

Michele Chiarlo Barbera d'Asti (Italy)

Cline Red Truck (California)

Cline Syrah (California)

Columbia Crest Cabernet Sauvignon (Washington State)

Columbia Crest Merlot (Washington State)

Concha y Toro Cabernet Sauvignon Casillero del Diablo (Chile)

Concha y Toro Merlot Casillero del Diablo (Chile)

Conde de Valdemar Rioja Crianza (Spain)

Georges Duboeuf Beaujolais-Villages (France)

Georges Duboeuf Morgon, Fleurie, or Moulin-à-Vent (France)

Fairview Estate Goats do Roam Red (South Africa)

Falesco Vitiano (Italy)

Gallo of Sonoma Pinot Noir (California)

Guigal Côtes-du-Rhône (France)

Hess Select Cabernet Sauvignon (California)

Jaboulet Côtes-du-Rhône Parallèle 45 (France)

Louis Jadot Beaujolais-Villages (France)

Lindemans Bin 45 Cabernet Sauvignon (Australia)

Marqués de Riscal Rioja Crianza (Spain)

Meridian Pinot Noir (California)

Paringa Shiraz (Australia)

Pepperwood Grove Merlot (California)

Pepperwood Grove Syrah (California)

R.H. Phillips Syrah EXP (California)

Prunotto Barbera d'Asti Fiulot (Italy)

Rancho Zabaco Zinfandel Dancing Bull (California)

Ravenswood Zinfandel (California)

Rosemount Grenache-Syrah-Mourvèdre (Australia)

Rosemount Shiraz (Australia)

Rosemount Shiraz–Cabernet Sauvignon (Australia)

Santa Rita Cabernet Sauvignon 120 (Chile)

Taurino Salice Salentino (Italy)

Torres Penedes Sangre de Toro (Spain)

Trapiche Malbec (Argentina)

La Vieille Ferme Côtes du Ventoux (France)

OUTSMART THE TABLE

Also look for these emerging red wine "value regions":

Languedoc-Roussillon (*Lahn-guh-DOCK Rue-see-YOHN*): Insiders agree that this vast region straddling France's Mediterranean coastline is France's most exciting locus for value, where many of the wines are soft, spicy reds from Rhône-style grapes, though some are straight varietals such as Merlot; two key districts are Costières de Nîmes and Coteaux du Languedoc.

Stellenbosch (*Stel-un-BOOSH*): As it has with white wine, South Africa's Stellenbosch region is making impressive strides with simple, eager-to-please Shiraz, Bordeaux-style blends, Pinotage, and the country's indigenous Rhône-type grape.

Sicily and Sardinia: Infusions of new technology and expertise have made these Italian islands capable of something more than bulk wine, as demonstrated by the big, ripe plummy Argiolas Perdera (from Sardinia) listed here.

On My Table | **ERIC CINNAMON** is the winemaker of Sonoma's Rancho Zabaco, a wellspring of rich, gutsy Zinfandel.

Zinfandel
Ridge, Rosenblum, Rancho Zabaco

Sauvignon Blanc—Sonoma and New Zealand
Rochioli, Rancho Zabaco

Pinot Gris from Alsace—"Broad, rich fig, spice, perfume—a meal in a glass; not Italian Pinot Grigio style."
Zind Humbrecht, Hugel

Pinot Noir from California
Williams Selyem, Saintsbury, MacMurray Ranch

102 More Faithful Friends at $15 and Under: Bubbly, Rosé, and Dessert Wine

BUBBLY

Bouvet Brut Signature (France)
Chandon Brut Fresco (Argentina)
Cristalino Cava Brut (Spain)
Domaine Ste. Michelle Brut Blanc de Blanc
    (Washington State)
Freixenet Cava Brut (Spain)
Gruet Brut (New Mexico)
Mionetto Prosecco Brut (Italy)
Nino Franco Prosecco Brut (Italy)
Pacific Echo Brut (California)
Seaview Brut (Australia)
Segura Viudas Cava Aria Brut (Spain)
Zardetto Prosecco Brut (Italy)

ROSÉ

Bodegas Muga Rioja Rosado (Spain)
Bonny Doon Vin Gris de Cigare (California)
Cune Rioja Rosado (Spain)
Marqués de Cáceres Dry Rioja Rosé (Spain)
Mas de Gourgonnier Rosé (France)

DESSERT WINE

Ceretto Santo Stefano (Italy)
Michele Chiarlo Moscato d'Asti Nivole (Italy)
Fonseca Bin 27 Ruby Porto (Portugal)
Robert Pecota Moscato d'Andrea (California)
St. Supéry Moscato (California)

103 Gifts for Wine Novices: Six Exciting but Safely Exotic Options

The best type of gift for the casual wine drinker is something interesting but not *too* adventurous. The novice, for example, might not appreciate the sweetness of Spätlese-level German Riesling or the lychee-and-pepper character of Gewürztraminer. Here are some options that offer something different while staying within the gustatory comfort zone.

PROSECCO Bubbly, festive, and inexpensive, Prosecco makes a wonderful gift, especially if you introduce it as "Italian Champagne" (okay, so it's not technically Champagne, but you don't have to get into *that*). Similar choices include American sparkling wine and Spanish Cava.

MEURSAULT Legions love Chardonnay, but many have yet to experience the glorious expression of this grape from Burgundy's Meursault village. While it isn't cheap, a bottle of Meursault will provide the butteriness and tropical fruit that Chardonnay lovers crave but with the intriguing earthiness and acidity that makes white Burgundy so special.

VIOGNIER Chardonnay fans will also experience snatches of joy from the rich, creamy embrace of Viognier. It is generally pricey, but R.H. Phillips and Pepperwood Grove deliver Viognier's tropical ambrosia for less than $15.

***CRU* BEAUJOLAIS** For less than $15, a bottle of Morgon, Fleurie, Brouilly, or any of the other *cru* Beaujolais appellations will dial up berry flavor that's light in body and bitterness and heavy on charm.

BIG, LIKABLE REDS The rich, lush, likable charms of Zinfandel (the real stuff), Australian Shiraz, and Argentine Malbec are always a refreshing change from the usual suspects Merlot and Cabernet Sauvignon.

MUSCAT-BASED DESSERT WINE The recipients of your gift may not think they like dessert wine, but one sip of the delicate Moscato d'Asti (the Santo Stefano is packaged in a slender, cone-shaped bottle that never fails to impress) or the lush, peachy perfume of Bonny Doon's Vin de Glacière will forever change their outlook.

Alluring Labels

Here are several popular wines that look as good as they taste:

• Bonny Doon Le Cigare Volant (California)	UFO hovering above a wine estate
• Gundlach-Bundschu Bearitage (California)	Grizzly bear chugging a glass of wine
• Livio Felluga (Italy)	Beautiful antique map
• Frog's Leap (California)	Famous flying frog
• L'Ecole No. 41 (Washington State)	Watercolor of schoolhouse and a hot-air balloon made from grapes
• Rancho Zabaco Zinfandel (California)	Colorful dancing bull
• Ruffino Chianti Classico Ducale Riserva and Gold Label (Italy)	Courtly nobleman scene
• Valley of the Moon Zinfandel (California)	Haunting black-and-white moon

Label rendered by a different artist each year:

- Château Mouton-Rothschild (France)
- Kenwood Cabernet Sauvignon Artist Series (California)
- Peter Lehmann Barossa Queen of Hearts wines (Australia)

104 Gifts for Wine Snobs: Eight Ideas to Avoid the Chill of "BCD"

I *call it* BCD: barely concealed displeasure.

Such is the reaction of many wine snobs when they receive yet another ordinary bottle of wine. They may smile broadly and tell you: "How, *thoughtful!* I've always wanted this kind of Merlot," but what they really mean is "I wouldn't even stir this dreck into my *coq au vin.*"

Not to worry: the eight options that follow will delight and intrigue even the most discriminating grape nuts—and help you avoid the chill of their BCD:

GRÜNER VELTLINER If the recipient of your gift likes lighter white wines, food-friendly, citrusy Grüner Veltliner will cast you as an agent of good taste. It is moderately priced, and finer merchants usually carry a few different types.

LEBANESE LOVE Improbable as it seems, war-torn Lebanon can produce wines of quality and complexity. Ask your favorite wine shop to secure you a bottle of Château Kefraya (especially the Comte de M), Chateau Ksara, or Chateau Musar—all of which make Bordeaux-style wine from Lebanon's Bekáa Valley. The last, Musar, is Lebanon's most famous wine.

GROWER CHAMPAGNE Not all good bottles of Champagne are household brands. Finer wine merchants often have (or can order) examples of grower Champagne—that is, Champagne from small, privately owned producers that grow their own grapes instead of contracting to buy grapes from outside growers. The best grower Champagnes are prized for their individual personalities, often reflecting the winemaker and the quirky subtleties of the soil from which they derive. A little-known way to identify a grower Champagne is to look for the initials *RM* introducing the tiny license number on the bottom edge of a Champagne label. Top grower Champagnes include Jacques Selosse, Chartogne-Taillet, Paul Bara, René Geoffroy, Jean Milan, Egly-Ouriet, Pierre Gimonnet et Fils, and Larmandier-Bernier.

UNUSUAL DESSERT WINE While no self-respecting connoisseur would look askance at a fine bottle of French Sauternes, consider adding something new to her vinous arsenal. Track down a bottle of Hungarian Tokaji Aszú, Canadian ice wine, Italian Vin Santo, or—if you really want to dazzle—German Beerenauslese or Trockenbeerenauslese. The next two choices qualify as unusual dessert wines too.

PICOLIT I was first introduced to Picolit as a graduate student when the resident professor in Stanford's Italian-theme dormitory heard of my interest in wine and brought me a sample. "This is ah *veeery* special wine from my home-land," she said, referring to the northeastern region of Italy called Friuli. Picolit is a rich and satisfying dessert wine, with hints of honey, almond, and apricots. Ask your favorite merchant to order it, as it is rarely stocked on store shelves.

BANYULS *AND* DARK CHOCOLATE You'll win friends and influence people by giving the romantics in your life a bottle of the portlike French dessert wine Banyuls, along with a nice hunk of gourmet dark chocolate. Chocolate-scented Banyuls is one of the few wines that isn't overwhelmed by the sweetness of chocolate—and the sheer decadence of the two together creates the kind of harmonic convergence that most foodies fantasize about.

A MEANINGFUL YEAR If you look hard enough, and have a generous budget, you may be able to buy a special bottle from your recipient's birth year or anniversary year. Online and conventional auctions are your best bet for locating old wine like this. A related and easier-to-find gift is a recent release to recognize a newborn's birth year or someone's graduation. The English have long bestowed bottles of vintage port on a newborn, but any wine with serious longevity will do, such as the best vintages of a top red Bordeaux or Italian Barolo. Note that the recipient will typically have to wait years before a new release of such wine comes to market.

OTHER SINGULARLY SPECIAL GIFTS Didier Dagueneau Pouilly-Fumé (see Shortcut 24); Côte Rôtie from the Rhône Valley (see Shortcut 37), Condrieu from the Rhône (see Shortcut 46), Super Tuscans (see Shortcut 41), Vendange Tardive or Sélection de Grains Nobles wine from Alsace (see Shortcut 25), Penfolds Grange (see Shortcut 44).

105 Supersize Your Generosity and Six Other Strategies for Gift Giving

Given the popularity of wine as a gift, let's consider seven more strategies to ensure your vinous generosity makes a big impact.

SUPERSIZE YOUR GENEROSITY There's something inescapably impressive about an oversized bottle. Its larger-than-life appearance so shouts "generosity" that it looks like it contains more wine than it actually does. Such large-format bottles are also special because of their rarity, as wineries produce only tiny quantities, much of which goes to restaurants. Their size makes them ideal for parties and celebrations. And many experts believe that wine ages more slowly in large bottles—an advantage if the wine is ageworthy and you want to cellar it for many years. Track them down through auctions and high-end merchants.

Oversized bottle sizes for regular, nonsparkling wine are magnum (two bottles), double magnum (four bottles), Jeroboam (Jer-uh-BOE-uhm; six bottles), Imperial (eight bottles), Salmanazar (Sal-muh-NAZ-uhr; twelve bottles), Balthazar (sixteen bottles), Nebuchadnezzar (Neb-uh-kuhd-NEZ-uhr; twenty bottles). Size names for Champagne bottles are somewhat different.

BAG IT Nothing adds festivity to the gift of wine like encasing it in a special bag. Home furnishing stores such as Pottery Barn and fine wine merchants usually carry various wine satchels; they come in a variety of fabrics (e.g., velvet, silk, cotton) and often have a corded tie at the top. Some of the sleekest are the Built NY Bottle Totes made of clink-proof wet-suit material that fits snugly around your bottles. Available in a variety of colors, they retail for less than $20 (see www.builtny.com).

IT'S THE *EXTRA* THOUGHT THAT COUNTS You'll make a wine gift more special by attaching a brief note about the wine. It need not be anything elaborate—in fact, it can just be a sentence or two paraphrasing a description from this book, such as: "Enjoy this Albariño—it is an aromatic, creamy white wine that comes from a mysterious Spanish region called Rías Baixas." In a crowded party, a note also assures that your generosity does not go unrecognized. Some paper goods shops sell blank tags designed to attach to a bottle neck.

ATTACH A SIX-MONTH "CONSUME BY" DATE   Because most people save their wine far too long (remember: 98 percent of wine doesn't get better with age), you might also attach a cheeky "consume by" instruction, such as: "Kate and Bill: You are *Required* to Drink This Within Six Months." Such a note will not only encourage them to seize the day, but it will ensure that the wine tastes fresh and fruity, especially with delicate types like Beaujolais, dry rosé, Pinot Gris, and Dolcetto.

DON'T EXPECT YOUR HOST TO SHARE   Taking a gift of wine to a friend's house isn't like taking a salad to a potluck dinner: the host isn't obligated to share it with you. Unless you've been asked to contribute wine, you shouldn't assume that your wine will be used—the host may already have planned the wine for the night. I make this clear by giving a bottle with the directive "This is for you to enjoy later." That said, if *you* are the host, it displays admirable bonhomie to offer to open your donors' bottle and share the gifts with them.

SPOT ON   For the shameless spillers in your life, I highly recommend the Wine Away stain remover. This little bottle has been my savior, single-handedly rescuing dress shirts, pants, and even my couch from red-wine stains. Its manufacturer, Evergreen Labs, is a bit vague about its ingredients, revealing only that it's nontoxic and contains fruit and vegetable extracts. But it really works—and a 12-ounce bottle is available for about $10 at many houseware stores.

EXPERTS-ONLY GIFTS   To outsmart connoisseurs who think they have everything, track down a:

Tastevin (taht-VAHN): The small, shallow silver cup that sommeliers and old-school servers use for sampling wine. Its surface is usually dimpled, to help reflect light into the wine in a dimly lit cellar, and some come with a chain so you can wear it around your neck. eBay and antiques dealers usually have a variety of styles, including pewter and silver versions. To make it really over the top, have it engraved.

Wine Thief: The long glass tube that winemakers use for sampling wine out of the barrel—not unlike an overgrown turkey baster. It makes for a spectacular conversation piece or an unusual way to transfer wine from a decanter. You can usually find them on eBay (I recently located several in the $30 range) or at online winery equipment sites.

Antique Wine Barrel: A smaller barrel makes a nifty countertop conversation piece or wastebasket, while a larger one brings viticultural charm to a walk-in wine cellar or backyard. Scour eBay or consult an antiques dealer.

DON'T FORGET Wine glasses (see Shortcut 87), decanters (see Shortcut 86), and fancy corkscrews such as the traditional French Laguiole and the high-tech Screwpull Lever (see Shortcut 81).

Three for the Road

We *conclude with* three subjects that inevitably arise in my wine classes. The first, headaches and wine, is a phenomenon not fully understood by modern medicine but one that can be minimized with certain measures. The next, visiting wine country, is a glorious pursuit that can be even more satisfying if you make yourself a VIP. And, finally, we cover the best resources to use in your continuing quest to outsmart wine. ∎

106 No One Has Figured Out Headaches and Wine, but Don't Blame Sulfites

Everybody seems to have a different theory about headaches and wine. Many blame red wine, some point to white, and a few swear the culprit is drinking both in the same night. My neighbor maintains that the bubbles in Champagne do her in, while eco-warrior friends are leery of any bottle carrying a sulfites warning. And it's hard to dispute the idea that anything in a box, jug, or pouch is an express ticket to a nasty hangover, not to mention scorn from wine snobs.

If you've already discovered your vinous downfall, there's no arguing with that. Just know that modern medicine isn't absolutely certain about which wine types give people headaches or exactly why they do. What we do know is that the leading suspect in the headache mystery is histamines. Naturally occurring substances in wine, histamines are said to dilate the blood vessels in the head and be a problem for people who lack the enzyme that helps metabolize this compound. Many studies have indicated that red wine is much more likely to contain histamines than white wine, which might explain why that bottle of Cabernet was such a pain in the membrane. Taking an over-the-counter antihistamine before imbibing may help.

In addition to histamines, possible causes of wine-induced headaches are the tannins predominant in certain varieties of red wine, aberrant strains of bacteria and yeast from grape skins, and, of course, drinking to excess. Heavy drinking can be especially painful with cheap wine, which is sometimes fortified with sugar to boost its alcohol content and results in an inferior kind of alcohol that some say is more likely to make heads pound.

Contrary to popular belief, one substance that most doctors are certain doesn't lead to headaches is sulfites, despite their infamous warning label. Sulfites are present in all wine, coming from the skins of the grapes and also from the traces of sulfur dioxide that winemakers add to prevent oxidization and kill bacteria. Sulfites won't affect you unless you're one of the rare people allergic to this compound, and even if you are, it will cause asthma symptoms, not head pain.

Here are two general recommendations that have helped my students.

1. **Give Your Downfall Another Chance:** Don't let a few hangovers cause you to write off an entire category of wine. Many people do this, as did I, when a few head-pounding sessions in college prompted me to conclude wrongly that Champagne gave me headaches. It was several years before I even touched the stuff again, but once I gave it a few more chances, headaches were no longer an issue. Sometimes you need to try a better producer or even a different context in which to drink a particular wine. If you give your vinous downfall a second, third, or even seventh chance, you might find it suits you just fine.

2. **Hydrate Yourself:** Always drink copious amounts of water throughout a night of heavy drinking and before bed. Water will counteract the dehydration and resulting headaches you experience as your body works to remove the toxins present in your blood after drinking. Water is the number-one weapon my wine-pro friends and I use to survive wine-saturated nights.

On My Table | **JEAN-GUILLAUME PRATS**, a former French champion in court tennis, is CEO of Château Cos d'Estournel, a top Bordeaux château.

Manzanilla [a dry Spanish sherry]—"To start a meal."
    Hidalgo

White Bordeaux—"For my birthday."
    Haut-Brion

Sauternes—"With Arcachon oysters."
    Château de Fargues

Ribera del Duero
    Vega Sicilia

Vintage port—"For the dark winter of the Médoc."
    Quinta do Vesuvio

107 For VIP Treatment in Wine Country, Make Reservations and Take Notes

"IF YOU CAN, GO TO THE SOURCE . . . SEEING THE WINERY, THE VINEYARDS, MEETING THE PEOPLE, WILL CHANGE YOUR PERCEPTION AND ADD ANOTHER DIMENSION NEXT TIME YOU DRINK THAT WINE."

—*Mireille Guiliano, president, Clicquot, Inc.*

If, like most people, visiting wine country finds you elbowing your way through a noisy hospitality room only for a $7 glass of mediocre Merlot, take heart: VIP treatment is easier to get than you think. Here are two insider ways to get better treatment at wineries—especially in bustling locales like Napa Valley.

MAKE RESERVATIONS The most interesting experiences are at the wineries that recommend or require appointments to visit. Worry not: these wineries aren't like those high-roller suites at Las Vegas hotels that cater to the Gulfstream and Beluga set. Appointment-only policies are less a function of exclusivity than they are of the wineries' small size and inability to accommodate heavy traffic, both in the winery itself and on the often windy mountain roads leading there.

The beauty of prearranging a visit is that it immediately separates you from the gaggle of yahoos scoping out their next boozy pit stop. It sends the message that you're making a special effort to visit that particular winery. The winery will often respond in kind, giving you a personal tour, tastes of rare wine, and perhaps barrel samples—sometimes conducted by the vintner herself.

It is also helpful to have your hotel's concierge or local distributor or merchant make the reservation, as you are more important to the winery when you are connected to a hotel or distributor that has an ongoing business relationship with the winery. And if you have any connection to the wine business, be sure that it gets mentioned too: the wine trade prides itself on taking care of its own.

TAKE NOTES Another way to differentiate yourself from the dreaded throngs of winery hoppers is to express a special interest in learning about the wines served. Take notes, whether in a journal, on a PDA, or even on a paper place mat. Most people never bother to record their impressions, but those who do sometimes find that a Reserve bottle magically emerges from underneath the tasting counter. By taking notes, you'll telegraph that you're serious enough to be served the winery's rare and wonderful stuff. It will also help you piece together the highlights of a long, merry day of sampling the vintner's art.

MORE STRATEGIES FOR OUTSMARTING VISITS TO WINE COUNTRY

- Avoid the summer and weekends to dodge the crowds.
- Before your trip, buy a map and plot your journey, as most wine regions are spread out and you'll probably be able to comfortably visit only three or four wineries in a day. Try to visit sites that are relatively close to each other. When touring Napa or Sonoma, I'm rarely without *The Quick Access Napa-Sonoma Wine Country Map and Guide* (Wine Appreciation Guild), a user-friendly, laminated foldout map that pinpoints over four hundred wineries and includes their contact information.
- Go early in the day. Winery staff is more likely to open a special bottle if they think there's enough time for the bottle to be finished that day.
- Buy something. Some wineries break out better stuff for paying customers.

CHEAT SHEET

Making reservations and taking notes differentiate you as a serious wine visitor and can bring about friendlier service and better wine.

OUTSMART THE TABLE

- "Adopt a winery" and follow it through the years, noticing the differences and similarites in its wines. Also, join the winery's club, if available; special deals and allocations of limited-run wines are offered to club members.
- When buying wine during winery visits, show it the care you would a beloved basset hound—protect it from the sweltering sun by parking in the shade, using a sunshade, or storing it in an ice cooler.
- To order Mark's exclusive *Guide to Outsmarting Napa Valley*, as well as insider booklets on other wine regions, please visit www.MarkOldman.com.

On My Table | **MICHAEL BROADBENT,** legendary wine writer and head of Christie's wine department, holds the title Master of Wine and virtually every other vinous honor.

Red Bordeaux—"I'm a Médoc man [for high-end Bordeaux] . . . but I rarely buy Pomerol because it's overpriced. . . . Lately I also am quite fond of Château Latour de By—a *cru* Bourgeois."

Champagne—"For breakfast, I always have two-thirds fresh orange juice and one-third Champagne."

Chianti Classico—"Like Bordeaux, a great food wine."

Riesling—"We will do an Auslese at 11:00 A.M. in the country."
     Weil

Sherry—"The best aperitif . . . I keep it in my refrigerator, next to the milk. . . . Recently had it with fish and chips."
     Tio Pepe

Tokaji Aszú—"I enjoy it after I go to the theater . . . also with dessert or as dessert."
     Arvay

Port—vintage and tawny—"Tawny port is soft, mellow, easy to enjoy, and a surprisingly good value."
     Warre's, Fonseca

108 More Resources to Outsmart Wine

Internet

Wine Spectator Online (www.winespectator.com)
The Web property of *Wine Spectator* magazine offers a vast database of wine reviews and straightforward searchability, accessible by subscription. Non-subscribers can look up articles on almost every conceivable wine subject, including top wine values, regional profiles, and an annual restaurant report identifying the world's most wine-friendly eateries.

Robert Parker Online (www.erobertparker.com)
Simultaneously an unobfuscating ex-lawyer, incorruptible consumer reporter, and unrepentant sensualist, Robert Parker's taste—as dispensed by his books, newsletter, and Web site—affects consumers with an influence second only to Oprah. A yearly subscription to the Web site affords access to thousands of Parker's wine reviews, making this a key resource for obtaining detailed critiques of specific wines. The search engine is sleek and user friendly, allowing the user to query wines by standard criteria like grape variety, price, and region, as well as by any words in Parker's tasting notes. You also get articles from his newsletter, *The Wine Advocate*, as well as a vintage chart so detailed it belongs at NASA Mission Control.

Stephen Tanzer's International Wine Cellar (www.wineaccess.com/expert/tanzer)
A senior editor at *Food & Wine* magazine, Stephen Tanzer is known for his lucid, detailed wine reviews, which, along with those of Robert Parker and *Wine Spectator*, form a "big three" of wine evaluators. His site affords subscribers access to articles from his bimonthly IWC newsletter as well as a searchable database of over twenty-five thousand tasting notes. Many of the wines reviewed can be purchased through links to partner site www.wineaccess.com.

Robin Garr's Wine Lovers' Page (www.wineloverspage.com)

This site's homespun appearance belies its king's ransom of free wine information, with thousands of articles (written by both Garr and several guest columnists), travel information, glossaries, food-and-wine matching ideas, and online discussion groups.

Allen Meadows's Burghound (www.burghound.com)

For an annual fee, this site provides online access to Burgundy expert Allen Meadows's masterful insights and tasting notes on the wines of this complicated region. Meadows's quarterly newsletter is also available in paper form.

Wine Searcher (www.Wine-Searcher.com)

A secret weapon for tracking down specific bottles, this ingenious database allows you to type in the producer, name, and year of a wine and then returns links to wine shops around the world that stock the wine, listed by price. Subscribing to a "Pro Version" increases the number of listings supplied.

Newspapers

The *Wall Street Journal*'s "Tastings" column

It's worth a subscription to the *Journal* just for Dorothy Gaiter and John Brecher's warm-spirited weekly column on wine. Joyful and nonjudgmental, it covers major wine topics with a clarity and folksy charm unique in wine writing.

The *New York Times*' "The Pour" column and more

Longtime "cheap eats" restaurant critic Eric Asimov is now lending his incisive wit and populist spirit to "The Pour," a column in the *Times*' weekly "Dining" section. Asimov also oversees the section's panel tastings, which provide useful feedback on currently available wines of a particular category, such as Dry Creek Zinfandel or wine from France's Mâconnais region. Veteran wine columnist Frank Prial also occasionally pens his crisp, colorful "Wine Talk" column for the paper.

Magazines

Wine Spectator (www.winespectator.com)

Excellent journalism meets the sheen of *Vanity Fair* in this glossy, oversized monthly, filled with up-to-date wine news, columns written by top wine writers, profiles of growing regions and winemakers, and copious tasting notes. This over-the-top publication is essential reading for both novices and serious collectors.

Decanter (www.decanter.com)

Published in the UK, this well-written monthly magazine provides a more international perspective on wine regions and trends. Stocked at better newsstands.

Wine & Spirits (www.wineandspiritsmagazine.com)

Published eight times a year, this practical publication is another quality source for topical information and wine news for consumers. As its name suggests, it also features articles on, and reviews of, other kinds of alcohol, such as premium vodka.

Newsletters

The Wine Advocate (Robert Parker)

The heart of Robert Parker's media empire, this unadorned, bimonthly newsletter continues to be the gold standard for ratings of specific wines. Using a 100-point scale similar to a grammar school report card, Parker gives each wine he tastes a score, followed up by a written justification for that rating. The advantage of the print newsletter over Parker's Web resource is that newsletter subscribers get the scoop on the latest wines weeks before it is published online. (www.erobertparker.com; The Wine Advocate, Inc., P.O. Box 311, Monkton, MD 21111; 410-329-6477)

International Wine Cellar (Steven Tanzer)

Each bimonthly issue of this print newsletter provides Tanzer's conscientious tasting notes on over five hundred wines, as well as articles on vineyard regions, vintage evaluations, and interviews with wine pros. Subscribers may also buy a joint print and Web subscription. (www.wineaccess.com; P.O. Box 20021, New York, NY 10021; 800-WINE-505)

Books

REINFORCING THE BASICS

Kevin Zraly, *The Windows on the World Complete Wine Course* (Sterling Publishing)
This book provides a country-by-country tour of the world's major wine-growing areas, accompanied by wine trivia and maps. A former sommelier, author Kevin Zraly writes with economy, presenting the information in manageable, memorable lists and modules.

Andrea Immer, *Great Wine Made Simple* (Broadway Books)
An unpretentious guide to wine components (e.g., oak, acidity, tannin) and major wine regions. The book really shines in its comparative tasting charts, which detail the finer distinctions between two similar wines (e.g., French Champagne and American sparkling wine).

Jancis Robinson, *How to Taste: A Guide to Enjoying Wine* (Simon & Schuster)
This was my first wine book, back in the 1980s when it was published in the UK as *Masterglass*. Written in breezy, reassuring prose, it remains one of the most useful overviews of wine, providing a satisfying mix of theory, practical advice, and tasting exercises. (Robinson's *World Atlas of Wine*, written with fellow Brit Hugh Johnson, is also a classic.)

GENERAL REFERENCE

Jancis Robinson (ed.), *The Oxford Companion to Wine* (Oxford University Press)
An essential reference for the serious drinker (but perhaps overwhelming to the neophyte), this 820-page, six-pound leviathan feels like an anthology of literature, with its extensive explanations (in small type), pervasive cross-references, and overall air of unassailable authority. If Dionysus won't answer your wine query, this book will.

Karen MacNeil, *The Wine Bible* (Workman)
At 910 pages, this mother lode of wine information is the ultimate encyclopedia for wine. It is a spectacular effort, written with the kind of lucidity and passion that one rarely sees in reference guides.

Oz Clarke's *Encyclopedia of Grapes* (Harcourt)

An effervescent chap who really knows his wine, Brit Oz Clarke is a far cry from the typical stuffy wine authority. His books are as rich and colorful as his writing, including the beautifully illustrated *Encyclopedia of Grapes*, which contains useful "maturity charts" for estimating the ageability of particular grape types.

Alexis Bespaloff, *The New Frank Schoonmaker Encyclopedia of Wine* (William Morrow)

This classic has served me so well in the past decade that its spine is now in tatters. Designed in a linear, text-only format that makes it more like a dictionary than an encyclopedia, it is one of the best quick-reference wine books on the market.

CHECK OUT

Michael Broadbent's Vintage Wine (Harcourt)

This unapologetically patrician diary recounts auction legend Michael Broadbent's fifty years of sampling the best and oldest wine with some of the world's wealthiest oenophiles. If you're curious about the taste of a Margaux 1791 ("remarkable") or a Romanée-Conti 1999 ("like an unexploded bomb"), this is essential reading.

Jay McInerney, *Bacchus & Me* (Vintage)

Derived from the novelist's wine column in *Home & Garden* magazine, this book is a stylish and eminently readable departure from the typical sleep-inducing wine guide. The book is laced with sly asides, such as "Like boys and girls locked away in same-sex prep schools, most wines yearn for a bit of flesh."

Kermit Lynch, *Adventures on the Wine Route* (Farrar, Straus & Giroux)

Creep inside the mind of an importer *extraordinaire* as he travels the back roads of France scoping out fine wine made by small, idiosyncratic producers. This candid narrative serves as a manifesto for understanding what quality wine is all about.

Select Bibliography

Coates, Clive. *Côte d'Or: A Celebration of the Great Wines of Burgundy.* Berkeley, California: University of California Press, 1997.

Jenkins, Steve. *The Cheese Primer.* New York: Workman, 1996.

Kramer, Matt. *Making Sense of Burgundy.* New York: William Morrow, 1990.

McCarthy, Ed, and Mary Ewing-Mulligan. *Wine for Dummies,* 2nd edition. Foster City, California: IDG Worldwide, 1998.

Norman, Remington. *The Great Domaines of Burgundy: A Guide to the Finest Wine Producers of the Côte d'Or.* London: Kyle Cathie, 1998.

Parker, Robert, Jr. *Bordeaux,* rev. 3rd edition. New York: Simon & Schuster, 1998.

Parker, Robert, Jr., and Pierre-Antoine Rovani. *Parker's Wine Buyer's Guide,* 6th edition. New York: Simon & Schuster, 2002.

Acknowledgments

A *pop* of the cork to the extraordinary efforts of:

David Cashion: a prince of perspicuity and editorial excellence—his professionalism and keen judgment are unmatched. Thanks also for the fine work and kind support of Kathryn Court, Sarah Manges, Ann Mah, and Stephen Morrison, as well as Bruce Giffords, Acadia Wallace, Maureen Donnelly, and Christine Benton.

Stephanie Abou: France's leading export, an ace agent and strategizer, who "got it" from our first glass of Prosecco; all at the Joy Harris agency; and Jo Maeder: the coolest radio goddess ever to venture south of the Mason-Dixon.

Jane and Clark Emery: my "Rexian" and literary inspiration, the queen of the constructive zigzag, and a true pioneer.

Denele Benhoff: the lovely Crock-a-Dee, an unflagging source of inspiration, always exhorting me to "dooo it, dooo it."

Burt and Deedee McMurtry: elegant expeditionists of gastronomy, geography, and goodwill. You instilled the big *B* in my Burgundian education.

Rob Schipano, a longtime dean of design, always up for the next caper. And Juliette Borda, a goddess of gouache.

Samer Hamadeh and Mark Hernandez, longtime trusted comrades-in-arms and occasional wine-seminar security detail.

A raise of the chalice to (in no particular order): Alan Chin and Vanessa Rocco, Danny Ko, Tony Goldman, M. Alexander Hoye, Peta Hartmann, Rose-Anna and Jeremy Stanton, Bill Landreth, Marty Higgins, all Vault staffers, Helen Bing (supreme orchestrator of "general joy"), the SU BoT and the SU SAA BoD, Tom "Nellie" Nelson, Rob "Full" Nelson, James Corl, Adrian "Lemons" Jasso, Dr. Andrew Frutkin, Léa Droessaert, Wendy Munger, Lee and Cece Black, Her Excellency Price Hicks, Heidi Roizen, Jim Canales, Laura Locke, Joan Lane, Theodore Allegaert, Kevin Hartz, Kasia "Jan 5" Moreno, "Cab for" Cory Booker, Julie Horowitz, Matthew Doull and Vicky Ward, Joey Raguso, Jeanne Krier, Maddy and Isaac Stein, Erik Charlton, Steve Olson, Ole Tustin,

Richard Rubenstein, Mary Cook and the SAA Wine Program, Fiona Smith Singer, Sarah Griffith, Pam Brandin, Magelonne Durand de Fontmagne, Dillon Cohen, G. Gordon Bellis, Ed Shen, Marcy Lerner, Gary and Greg Butch, Jon Damashek, Erika Seidman, Dan Beltramo, John Kirks, Roy Johnson, the Meateaters, Vicki Sant, the Oxford Wine Circle, the Georgetown Club of New York, Nascar C. Philips, Bill Seeson, Rock Tang, Carter Weiss, Chloé and Lalo de Smet, Leslie and George Hume, Marko Lehtimaki, John Abbott, Ahovi Kponou, K. Don Cornwell, Phil Melconian, Jen and Bobby Peters, Kevin and Jane Warsh, Dixon Robin, Mitchell Fenster, Bart Araujo, Walter Hewlett, Eileen Foliente, Marcy Lerner, Erik Jorgensen, Matt Paige, Steve Apfelberg, Mike Wyatt, Nick Orum, Al and Boots Braunstein, Raoul Bhavani, Rick Holmstrom, Mel Penn, Riccardo and Karen Bracco, Howard Wolf, Edie Barry, Amy Paulson, Linda McCarthy, Jeremy Seysses and family, Karena Bullock, Five Points restaurant of New York, Harris' Restaurant of San Francisco, Jon Damashek, the Mulner family, and Bobby Wong.

A general's salute to all eighty-three On My Table participants (full list in the Appendix), with an extra thumbs-up to the passionate efforts of Heather Willens, Mireille Guiliano, Geddy Lee, Mike Havens, Terry Theise, Jay McInerney, Rémi Krug, Jack Stuart, Daniel Johnnes, David Andrew, Larry Stone, John Kapon, Michael Broadbent, and Eric Ober.

A high-five for the fine assistance of Luke Hasselhof, Pegi Cecconi, Kathleen Talbert, Marvin Shanken, Dixie Lee Gill, Jana Fleishman, Sandy Timpson, Fern Berman, Kylene Keith, Chris Shipley, Kevin Tedesco, Mark Hawley, Elizabeth Faulkner, Ann Pickett, Benedetta Roux, Michele Connors, Jochen Becker-Köhn, Cécil Brodard, and Christian Holthausen.

And finally, my gratitude to the good cheer and continuing kindnesses of Mrs. Saylor and all of the family, especially the doctors Oldman: Elizabeth, Marilyn, and Elliott.

"Pull the lever, get the egg."

Appendix:
On My Table Survey Results

The *On My Table* survey conducted for this book comprises the personal wine preferences of eighty-three accomplished wine enthusiasts, from leading winemakers and sommeliers to renowned chefs and celebrity collectors. Survey respondents range in age from twenty-four to ninety-five and represent thirteen countries and more than twenty wine regions therein, from the backwoods of the Pacific Northwest to the grandest châteaux of Bordeaux to Lebanon's Bekáa Valley, the "bread basket" of ancient Rome. A full list of participants appears at the end of the Appendix.

The Ten Most-Often-Cited Wine Types in the On My Table Survey

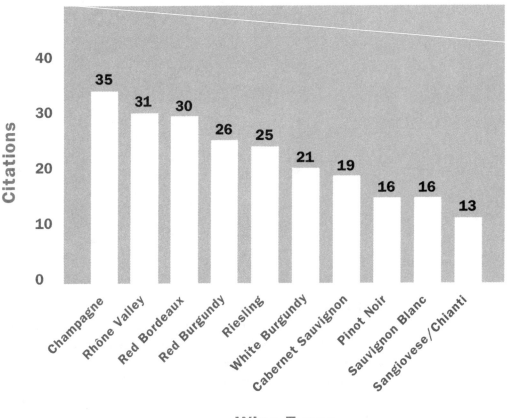

Interesting Patterns from the On My Table Survey

CHAMPAGNE WINS About half of the survey respondents put Champagne—the real stuff from France—on their list of favorites.

TRIUMPH OF THE RHÔNE VALLEY In an upset, the Rhône Valley emerged as the most popular source of nonsparkling wine, edging out more famous red Bordeaux and red Burgundy. The northern Rhône was cited sixteen times, while wine from the southern Rhône had fifteen mentions.

RIESLING AND CABERNET SAUVIGNON LEAD, CHARDONNAY LAGS

The top varietal wine was Riesling—reflecting the fact that insiders continue to relish this wine, while most casual wine drinkers ignore it. Varietal Cabernet Sauvignon came next, occupying the seventh spot, while varietal Chardonnay lagged behind with only ten votes. (In fairness to this wonderful grape, Chardonnay from France's Burgundy region—i.e., white Burgundy—rated the sixth most popular.)

CHAMBOLLE-MUSIGNY TOPS IN RED BURGUNDY The most cited village of Burgundy was Chambolle-Musigny, the Côte de Nuits village known for expensive, elegant wine such as the *premier cru* Les Amoureuses.

GIGONDAS POPULAR IN SOUTHERN RHÔNE Among those who cited southern Rhône appellations, the district of Gigondas was mentioned several times. An affordable alternative to Châteauneuf-du-Pape, Gigondas is a sturdy, spicy wine with plenty of the region's characteristic dark berry earthiness.

NEW ZEALAND WINS FOR SAUVIGNON BLANC The most popular country for Sauvignon Blanc was New Zealand—beating out the old guard of France and America.

LANGUEDOC BEATS MERLOT In one of the more dramatic upsets, the backwoods locale of the Languedoc-Roussillon (six citations) triumphed over the world-famous varietal Merlot (four). This reflects the fact that experts increasingly view the Languedoc as one of the world's most exciting regions for value, where many of the wines are soft, spicy reds from Rhône-style grapes.

DID SOMEBODY SAY MADIRAN? One of the biggest surprises was the popularity of wine from Madiran, an obscure viticultural area of southwestern France that makes rich, earthy, full-bodied red wine. It was mentioned four times—the same score as varietal Merlot.

Survey Respondents

Locations of Survey Respondents

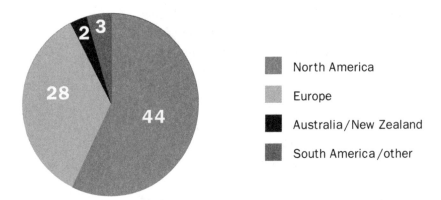

- North America
- Europe
- Australia/New Zealand
- South America/other

Occupations of Survey Respondents

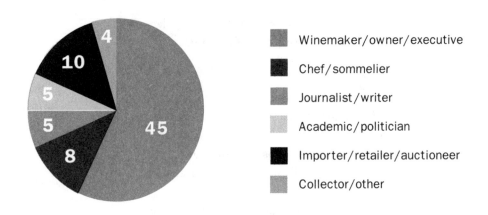

- Winemaker/owner/executive
- Chef/sommelier
- Journalist/writer
- Academic/politician
- Importer/retailer/auctioneer
- Collector/other

On My Table Survey Participants

PERSONALITY AND *TERROIR*

Tori Amos, music star and Bordeaux lover, Devon, England

David Andrew, former global wine buyer, Costco, Seattle, WA

Piero Antinori, owner, Marchese Antinori, Tuscany, Italy

Robert Lawrence Balzer, wine writer and educator, Los Angeles, CA

Mario Batali, celebrity chef, restaurateur, and TV personality, New York, NY

Michael Bonaccorsi, the late vintner and master sommelier, Santa Barbara, CA

Daniel Boulud, celebrity chef and restaurateur, New York, NY

Michael Broadbent, wine writer and head of Christie's wine department, London, England

Regis Camus, winemaker, Champagne Charles Heidsieck, Champagne, France

Jean-Michel Cazes, owner, Château Lynch-Bages, Bordeaux, France

Alessandro Ceretto, winemaker and co-owner, Piedmont, Italy

Eric Cinnamon, winemaker, Rancho Zabaco, Sonoma, CA

Francis Ford Coppola, legendary filmmaker and vintner, Napa, CA

Didier Depond, president, Champagne Salon, Champagne, France

Frédéric Drouhin, manager and family proprietor, Maison Joseph Drouhin, Burgundy, France

Georges Duboeuf, proprietor, Les Vins Georges Duboeuf, Beaujolais, France

Alvaro Espinoza, winemaker, Haras de Pirque, Maipo Valley, Chile

Pierre-Henry Gagey, president, Louis Jadot, Burgundy, France

Lane Giguiere, cofounder and manager, R.H. Phillips, Dunnigan Hills, CA

Peter Granoff, wine merchant, e-commerce pioneer, and master sommelier, San Francisco, CA

Mireille Guiliano, president, Clicquot, Inc., New York, NY

Fritz Hasselbach, winemaker and owner, Gunderloch, Nackenheim, Germany

Mike Havens, winemaker and owner, Havens, Napa, CA

Paul Henderson, owner, Gidleigh Park, Devon, England

Serge Hochar, winemaker and owner, Château Musar, Beirut, Lebanon

Etienne Hugel, co-owner, Hugel et Fils, Alsace, France

Michel Jaboulet, president and owner, Paul Jaboulet Aîné, Rhône, France

Craig Jaffurs, winemaker and owner, Jaffurs Wine Cellars, Santa Barbara, CA

Daniel Johnnes, importer, author, and wine director, Montrachet, New York, NY

Kevin Judd, winemaker, Cloudy Bay, Marlborough, New Zealand

John Kapon, co-owner, president, and auction director, Acker, Merrall & Condit, New York, NY

Karen King, wine director, Gramercy Tavern restaurant, New York, NY

Rémi Krug, co-owner, Champagne Krug, Champagne, France

Fran Kysela, importer and owner, Kysela, Père et Fils, Winchester, VA

Mészáros László, director and winemaker, Domaine Disznókő, Tokaj, Hungary

Geddy Lee, collector and rock musician, Toronto, Canada

Ludacris, rap star and Champagne lover, Atlanta, GA

Kermit Lynch, importer, owner, and author, Kermit Lynch Wine Merchant, Berkeley, CA

Sirio Maccioni, owner, Le Cirque 2000 restaurant, New York, NY

Cristina Mariani-May, owner, Castello Banfi, Tuscany, Italy

Jay McInerney, bestselling novelist and wine writer, New York, NY

Allen Meadows, owner, Burghound.com, Los Angeles, CA

Corinne Mentzelopoulos, co-owner and managing director, Château Margaux, Bordeaux, France

Robert Mondavi, founder, Robert Mondavi Winery, Napa, CA

Christian Moreau, winemaker and owner, Domaine Christian Moreau, Chablis, France

Stephen Mutkoski, professor and creator of Cornell's "Intro to Wine" course, Ithaca, NY

Ann Noble, professor emerita of enology and inventor of the Wine Aroma Wheel, Davis, CA

Greg Norman, golf legend, winery owner, and collector, Jupiter, FL

Eric Ober, former president, Food Network, New York, NY

Chester Osbourn, chief winemaker, d'Arenberg, McLaren Vale, Australia

Georges Pauli, winemaker, Château Gruaud-Larose, Bordeaux, France

François Perrin, winemaker and owner, Château de Beaucastel, Rhône, France

Jean-Guillaume Prats, CEO, Château Cos d'Estournel, Bordeaux, France

Don Quattlebaum, importer and owner, New Castle Imports, Myrtle Beach, SC

George Radanovich, U.S. congressman and former winery owner, Washington, DC

Alan Richman, food and wine writer, *GQ* magazine, New York, NY

Jean-Claude Rouzaud, president and owner, Champagne Roederer, Champagne, France

Morley Safer, correspondent and co-editor, *60 Minutes,* New York, NY

Garen Staglin, owner and vintner, Staglin, Napa, CA

Park Smith, collector and co-owner, Veritas restaurant, New York, NY

Larry Stone, master sommelier and wine director, Rubicon, San Francisco, CA

Jack Stuart, general manager and winemaster, Silverado, Napa, CA

Serena Sutcliffe, M.W., head of Sotheby's International Wine Department, London, England

Dominic Symington, managing director, Symington Port Companies, Vila Nova de Gaia, Portugal

Rupert Symington, managing director, Symington Port Companies, Vila Nova de Gaia, Portugal

Claude Taittinger, director and family proprietor, Taittinger, Champagne, France

Felipe González-Gordon Terry, family proprietor, Gonzalez Byass, Jerez de la Frontera, Spain

Terry Theise, importer and owner, Therry Theise Selections, Washington, DC

Mike Thompson, U.S. congressman, Washington, DC

Miguel Torres Jr., president, Jean León winery, and fifth-generation winemaker, Penedes, Spain

Charlie Trotter, celebrity chef, restaurateur, and author, Chicago, IL

Madeline Triffon, wine director, Unique Restaurant Corporation, Detroit, MI

Neil deGrasse Tyson, collector, astrophysicist, and director, Hayden Planetarium, New York, NY

Delia Viader, owner, Viader, Napa, CA

Arthur von Wiesenberger, collector, "water master," and food and wine writer, Santa Barbara, CA

Ray Walsh, chief winemaker, King Estate, Eugene, Oregon

Wilhelm Weil, estate director and winemaker, Weingut Robert Weil, Rheingau, Germany

Jamey Whetstone, assistant winemaker, Turley Wine Cellars, Napa, CA

Heather Willens, import sales director, Jeroboam Wines, New York, NY

Craig Williams, winemaker, Joseph Phelps, Napa, CA

Wade Wolfe, general manager, Hogue Cellars, Prosser, WA

Phil Woodward, cofounder, Chalone Wine Group, Napa, CA

Donald Ziraldo, cofounder, Inniskillin Wines, Ontario, Canada

Note: To ensure a wide selection of recommendations, the picks of Amos, Coppola, Ludacris, Meadows, Norman, and Pauli were not included in the final calculation of preferences because each of their responses offered fewer than four different wines.

Index

acidity, 6, 12, 23
    age of wine and, 17, 20, 295
    fermentation and, 16–17
    food and, 17, 222, 235–36
aeration, 12, 21, 275
    see also decanting, decanters
aftertaste, *see* finish
aged tawny port, 199
ageworthy wines, 294–99
Albariño, 148–49
alcohol content, 6, 15, 22, 23
Alsace, 75–77, 153
Alsatian wines, 75–77, 153–54
American Viticultural Area (AVA), 310
American wines, *see specific states*
Amos, Tori, 23, 94
Andrew, David, 64
Anjou, 141
Antinori, Piero, 124
aperitif wines, 215, 232
appellation, 51, 67, 107, 309
appreciation of wine, 5–27
Argentine wines, 165–66, 188
aroma, 9, 12, 18, 19, 23
    see also nose, of wine
artichokes, 235
Auslese, 38
Australian wines, 3, 15, 22, 188, 298
    bin number on, 137
    climate and, 60
    winemakers' practices for, 60–61, 136–37
    see also Shiraz; *specific types of wine*

Austrian wines, 39, 156–57, 196, 202

bachelor parties, 217
balance, 12, 23
Balbo, Susana, 166
Bandol, 141
Banyuls, 327
Barbaresco, *see* Barolo and Barbaresco
barbecues and picnics, 212
Barbera, 172–73
    grapes, 141
Barolo and Barbaresco, 130–31, 294
barrels, 18–19, 330
Batali, Mario, 4, 103, 112, 125, 170, 186
Beaujolais, 160–61, 211, 324
    alternatives to, 172–73
    cru Beaujolais, 114, 160–61, 211, 324
    as fail-safe restaurant choice, 250
Beaujolais Nouveau, 113–14, 304
    alternatives to, 160–61
Beerenauslese, 38
best buys, 317–23
Best Cellars, 307
birthday parties, 213–14
bistro wines, 215–16
Bize, Simon, 109
blush wines, 57
body of wine, 12, 13, 22
Bonaccorsi, Michael, 122, 209
Bordeaux:
    dominant grapes in, 45, 82–83

Bordeaux (*cont.*)
    1855 classification and, 86–87, 89–91
    purchasing futures in, 90–91
    see also red Bordeaux; white Bordeaux
Bordeaux region, 26, 44, 98
    climate of, 83
    see also specific subregions and types of
       wine
Boulud, Daniel, 27, 223
bouquet, *see* aroma
Bourgeuil, 163
brandy, 22, 198
Broadbent, Michael, 82, 199, 338
Brunello di Montalcino, 125–26
bubbles:
    Champagne, 180, 181
    inebriation accelerated by, 191
    judging sparkling wines by, 180
Burgundy, 107–10
    see also red Burgundy; white Burgundy
Burgundy region, 141
    climate of, 100, 110
    group ownership of vineyards in,
      109–10
    importance of *terroir* in, 25, 103
    producers as paramount in, 109–10
    subregions of, 68–72, 103–6
    see also specific subregions
business meals, wine for, 252, 254
BYOB, 259–60

Cabernet Franc, 163–64
    grapes, 82, 202
Cabernet Sauvignon, 42–43
    alternatives to, 163–64
    grapes, 20, 30, 45, 48, 60, 73–74, 82–83,
      87, 92, 128, 133, 134, 163, 295
Cahors, 165
California wines, 2–3, 15, 16, 22, 298
    climate and, 60
    winemakers' practices for, 60–61
    see also specific regions and types of wine
Canadian wines, 202, 203
Carmenère grapes, 44
Carneros, 46

Cava, 187–88, 250
caviar, 232
Cellars International, 313
Ceretto, Alessandro, 132
Chablis, 16, 68–69
Chambolle-Musigny, 105
Champagne:
    alternatives to, 186–87
    body of, 180–81
    deciphering labels of, 180
    dry vs. sweet, 179
    fermentation of, 178
    French regulations for, 177–78
    grape blend used in, 177–78, 180
    grower, 326
    judging of, 180–81
    prestige cuvée, 183–85
    production of, 177–78
    rosé, 210
    serving temperature for, 271–73
    styles of, 181
    vintage vs. nonvintage, 178–79
    see also sparkling wines
chaptalizing, 22
Chardonnay, 15, 23, 32–34, 36, 37, 38, 67
    alternatives to, 146–49
    from Australia, 18, 33, 67
    from California, 18, 32–33, 67
    as fail-safe restaurant choice, 250
    grapes, 30, 60, 67, 68, 71, 177
    oak used in, 15, 32–33
    popularity of, 32, 65
Chassagne-Montrachet, 68, 70–72
Château Haut-Brion, 89–90
Château Lafite-Rothschild, 89–90
Château Latour, 89–90
Château Margaux, 89–90
Château Mouton-Rothschild, 89–90
Châteauneuf-du-Pape, 120, 167–68
cheese and wine, 229–31, 234
Chenin Blanc, 226
Chianti, 17, 60, 122–23
    alternatives to, 170–71
    Italian laws regarding, 128
Chianti Classico, 123

labels, labeling:
  of Bordeaux, 64, 65
  of Burgundy, 68–69, 71,
    106–7
  buzzwords on, 309–10
  good-looking, 325
  importer names on, 311
  New World vs. Old World method of, 30,
    51, 60, 67
lactic acids, 17
Languedoc-Roussillon region, 321
late-bottled vintage port, 199
late-harvest wines, 195–96
  see also dessert wines
Lebanese wines, 326
Lee, Geddy, 64, 102, 112, 160
Left Bank, see Graves region; Médoc
  region
leftover wine, 285–88
legs, of wine, 11, 13
LoCascio, Leonard, 313
Loire Valley region, 35, 65, 73, 141
  see also specific subregions
long-term storage, 291–93
look, of wine, 11
Ludacris, 190, 191
Lynch, Kermit, 312, 314

Maccioni, Sirio, 27, 258
McInerney, Jay, 18, 48, 111, 112,
  119, 146
Mâconnais, 68, 69, 73
Mâcon-Villages, 69
Madeira, 201
Malbec, 165–66
malic acids, 17
malolactic fermentation, 16–17, 35
Malvasia grapes, 202
Margaux, 87
Mariani-May, Cristina, 127
Marlborough, 16
marriage proposals, 217
Marsala, 201
Marsannay, 141
Meadows, Allen, 15, 72, 106

Médoc, 83, 86–88
  cru bourgeois wines of, 86, 87, 95–96
  cru classé wines of, 86, 87–88
  1855 classification and, 87, 89–91
Mendoza region, 165
Mentzelopoulos, Corinne, 91
Mercurey, 106
Meritage, designation as, 310
Merlot, 42, 44–45, 51, 131
  alternatives to, 165–66
  grapes, 30, 82, 83, 92–93, 128, 134
méthode champenoise, 178
Meursault, 68, 70–72, 324
mold, 258, 267
Mondavi, Robert, 26, 35–36, 50
Montalcino, 125, 126
Montesquieu, Charles, 64
Morey, Bernard, 109
Moscato d'Asti, 202–3, 226
Mourvèdre grapes, 119, 167
Muscadet, 318
Muscat grapes, 202, 325
mushrooms, 26, 47, 99, 100, 131, 187, 221,
  233, 295
Mutkoski, Stephen, 265

Napa Valley, 16, 46
Nebbiolo grapes, 131
négociants, 110
Negroamaro grapes, 171
New Castle Imports, 313
newsletters, 303
New World wines, 29–57, 60
  labeling of, 30, 51, 60, 67
  vintage as less of an issue in, 60–61, 298
  see also specific countries and types of wine
New Zealand wines, 35, 151–52
Noble, Ann C., 8, 11
Norman, Greg, 32, 34, 317
nose, of wine, 11–12
nose, training of, 6, 7–10
Nuits-Saint-Georges, 105

oak, 6, 23
  American vs. French, 18–19, 133, 134

oak (cont.)
    aroma and, 18, 19
    and cost of barrels, 18–19
    fermentation using, 18–19, 35, 133
    tannin in, 28, 20
Ober, Eric, 129
off-dry wines, 15, 16, 222
old vines, 49, 310
Old World wines, 59–141
    labeling of, 30, 51, 60, 67
    tastes in wine, 60
    see also specific countries and types of wine
opened wine, lifespan of, 285–86
ordering, at restaurants, 249–55
Ordoñez, Jorge, 312
Oregon State wines, 78, 79
Osbourn, Chester, 138, 294
oversized bottles, 328

pacing, of wine service, 247
palate, 12
    see also taste
Parker, Robert, 9, 25, 295
Passover, 213–14
Pauillac, 87
pepper, as wine friendly, 222
Perrin, François, 169
Pessac-Léognan region, 64, 65, 87, 88
Petite Sirah grapes, 51
Petite Verdot grapes, 82
Philips, Dan, 312
Picolit, 327
Piedmont region wines, 123, 130–31, 141,
    172–73, 202
pink wines, 55–57
    see also white Zinfandel
Pinot Blanc, 77
    grapes, 76, 77
Pinot Grigio, 37, 65, 76, 78–79
    alternatives to, 156–57
    as fail-safe restaurant choice, 250
Pinot Gris, 76, 78, 79
Pinot Meunier grapes, 177
Pinot Noir, 46–47, 99
    as fail-safe restaurant choice, 250, 254

grapes, 30, 60, 99–101, 104, 110,
    140, 177, 295
pizza, 213
plastic stoppers, 264
Pomerol district, 45, 83, 92–93
port, 22, 198–201
Portuguese wines, 198, 201
Pouilly-Fuissé, 69, 73
Pouilly-Fumé, 36, 73–74
Prats, Jean-Guillaume, 335
preferences, communicating of, 12, 249, 253
premiers crus, see Bordeaux, 1855 classifica-
    tion and
prestige cuvée Champagne, 183–85
price:
    quality not indicated by, 306
    restaurant markups on, 239–40, 244
Primitivo, 170–71
    grapes, 49, 170
Priorato, 135
producers, as paramount in Burgundy,
    109–10
Prosecco, 186–87, 250, 324
"puffing," opening sparkling wine by,
    281–82
Puglia region, 71, 170
Puligny-Montrachet, 68, 70–72
purchasing wine, 301–30
    by the case, 307
    online research for, 307–8
    strategies for, 306–8
    trends vs. reliables in, 307
    from wine merchants, 303–8

Quattlebaum, Don, 116, 313

recorking leftover wine, 287, 288
red Bordeaux, 42, 60, 82–98
    ageability of, 83, 294, 295
    alternatives to, 95–99
    decanting of, 84
    grape blending in, 45, 64, 82–83, 87,
        92–93
    labeling of, 84, 86–87
    off-vintages, 95

second wines of, 97–98

vintage and, 84

see also specific subregions

red Burgundy, 60, 99–112

   ageability of, 47

   American Pinot Noir wines compared
      with, 46–47, 99

   complexity of, 23, 100

   decanting of, 101

   as inconsistent, 47

   see also specific subregions

red wines, 41–52, 81–137, 324

   age of, 11, 17, 294–96

   alternate selections for common, 159–73

   best buys in, 320–21

   emerging regions for, 321

   fermentation of, 20, 48, 83

   histamines in, 333

   serving temperatures for, 22, 268–73

   short-term storage of, 289–90

   tannins in, 16, 17, 20–21

   for Thanksgiving, 208–9

   weight of, 225

   see also specific types of red wine

refrigeration:

   of leftover wine, 287, 288

   for short-term storage, 290

regional styles of wine, 59–141

reserva, 134

reservations, at wineries, 336

"reserve," on label, 309

residual sugar, 15

resources, 339–43

restaurants, 237–60

   bottle stranding at, 248

   business meals at, 255

   BYOB at, 259–60

   discretion in ordering at, 249, 253, 254

   fail-safe choices at, 250–51

   finding good values at, 239–40

   food-wine pairing recommendations at,
      243–44

   off-vintages at, 240

   ordering by glass or bottle at, 244

   previewing wine lists of, 244, 255

price markups at, 239–40, 244

seeking selection help from staff at,
   249–50

sending back bottles at, 257–58

servers at, 246–47, 249–50

simple ordering phrases for, 253

upsell at, 246–47

wine presentation at, 247

see also wine lists

Rhône Valley, 51, 116–21, 141

   northern, 116–18, 136

   southern, 119–21

Rías Baixas, 148

Ribera del Duero, 134–35, 229

Richman, Alan, 14, 270

Riesling, 15, 37–39

   Alsatian vs. German, 76

   grapes, 30, 37–39, 75, 76, 195, 202

   see also German Rieslings

Right Bank, *see* Pomerol district; St.-
   Emilion

Rioja, 18, 60, 133–34

ripeness, 38

   alcohol content and, 15, 22

   sweetness and, 15, 202

romantic interludes, 212

rosé, 57, 140–41

   best buys for, 323

   Champagne, 210

Roussanne grapes, 168

ruby port, 198–99

Russian River Valley, 46

Safer, Morley, 24

salad dressing, 235–36

Salice Salentino, 171

salty foods, 233

Sancerre, 35, 60, 65, 73–74

Sangiovese grapes, 60, 122–23, 125, 126

Santa Barbara, 46

Santenay, 106

Saumur-Champigny, 163

Sauternes, 65, 195–96

Sauvignon Blanc, 35–36

   alternatives to, 151–54

Sauvignon Blanc (*cont.*)
 grapes, 30, 35–36, 60, 64, 195
 New World vs. Old World styles of, 151–52
Savigny-lès-Beaune, 105
Screwpull, 263–64
screw tops, 264
seafood, 216, 233, 318
second-seat wines, 240
second wines, 97–98
sediment, 275–77
Sélection de Grains Nobles (SNG), 76
Sémillion grapes, 35, 64–65, 195
sensory vocabulary, 8
serving of wine, 266–82
serving temperatures, 247–48, 268–73
 chart, 272
 for dessert wines, 17
 for red wines, 22, 268–73, 288
 for white wines, 268, 270–73
shelf talkers, 303
sherry, 200–201
Shipley, Chris, 56, 292
shippers, 110
Shiraz, 15, 18, 51, 116, 131, 136–37
 as fail-safe choice at restaurant, 250
 sparkling, 137
 see also Syrah
short-term storage, 289–90
smell, *see* aroma; nose, of wine
Smet, Chloé de, 109
Smith, Park, 113, 291
Solomon, Eric, 312
Sonoma Coast, 46
South African wines, 35, 318, 321
Spanish wines, 18, 141, 187–88, 200–201, 309
 see also specific types of wine
sparkling wines, 175–91
 affordability of, 190
 American vs. French, 186–87
 best buys for, 323
 for everyday meals, 190–91
 judging of, 180–81

opening of, 248, 281–82
serving temperature for, 271–73
 Shiraz, 137
 storage of, 289–90
Spätlese, 38
special occasions, 205–18
sprung-from-prison wines, 218
stain remover, 329
steakhouse wines, 215
Stellenbosch wines, 318, 321
St.-Emilion, 45, 83, 92–93
St.-Estéphe, 87
St.-Julien, 87
St. Patrick's Day, 214
Stone, Larry, 156, 245, 311
stoppers, 264, 288
storage, 283–94
 conditions for, 289–90
 of leftover wine, 285–86
 long-term, 291–93
 short-term, 289–90
 by wine merchants, 304
Stuart, Jack, 16, 46
sulfites, 333
summer wines, 217
Super Tuscans, 128–29
Sutcliffe, Serena, 27, 85, 112
sweet wines, *see* dessert wines
swirling, 6, 12, 13
Symington, Dominic, 286
Symington, Rupert, 201
Syrah, 51–52, 136
 grapes, 30, 51–52, 116, 117, 119, 128, 136, 137, 167
 see also Shiraz

Taittinger, Claude, 179
tannins, 6, 12, 16, 20–21, 23, 48, 295
 decanting and, 275
 fermentation process and, 20
 foods that neutralize, 222, 226
 in oak wood, 18, 20
 other uses of, 21
 as "structure" of red wine, 17, 20

white wines (*cont.*)

    fermentation of, 20, 48, 56, 64

    histamines in, 333

    serving temperature for, 268, 270–73

    short-term storage of, 289–90

    weight of, 225

    see also specific types of white wine

white Zinfandel, 56–57

    red Zinfandel compared with, 48

    sweetness of, 37, 38, 140

Wiesenberger, Arthur von, 27

Willamette Valley, 46

Willens, Heather, 189

Williams, Craig, 146, 155

Wine Aroma Wheel, 8, 9

Winebow, 313

wine cellars, 292

wine country, trips to, 336–37

wine glasses, 278–79, 330

    caring for, 279

    holding of, 12

wine lists, 242–44, 255

winemaking technology, 297–98

    Old World vs. New World, 60–61

wine merchants, 303–8

wine novices, gifts for, 324–25

wine racks, 290

wineries, visiting, 336–37

wine satchels, 328

wine snobs, gifts for, 326–27, 329–30

Wine Spectator, 9, 79, 295

wine storage units, 292

wine tasting (s), 8, 303

wine thief, 330

wing-type corkscrew, 264

winter wines, 216

Wolfe, Wade, 280

wood-aged port, 198–99

Zinfandel, 15, 22, 30, 48–50

    alternatives to, 167–68

    as fail-safe restaurant choice, 250

    grapes, 48–50, 140, 170

    see also white Zinfandel

Ziraldo, Donald, 204